PETER FENWICK is a Fellow of the Royal College of Psychiatrists. He holds a research post as a senior lecturer at the Institute of Psychiatry in London. He has a special interest in sleep and has been involved in research into lucid dreams.

ELIZABETH FENWICK is a professional writer on health and family matters. She has had books on health and child care published by Family Doctor Publications, and coauthored several others with her husband, Peter.

Also by Peter and Elizabeth Fenwick

THE HIDDEN DOOR: UNDERSTANDING AND CONTROLLING DREAMS

THE TRUTH IN THE LIGHT:
AN INVESTIGATION OF OVER 300 NEAR-DEATH EXPERIENCES

PAST LIVES

An Investigation into Reincarnation Memories

Peter and Elizabeth Fenwick

BERKLEY BOOKS, NEW YORK

For
James and Sarah
June and Hugh
and
Benjamin Brooke

PAST LIVES

A Berkley Book / published by arrangement with
the authors

PRINTING HISTORY
First published in Great Britain in 1999 by Headline Book Publishing
Berkley edition / July 2001

The Penguin Putnam Inc. World Wide Web site address is
www.penguinputnam.com

ISBN: 0-425-18075-1

BERKLEY®
Berkley Books are published by The Berkley Publishing Group,
a division of Penguin Putnam Inc., 375 Hudson Street,
New York, New York 10014.
BERKLEY and the "B" design
are trademarks belonging to Penguin Putnam Inc.

PRINTED IN THE UNITED STATES OF AMERICA

10 9 8 7 6 5 4 3 2 1

CONTENTS

Introduction   vii

CHAPTER

1   Some Classic Cases   1
2   Glimpses of the Past   16
3   Culture and Reincarnation   46
4   The Tricks That Memory Plays   64
5   Taken Over by the Past   77
6   Dreams of Forgotten Lives   92
7   Searching for a Past Life   115
8   The Case of the Spanish
    Adventuress   129
9   A Question of Fraud and a Case
    of *Folie à Trois*   146
10 Soul Mates   163
11 Using the Past to Heal the Present   177
12 Hidden Talents   194
13 "My Other Mummy"   219
14 Children Who Remember   243
15 Stretching Coincidence   270
16 The Psi Hypothesis   293
17 Science and the Soul   309

    Bibliography   322
    Index   326

CONTENTS

Introduction

Introduction

I hold that when a person dies
His soul returns again to earth;
Arrayed in some new flesh disguise,
Another mother gives him birth.
With sturdier limbs and brighter brain
The old soul takes the road again.

John Masefield

FROM the time he was a small child Alan Pring knew that he wanted to fly. When he was only five or six he bewildered his parents by the intensity of this wish and by his determination that one day he would become a pilot. His chance came when he joined the RAF during the Second World War.

When I began flying in 1943 my instructor was convinced that I had piloted aircraft before. I just knew how to fly and every "new" experience to which I was introduced in the air was already a memory. Similarly, the first time I encountered the smell of aircraft-fabric dope I knew that I had experienced it previously. The odour gave me the most peculiar sense of pleasure, as if it was associated with very happy memories. My love of flying has never faded, but it is directed always in my memory towards biplanes. I feel that I flew Sopwith aircraft.

When the war ended in 1945 I was grounded, but in 1947 I rejoined the Royal Air Force Voluntary Reserve (RAFVR) and resumed flying, albeit in Tiger Moths, which was the only aircraft that the RAFVR had until the arrival of the Chipmunk in 1950. I flew at weekends and at summer camps with other pilots from Pengam

Moor airfield (now a housing estate) at Cardiff. One day six of us decided to have a dogfight. The planes had no radios, so all flying, including formation flying, was done using hand signals. We took off in formation and then split up to climb to altitude and rendezvous over a specified landmark at a specified time. The object was to gain as much height as possible and to remain out of sight of the other pilots until the dogfight began. To get on the tail of another aircraft constituted a "kill"; but the range had to be not more than 20 yards. The eventual overall victor would benefit from his "kills" in the mess.

We drew lots for particular aircraft because although outwardly identical they all had their own characteristics. I drew the prize "Tiger," which had a different propeller to all the others in that its pitch gave the aircraft a much greater rate of climb.

I had a huge advantage, because in the set time I would be able to climb higher than my five opponents and be able to conceal myself in the sun and have the extra speed that a dive would give. In the allotted time of 15 minutes I had climbed to over 9,000 feet, and over the selected map reference I looked down, in confident anticipation, for my opponents. Soon I spotted four of them at least 1,000 feet below me. Secure in the knowledge that no other "Tiger" could be near my height I concentrated on searching for the fifth aircraft. Suddenly, with an ominous sinking feeling in my stomach, I twisted in my tight harness and looked behind me. There, not five yards from my tail, was the whirring propeller of the fifth Tiger. The pilot had a huge grin on his face as he pointed one hand around his windscreen and "fired his guns." At that moment I experienced a horrendous feeling of doom. In an almost subliminal flash it was no longer a Tiger Moth behind me but a Fokker triplane, and above its round engine cowl I saw the flashes of its two machine guns and immediately felt terrible blows in my back and momentarily everything went black. It lasted only a second or two, and then I watched as the other pilot broke away to dive on other victims. For a while I was in a state of shock, and I must admit that I was quite emotionally upset as I descended to fly back to the airfield. It was not losing the contest that upset me, but the conviction that it had all happened before and that I had been killed through carelessness and over-confidence in a dogfight in the First World War.

Later, in the bar, the other pilot explained how he had out-climbed me. He had used a thermal up-current from the cooling towers of a nearby power station. I had made a fatal assumption that my plane would be the highest.

Alan has never had any other specific memory of a previous existence and remains dubious of most tales in which people recount details of other lives. But many years after this experience, while undergoing surgery in Manchester Royal Infirmary, he had a near-death experience which had a profound effect on him. It convinced him that it was impossible to cease to exist. Given this belief, he says, it would seem plausible, if not logical, that reincarnation is a possibility.

Alan's conviction that it is impossible for man to cease to exist lies at the heart of a belief in reincarnation. Reincarnation assumes that man has a component that can survive the death of the body and contains elements of both memory and personality. It is one of the oldest and most widely held of mankind's spiritual beliefs. Henry Ford, Gustav Mahler, Richard Wagner and David Lloyd George are among those who have expressed a belief in reincarnation. So too did General Patton and Lord Dowding, who directed the Battle of Britain in the Second World War. Napoleon was convinced that he had a previous existence as the Emperor Charlemagne. The actress Shirley MacLaine recounted several vivid past-life experiences in her book *Out on a Limb*. And Diana, Princess of Wales, is said to have told friends that she believed she was a nun in a previous life.

Even today, and even in the West, when we say "He's his grandfather all over again," we seem to be arguing for more than just the supremacy of the genes. An essential part of the belief in reincarnation is that some features of the person who dies survive death and are transmitted to an unborn child. Conceptually, there has to be a vehicle to carry these qualities, a vehicle that is able to carry aspects of the donor's experience, memories and personality, hold them independently of the donor after death, and then transfer them into a developing brain so that the "reincarnee" takes on some or all of the characteristics of the donor and may have access to some of the donor's memories. This vehicle is often called the soul. The concept of soul is a complicated one and contains wide differences between cultures, but throughout this book it will be used in this very general sense. This concept is also based on the implicit assumption that there is a linear time to which the soul is bound—that there is a before and an after, a future life and a past life—a concept that fits satisfactorily the current popular Western view of the world. However, Western physics no longer defines time in a literal linear fashion, and so the idea of flowing from one lifetime to another in a linear sense is already flawed.

Although in most people's minds a belief in reincarnation is associated particularly with Buddhism and Hinduism, it is far older than either of these. Belief in reincarnation—the transmigration of the soul after death to another living body—has recurred in some form in almost every human society and in almost all the major world religions except Judaeo-Christianity and most Muslim groups. The ancient Egyptians were said to have used embalming as a method of preventing or delaying reincarnation by holding the soul in the body, as they assumed that so long as the body did not decay, the soul would not be freed.

In the Western world, the first mentions of reincarnation are in Greek writings from around the sixth century BC. These describe the origin of man, springing from the soot of the burning bodies of the Titans—in Greek mythology the children of Uranus (heaven) and Gaea (earth). The Titans were destroyed by Zeus's thunderbolts as punishment for murdering and eating his son, Zagreus. Man therefore had within him a small divine spark (Zagreus) but a much larger Titanic component of evil (original sin). Man's worldly task was to conquer the evil "Titanic" element within himself so that he could achieve divine status. His soul survived bodily death, and in some doctrines was rewarded or punished in another world before being recycled in another human or animal body. In this way the soul was recycled until its ultimate happy release into a state of bliss.

In ancient Greece, Plato believed that the soul was immortal and that there was a fixed number of souls, which regularly reincarnated (clearly, he had not foreseen the population explosion of today). There is some (rather dubious) evidence that Pythagoras may have taught reincarnation, and there are certainly references to reincarnation in Roman literature. The poet Ennius described a dream in which he met Homer, who told him that they were both incarnations of the same soul, which had once belonged to a peacock. Virgil, in the *Aeneid*, introduced the idea of reincarnation into his account of the Underworld.

In its most primitive form the idea of reincarnation is independent of any moral teaching. An individual had a soul, or sometimes even several souls, one of which could separate from the body during sleep, passing in and out of it through the mouth or nostrils. It stands to reason that a soul able to make its exit in this manner must be small; in India, for example, it appeared as a manikin or an insect, and in Germany as a snake, weasel or mouse (not quite small enough, one would have thought). Commonly, the soul is spoken of as "flying" in Greece, and indeed it is often depicted as a bird; in Egypt and Assam a hawk, in Europe most commonly a dove; in Lombardy poles bearing pigeons were often erected over graves.

From this belief that the soul can separate from the body during life, it followed quite naturally that on the death of the body the soul, having made its final exit, might be able to enter and be reborn in another individual. In Germany the essence of a dying man's heart was said to pass into his brother, doubling his courage. This belief in the separation of the soul is probably also responsible for the common taboo among some primitive cultures of giving children names already held by living family members—identity of name implies identity of personality; it suggests that if two people in the same family bear the same name, they share the same soul, and one might die.

Druidism, the faith of the Celtic population of Gaul and the British Isles until the arrival of the Romans and the introduction of Christianity, taught that the human soul was immortal and passed into other bodies after death. However, there is no evidence that the Druids believed that the purpose of this chain of successive lives was to purify the soul, or that reincarnation was linked in any way with moral retribution.

The notion of transmigration of the soul lies at the heart of many myths and legends, in the belief that witches or magicians, for example, could make themselves invulnerable by separating their soul and keeping it safe in some far-distant place—in an animal or plant in the forest, for example, or an egg beneath the sea. While the soul was safe, its owner could not be destroyed.

In legend, humans may reincarnate in plant or animal as well as human form. Trees may grow from the graves of lovers, such as Tristan and Iseult, twining around each other together as in life the lovers themselves were intertwined. In the story of the Greek hero Ajax, flowers sprang from drops of his blood, suggesting that his soul was in his blood and had flowed out of his body with it. In parts of Asia it is thought that the soul goes into the crops. If necessary, the soul can be held within the body by preserving the corpse by smoke-drying; then, at a more agriculturally propitious time, the funeral ceremony is held and the soul released.

Beliefs in magic, spirits, witchcraft and reincarnation, like beliefs in Communism or Thatcherism, come and go within particular cultures and societies (though the former are more robust and longer-lasting than the latter). The early Jewish philosopher Philo Judaeus (30 BC to AD 40) believed that the soul came from God and at death only those who on earth kept themselves free from attachment to the world of the senses would return to God. All others (which is to say almost everyone) must at death pass into another body.

The doctrine of reincarnation was tolerated in some southern European Christian societies, for example the Gnostics and the Manichaeans, until the mid-sixth century. It was finally declared unacceptable by the Council of Nice in 553. Even so it lingered as a heresy for many centuries. In Europe in the Middle Ages this heretical belief continued to be held by numerous sects known collectively as the Cathars.

The Cathars' view of reincarnation was something of a lottery. They believed that only if man had received the gift of the Paraclete, the holy spirit, could he escape his earthly flesh and be reconciled to God. Otherwise, after death the soul fled into the first earthly lodging it could find, which might, according to the luck of the draw, be either animal or human. The Cathars fell into two classes: the Perfect, who had received the gift of the Paraclete, and the Believers, who had not. The Perfect formed the ordained priesthood and controlled the Church; the mere Believers had to give them unquestioning obedience and total adoration.

However, the life of a Perfect was not an easy one. The Perfects had to reject their families and follow Christ, fast frequently, and follow a virtually vegan diet on the grounds that everything that was sexually begotten was impure (a very sketchy knowledge of natural history, however, led them to believe that fish were the product of virgin births). They had also to remain celibate. Moreover, thanks to the Inquisitors, their lives were fraught with danger. Not surprisingly, most Believers preferred not to seek the gift of the Paraclete until they were on their deathbed. As a sect the Cathars had virtually disappeared by the end of the thirteenth century, eradicated by the combined might of the state and the Catholic Church, and perhaps also by their dedication to a celibate life.

In more modern times, reincarnation according to the laws of karma is the cardinal tenet of the Theosophical Society, founded in 1875 by Madame Blavatsky. The spiritual leader Sai Baba is said to be in his second incarnation and to have strong memories of his previous incarnation as Sai Baba of Shirdi, a Muslim saint who lived from 1840 to 1918. Some of his devotees claim that Sai Baba in this life has simply continued conversations that he had been having with them in his previous life: he is even said to have told one man (correctly) "You owe me 14 rupees!" Sai Baba foretells his own death in the year 2020 and a third incarnation eight years later as Prema Sai Baba, which means "the embodiment of love."

In some cultures—Buddhism and Hinduism, for example—reincarnation is associated with retribution. In all the indigenous religions of India—Hinduism, Jainism, Buddhism, and, in part, Sikhism—the law of karma dictates that the physical conditions of each life are determined by the moral and religious character of the preceding one. In orthodox Hinduism, the belief is that if a man leads a good life he will be born again wealthy and in a high caste; if he sins, he will be born again in a low caste, or even as an animal. This continues until the soul attains salvation and is released from this cycle of birth and rebirth.

Buddhists deny any continuance of the soul. Karma, for the Buddhist, means that there is a continuity of moral consequences, each successive life being determined by the consequences of the previous one. The working of karma is maintained wholly by desire; karma dies when desires cease. In Buddhism the soul reincarnates until it reaches a state of nirvana—the cessation of desires, craving or passion. The enlightened Buddhist, it is said, can remember his past births and see the destinies of departed individuals.

Tibetan Buddhism is of special interest because of the unique part played by reincarnation in that religion. Buddhism reached Tibet from India between the seventh, and tenth centuries AD, and with it came a belief in reincarnation. But throughout the course of the next five centuries the Tibetans developed their own concept of reincarnation, which included the idea that spiritually advanced lamas (monks) sometimes have the ability to control their next incarnation. By the fifteenth century it had become generally accepted that when the principal of a monastery died, his true successor could be identified by finding his next incarnation. The reincarnating lamas are known as *sprul-sku*, or *tulkus*, and their number has grown dramatically since the fifteenth century, perhaps because the prestige of a monastery is greatly increased if it is known to have an "incarnation" as its head. There are now several hundred *tulkus*, of whom the Dalai Lama and the Panchen Lama are the most important.

Although a senior lama will often predict, or at least drop hints about, the circumstances of his next life, these utterances may take a rather Delphic form, and this can make it difficult for the monks who have the task of interpreting them and

finding his successor. Jeffrey Iverson, journalist and television producer, has described in his book *In search of the Dead*
the search for one such *tulku*, Ling Rinpoche, said to be the
reincarnation of the senior tutor to the Dalai Lama. The story
was told to Jeffrey Iverson by Lobsang Lungrig, who had
been the servant of the deceased senior tutor, had helped to
lead the search for his successor, and now acted as guardian
to Ling Rinpoche. The Dalai Lama and his tutor had been
very close, and in fact it was the Dalai Lama himself who provided the clues that led to the discovery of the little boy. He
revealed that a reincarnation had already been born in one of
the Tibetan settlements in India in 1985.

Two search parties set out to find the child, and in one year
had collected 690 names with all the special signs surrounding their births. From a study of these, His Holiness was able
to say that the child had been born at Bir, a two-hour drive
from Dharamsala, where ten children were on the list.

The searchers visited Bir again, but at first it seemed that
they would have no luck. Some of the children cried when
they were pulled close and none showed any signs of recognition. At the last minute they realised that one of the ten children on their list was absent. It transpired that this little boy
lived with his brother in the orphanage at the Tibetan Children's Village at Dharamsala. His mother was dead and his father too poor to support him.

The next day the search party went to the orphanage. And
here one little boy came out and approached them, taking the
hand of one of the attendants, and "showing extraordinary
cheerfulness." The child was only 21 months old, barely able
to walk and unable yet to talk. But asked if he recognised
them, the child nodded. They then showed the child four
rosaries, and unerringly he picked out the only one of the four
which had belonged to the former senior tutor. Not only that,
but he held it correctly and fingered correctly 20 of the 25
beads. The search party were convinced that their search was
ended. Their feelings were confirmed the following day when
the searchers and senior staff at the school gathered together
for some refreshments. This little boy, of his own accord, got
up and distributed sweets to everyone present, placing his

hand on each head as if in a blessing. Lobsang Lungrig takes up the story:

> We went to His Holiness and reported these incidents. He asked us to bring the child to His residence the next day . . . On the way, one attendant asked where the residence was, and the child is said to have pointed in the right direction. When he arrived the boy exhibited signs of recognition, reminiscent of a child meeting his parents. He sat for an hour on my lap and when he was led to His Holiness he did not show any trait of fear. His Holiness was impressed and even expressed surprise at the small child's acuteness . . . There were many occurrences that confirmed our belief. His behaviour while eating, his smiling. He does lots of things that are typical of the past master. I served the master ever since he was 34 until he died at 81. This child loves me more than his natural father. Every time I visited him he always insisted on accompanying me wherever I went. He always showed sensitivity in recognising past associates and students, especially Western students of the past master. He called some close students by their names.

In Tibetan Buddhist teachings, reincarnation is the means to the eventual end of enlightenment. So there is a special spiritual significance in the monks' traditional search for a reincarnated lama. It is testimony to their belief that someone who has already attained this end is still prepared to come back to earth to help others. However, the search has worldly significance too, because religious leaders in Tibet have always held political and economic power. And since the annexation of Tibet by China in 1950, the departure of the Dalai Lama to exile in India, and the unflagging efforts of the Chinese to destroy Tibet's social, cultural and religious order, what was once a spiritual quest has been transformed into a politically motivated power struggle.

The Panchen Lama (the title bestowed in the seventeenth century by the fifth Dalai Lama on the abbot of Tashilhunpo) is second only to the Dalai Lama in the hierarchy of Tibetan

Buddhism. The tenth Panchen Lama was an ambiguous figure, at first a friend of Mao Zedong and later, when he recognised and tried to protest against the erosion of the Tibetan way of life, tortured and imprisoned in Beijing for 17 years. After his release in 1979 he was careful to support the party line in public but argued in private that giving up the Tibetan claim to independence might be the price that had to be paid if Tibetan culture were to survive. On 28 January 1989, at the age of 51, the tenth Panchen Lama died—officially of a heart attack, though many of his followers claimed he had been poisoned.

In Tibet the search for the next Panchen Lama began. Reports of unusual boy children from all over Tibet were collected by Abbot Chadrel, head of the Panchen Lama's monastery. Dreams and signs were interpreted. To the Dalai Lama in exile was sent a short list of likely candidates, among them one Gendun Choeyki Nyima, the son of a doctor, born in Nagchu, a remote area of central Tibet. It was not until January 1995, six years after the search had begun, that the Dalai Lama made his final choice. Gendun Choeyki Nyima was recognised as the authentic incarnation, the eleventh Panchen Lama.

A far more difficult problem, however, was to gain acceptance of the new Panchen Lama by the Chinese government. After months of negotiation it became clear that Beijing was determined to nominate its own candidate. The Dalai Lama decided that he had no choice but to pre-empt them. On 14 May 1995 His Holiness made the official proclamation of reincarnation. He ended his statement thus:

> The search and recognition of Panchen Rinpoche's reincarnation is a religious matter and not political. It is my hope that the Chinese government, with whom I have kept contact regarding this matter through various channels over the recent years, will extend its understanding, cooperation and assistance to the Tashilhunpo Monastery in enabling Rinpoche to receive proper religious training and to assume his spiritual responsibilities.

This was, alas and predictably, a vain hope. There was tragically no question of this reincarnation being a purely religious matter. Within days, security police had arrived at the home of the little six-year-old boy who had just taken up his unenviable inheritance as the eleventh Panchen Lama. With his parents and brother he was flown out of the country and neither he nor his family have been seen since. The Chinese say he is alive and well, but they refuse to say where. In December 1995 another small boy, whose parents are rumoured to be Party members and who had the blessing of the Party, was proclaimed the official reincarnation of the Panchen Lama and enthroned.

The idea of reincarnation is attractive to many people either because with the concept of karma it seems to offer an explanation of the inequalities of life or because it suggests that there is a meaning and purpose to life. For others, like Alan Pring, the idea of a "past life" feels intuitively right because it helps to explain feelings, empathies, abilities, which seem to have sprung from some quite inexplicable source and for which there seems to be no logical explanation.

It is part of human nature to long for immortality, and this longing gets stronger the older you get. For some of us it is enough to be able to pass on our genes and our memories to another generation. For others, immortality implies personal survival in the form of some subtle life force or energy which we may call soul or spirit, which is separate from the body and survives death. But for many people the world over, immortality means the reincarnation of individual consciousness, recycling of a personality in another body and another time.

Mankind has always looked for some external proof of personal survival—ghosts and apparitions, out-of-body and near-death experiences, possession and spiritualism: we value these because they seem to provide objective confirmation of an inner conviction that death cannot mean the end, that we cannot just cease to exist. This is also why we look hopefully towards science for confirmation of these feelings. Science is in the business of proof. If science says we can survive, then at last we can relax and believe it.

Unfortunately, science as it now stands is of little help to those who want to believe. Science holds a simple and straightforward view on the subject of reincarnation. It is impossible. The death of the body means the death of the brain, which is responsible for the generation of personal consciousness. Without the brain there can be no survival of personal consciousness after death. If we want to speculate about the existence of, let alone the survival of, the soul, Western science, which deals only with the objective, external world, can do little to help us. Current Western science does not yet understand consciousness, and until we understand consciousness we can only speculate about reincarnation.

What science can do, despite its limitations, is to look at the personal experiences that have formed the basis of many people's belief in reincarnation. It can assess the quality of the evidence that they have indeed lived a previous life, and it can see how far the phenomenon of past-life memories can itself be explained within a scientific framework. If we find there is objective evidence, and if it seems there are phenomena which we can't explain easily without stepping outside the boundaries of current science, it will be up to the reader to decide whether this amounts to a clear case for reincarnation.

And if we don't? Will this invalidate the whole case for reincarnation? True conviction has to arise out of personal experience, and the one thing science can never measure or validate is the quality of subjective personal experience. For the overwhelming majority of people whose accounts are quoted in this book, belief in a past life arose from some very personal experience for which reincarnation seemed to them to be the only answer. For these fortunate few, the fragmentary echoes of past lives which stir their memories provide all the proof of personal survival that they need.

1

Some Classic Cases

If we cannot remember what we were doing or thinking last Monday, how on earth do we imagine it would be easy, or normal, to remember what we were doing in a previous lifetime?

Sogyal Rinpoche

SOME cases of past lives are so intriguing, so full of convincing detail, that for many people they have come to be regarded as absolute proof of reincarnation. What is nearly always lacking in a past-life memory is fact—names and dates and events that can be checked and which might provide either proof of identity or at least compelling evidence that the "reincarnee" really had experienced the events in another time and place which they claimed to have remembered.

The following three cases are notable for the amount of detail remembered—enough in one case to establish an identity, and in the others enough at least to suggest that the people involved had genuine knowledge of the life they described, however they may have obtained it. All three cases have been extensively investigated and the facts checked. So if we want to see whether there might be a prima facie case for reincarnation, they are probably as good a starting-point as we can get.

THE SEARCH FOR BRIDEY MURPHY

Bridey Murphy was one of the first and most publicised, personalities to emerge from the hypnotic exploration of past lives. The story of her regression, *The Search for Bridey Mur-*

phy, written by the man who regressed her, made a best-selling book and was made into a film. The Bridey Murphy case has been dismissed by many people as either fantasy or fabrication, but even if it provides little evidence for reincarnation, it still poses some intriguing questions, questions to which so far no one has produced satisfactory answers.

Bridey Murphy's incarnation in this life is an American woman, Virginia Tighe, the wife of Hugh Tighe, an insurance salesman. The couple lived in Pueblo, Colorado, and among their friends was a businessman, Morey Bernstein, who had taken up hypnotism as a hobby. One evening at a party, Virginia volunteered to be a subject for Bernstein. He discovered that she was a good hypnotic subject and persuaded her to allow him to try to regress her under hypnosis back even beyond her birth, an experiment he had long wanted to do.

Virginia underwent six regression sessions, with Bernstein, which both his own wife and Hugh Tighe witnessed, between November 1952 and October 1953. During the first session Bernstein instructed Virginia to go back and back in her mind until she found herself in some other scene, in some other place, in some other time. Then, he said, when he talked to her again she would tell him about it.

Suddenly Virginia began to talk in a soft Irish brogue. ". . . Uh . . . scratched the paint off all my bed. Jus' painted it, 'n' made it pretty. It was a metal [tape indistinct, probably "little"] bed and I scratched the paint off of it; dug my nails on every post and just ruined it. Was jus' terrible."

MB: Why did you do that?
VT: Don't know. I was just mad. Got an awful spanking.
MB: What is your name?
VT: Uh . . . Bridey.
MB: Don't you have any other name?
VT: Uh . . . Bridey Murphy.
MB: And where do you live?
VT: . . . I live in Cork . . . Cork.

Neither Bernstein nor Virginia had ever been to Ireland. And yet over the subsequent five sessions Bridey's Irish brogue grew stronger, and the picture of her life in eighteenth-century

County Cork became more detailed. Bridey said she was born on 20 December 1798, came from a Protestant family and was the daughter of a barrister, Duncan Murphy, and his wife Kathleen. She said that she lived at "the meadows" outside Cork—and gave details of her siblings, an older brother, Duncan, and a younger brother who had died in infancy.

Until she was 15 Bridey had gone to a school run by a Mrs. Strayne, whose daughter, Alice, married Bridey's brother Duncan. Bridey herself married Brian MacCarthy, the son of a Roman Catholic barrister, John MacCarthy. The couple went through two marriage ceremonies, one in Cork and a second, Roman Catholic ceremony, which was kept a secret from Bridey's parents, in Belfast, at the home of a priest, Father John Joseph Gorman. The couple had no children, and lived in Belfast until Bridey's death, at the age of 66, as a result of a fall in which she broke her hip. She was, (in her own words) "ditched," i.e. buried, in Belfast in 1864.

Bridey claimed that while they were living in Belfast her husband Brian wrote for the *Belfast News Letter* and taught at Queen's University. She mentioned the names of several places in Ireland, including Galway, County Limerick, Antrim, and a place called Baylings Crossing. She also mentioned various shops she had known in Belfast, including a food shop called Farr's and a greengrocer called John Carrigan. She described the currency used as pounds, tuppences and sixpences.

Before Bernstein published his book *The Search for Bridey Murphy* his publisher suggested that some independent research should be carried out in Ireland to check out as many as possible of the facts of Bridey's story. When this was done, many of the general facts she had given about life in Ireland did indeed prove to be correct. But it was impossible to prove the existence of Bridey herself, because records of births, deaths and marriages did not exist until after 1864, the year in which Bridey died.

Subsequently every statement made by Bridey Murphy has been scrutinised, checked and analysed, both by people who have wanted to demolish her story and those who have wanted to confirm it. Bridey Murphy's is certainly not a wa-

tertight case. It is still floating—just—but there are holes beneath the waterline.

Some of the facts that have been confirmed are more compelling than others. Many of the places she had mentioned—
Galway, Limerick and Mourne, for example—are celebrated
enough for most people to have known. But Baylings Crossing did not appear on any map, and only by chance was it discovered that it did exist, but only as a crossing point which
would not appear on a map. What did appear on an 1801 map
of Cork was an area just outside the city called Mardike
Meadows, which corresponded very well with Bridey's description of living with her parents at "the meadows." There
is no trace of a Roman Catholic barrister called John Brian
MacCarthy living at that time, though there was a book-
keeper of that name. It has been suggested that Bridey may
have been attempting some social upgrading of her family by
describing her father and husband as barristers. Either way,
this is not very persuasive—MacCarthy, is a common enough
Irish name. Neither has any trace been found of a St.
Theresa's Church in Belfast at that time, nor of a priest named
John Gorman. But there was a greengrocer called John Carrigan in Belfast at that time, and a William Farr who sold food,
and neither of these names are particularly common or obvious choices for someone drawing on a random store of Irish
names. And the "tuppence" that Bridey mentioned was a coin
only in circulation during her lifetime, between 1797 and
1850.

Bridey's use of colloquial and contemporary Irish language was also shown to be largely correct. During one session she sneezed violently, then opened her eyes and asked for
a "linen" (the word for a handkerchief), for example. She also
said that her mother had made her some "slips" (the word
used to describe a pinafore at that time) with sashes. However,
mixed with these convincing "Irishisms" were many modern
American words and expressions, such as "candy" and
"downtown." This isn't surprising. It's not unusual for hypnotised subjects to use some of their own current idiomatic
language. One would expect a mixture rather than consistent
use of one or other language.

Several of the criticisms that were made of her story at first were later shown to be unfounded, sometimes because of the difficulty in transcribing tapes of the hypnotic sessions, which were not always clearly articulated. In the first regression session, for example, she had mentioned a "metal bed." It was suggested first of all that this was not a word a child would use; secondly, that metal beds were unknown in Ireland at that time (in fact they were uncommon but by no means unknown). Bridey had also, when asked about the house she lived in, said that it was "A nice house . . . it's a wood house. . . ." Wood was scarce in Ireland and it was highly unlikely that any house she lived in would have been made of wood. In each case, however, more careful listening to the tapes showed that the contentious word was inaccurate: the "metal bed" was in fact a "little bed" and the "wood house" a "good house."

Many attempts were made to discredit Virginia Tighe and Morey Bernstein when the story first appeared in America. Bernstein's book was serialised in the *Chicago Daily News* and, not surprisingly, many of the attacks originated in other newspapers. The *Chicago American*, for example, pointed out that Virginia Tighe had an Irish aunt who had regaled her with tales of Irish life which provided the background to flesh out a fantasy. More damningly, they also claimed to have discovered "the real Bridey," an Irish woman called Bridie Corkell whose maiden name was Murphy and who had at one time lived in the same street as Virginia and her foster-parents in Chicago. Bridie Corkell had, the *Chicago American* claimed, talked to Virginia many times and knew her well. They also claimed that Virginia had been in love with Bridie Corkell's son. The Bridey Murphy story was exploded: it was all, apparently, a hoax. Various newspapers around the world published purported "confessions" to this effect by both Bernstein and Tighe, and on 25 June 1956 *Life* magazine, under the headline "Bridey Search Ends At Last," printed a picture of Bridie Corkell surrounded by her grandchildren.

That was by no means the end of the story. A further flurry of investigative journalism by the *Denver Post* showed that the aunt referred to by the *Chicago American*, Mrs. Marie Burns, although of Scottish-Irish descent, had been born in New York and had spent most of her life in Chicago, and that in any case Virginia had not met her until she was 18. A woman called Bridie Corkell had indeed lived opposite Virginia (which Virginia readily admitted) and had had a son, John, but Virginia denied knowing her well or ever having been in love with her son—he was seven or eight years older than she was, and married by the time Virginia had started to become interested in boys. It was difficult for the *Denver Post* to find out much more about Mrs. Corkell because she refused resolutely to answer any questions—which may have had something to do with the fact that her son John Corkell was in fact the editor of the *Chicago American*'s Sunday edition.

Virginia's own response to these claims and counter-claims was evident in a lecture she gave in 1976:

> *Life* magazine . . . took it upon themselves to write an exposé . . . and people were saying, "Oh well, she heard that all from a neighbour." May I say that the woman lived somewhere in the general vicinity of where I lived. I never said one word to that woman! It came out later, but was never printed, that the woman's son was the telegraph editor of the *Chicago Herald American*. Someone found a woman who would say that she was Irish and that her name was Bridey Murphy and that she'd talked to me. It is not true—my hand to God and my three grandchildren and my three children! Also—the parish priest of this particular woman would say that her first name was Bridey or Bridget, but would not sign any paper to the effect that her last name was Murphy . . .

On the face of it the most likely explanation of the Bridey Murphy story is that she had at some time acquired all the information she gave, forgotten it, and that these forgotten memories then resurfaced when she was under hypnosis. This phenomenon, known as cryptomnesia, is described in more detail in Chapter Four and is probably the basis for many apparent past-life memories. Little of what she says seems to have been so obscure that she couldn't have acquired the knowledge if she had set out to do so. But no one has produced a truly convincing explanation of where she might have acquired her knowledge of Ireland and Irish life in the nineteenth-century—the name Baylings Crossing, for instance—or why she should have done so. Books and films are one obvious source, but Virginia, according to Bernstein, had not the slightest interest in books, and certainly not in the kind of books that would have given her the detail needed to produce the Bridey Murphy story.

Neither did she seem either to welcome the publicity her story stimulated, or to profit by it. She appeared under a pseudonym in Bernstein's book, and after she was "outed" refused to make money by becoming a public personality. And there has never been any suggestion that she had any kind of special relationship with Bernstein, the hypnotist, and was either consciously or unconsciously trying to please him or to attract his interest and attention.

There seems to be general agreement that Bernstein himself acted in good faith. The worst charge that can be levelled against him is perhaps that he accepted too readily that what he heard in the hypnotic sessions was evidence of reincarnation. Most people now would probably agree that the story of Bridey Murphy does little either to prove or disprove the idea of reincarnation. But it may well suggest that sometimes in the hypnotic state people can apparently access memories that seem to belong to another time, another place or another person.

THE SEVEN LIVES OF JANE EVANS

Arnall Bloxham was a hypnotherapist with a lifelong interest in past-life research. In a lifetime of research he amassed tape recordings of 400 past-life regressions. One of his subjects was Jane Evans, a woman who initially had no interest in reincarnation but simply consulted Bloxharn in the hope that he could help her rheumatism. She agreed to be regressed and under hypnosis recalled seven lives. The most celebrated of these was her life as Rebecca, a young Jewish mother in twelfth-century York, a life that ended in 1190 with the massacre of Jews in the city.

While Jane was under hypnosis, Bloxham had suggested to her that she should go back in time to the twelfth century.

He then asked her the date, and she told him that it was "the Christian year 1189" and that she was living in York, the wife of a Jewish moneylender called Joseph and the mother of two children. She conveyed vividly what it was like to be a Jew in York at that time, just before the Third Crusade, when Christian religious fervour was at its height and anti-Jewish feeling was rife. She recalled, for example, how she had to wear a badge to indicate her religion. She talked from a very personal point of view, describing only the feelings and the fate of herself and her family, and making no mention of the historical details of the massacre.

As anti-Jewish feelings grew, Rebecca and her family considered fleeing from York but were reluctant to abandon their home and possessions. Then one evening an angry mob started to attack and fire the Jewish quarter. The family fled from the flames, chased by the mob. Joseph managed to distract their pursuers for long enough to enable them to get away, by throwing down a sack of coins. Eventually, exhausted, they entered a church, tied up the priest and hid in the crypt beneath the floor. The final moments of the tape make moving reading. Joseph and their son go out to search for food. Left in the darkness of the crypt, Rebecca and her daughter Rachel can hear horses coming nearer and nearer.

Bloxham: I expect your son and husband will be back soon?

Rebecca: Yes, they must be back . . . We're worried, we're frightened. We can hear them coming, we can hear the horses coming, we can hear the screaming and the shouting and the crying: "Burn the Jews, burn the Jews, burn the Jews" . . . Where is Joseph? Why doesn't he come back? (*She pauses, then almost screams.*) Oh God, they're coming . . . they . . . they are coming . . . Rachel's crying . . . don't cry . . . don't cry . . . don't cry. (*Pause.*) Aah, they've entered the church. We can hear them. They've entered the church . . . the priest is loose . . . he has told them we are here . . . they're coming down. (*Pause, and voice almost incoherent with terror.*) Oh not . . . not, not, not Rachel! No, don't take her . . . don't . . . stop. They're going to kill her . . . they . . . don't, not Rachel, no, no, no, no, no, don't take Rachel . . . no!

Bloxham (*shocked*): They're not going to take her, are they?

Rebecca (*grief-stricken voice*): They've taken Rachel, they've taken Rachel . . .

Bloxham: They are not going to harm you, are they? (*Silence.*) Are you all right? They have left you alone, have they?

Rebecca: Dark . . . dark . . .

The writer Jeffrey Iverson, while researching his book *More Lives Than One? The Evidence of the Remarkable Bloxham Tapes*, asked Professor Barrie Dobson, an authority on Jewish history at York University, to listen to the tapes and comment on them. Professor Dobson was impressed by the accuracy of much of Rebecca's memories.

However, there are serious flaws in Rebecca's story. From her description of the medieval city of York, Professor Dobson concluded that the church in which she had taken refuge was most likely to have been St. Mary's, Castlegate. But St. Mary's, in common with all of York's medieval churches except York Minister, had no crypt. Some months later, however, in the spring of 1975, workmen renovating the church found something that seemed to have been a crypt which from their description seemed to have been either Norman or Romanesque—which would mean that it predated the massacre of 1190. Unfortunately, it was blocked up again before it could be properly investigated.

For a while this seemed as near to "proof" as most cases of reincarnation can ever hope to get. But, alas, the later and considered view of this chamber is that, in the words of Professor Barrie Dobson, "it now seems overwhelmingly most likely that the chamber which workmen reported encountering when renovating St. Mary's, Castlegate, in 1975 was not an early medieval crypt at all, but a post-medieval charnel vault."

Then there is the question of Rebecca's badge, the badge that all Jews had to wear at that time to indicate their religion. The fact that she reported having to wear a badge initially made her story less convincing, because it was not until 1215, 25 years after Rebecca's death, that the Church authorities in Rome made the wearing of such badges by Jews in Christian kingdoms mandatory, However, Iverson's research showed that the wearing of these badges was, in fact, already common in England in the twelfth century, before the proclamation. A more sceptical view is that of Melvin Harris, a BBC writer and presenter, who pointed out in his book *Sorry, You've Been Duped!*, that Rebecca described these badges as yellow circles, which were worn "over our hearts." Harris maintains that the Jewish badge was not introduced until the next century, and in any case took the form of two oblong white strips of cloth—the yellow circle was the badge worn by Jews in France and Germany after 1215.

Unless one can discover the source of apparent past-life memories, it is almost impossible either to prove or to disprove an account of a past life. However, Jane Evans's memories of life as Rebecca seemed to offer powerful evidence for reincarnation. But, perhaps unfairly, these memories are made to seem more suspect when one considers another of her seven past-life regressions.

In this life Jane had moved slightly forward in time—to medieval France in about 1450. Here she recalled her life as Alison, a young Egyptian servant in the house of Jacques Coeur, a merchant prince of that period. She described Coeur's intrigues in some detail and his fall from the king's favour after the death of Agnes Sorel, the king's mistress. Coeur was arrested, but here Alison's recollections ended, as she came to yet another violent end, quaffing a poisoned draught given to her by Coeur.

At first glance this past life looked very convincing. Alas, a second and third glance reveal that it was much more likely that these memories had their origins in Jane's current life. Jacques Coeur was a historical figure, and his life was well documented. Cryptomnesia was an obvious explanation. But one of the things that puzzled even those willing to believe in young Alison was that she made no mention of Coeur's wife and five children—characters who must have impinged at least to some extent on the life of a member of the household. This omission was difficult to explain even for those who assumed the case was one of cryptomnesia, because Coeur's family are mentioned in every historical account of him.

Again, it was Melvin Harris, an inveterate browser in second-hand bookshops, who found a possible explanation, in the form of a historical novel published in 1948: *The Money-*

man by C. B. Costain. This, Harris found, contained all the detail and authentic-sounding touches in "Alison's" life. Moreover, it made no reference to his wife and children because, the author explained, "they played no real part in the events which brought his career to its climax."

Suspecting that cryptomnesia is probably the explanation for at least one of Jane Evans's lives, it is difficult to argue that the York life doesn't have a similar explanation, even though the source has not been found. There is no doubt that in her hypnotic trance Jane felt she was living the life of Rebecca—the emotion she showed was genuine emotion, the terror she felt was real. Indeed, the intensity of the emotions expressed is the very thing that convinces people who watch past-life regressions that they really are watching someone who is being taken over by his or her past.

And yet one cannot regard this deeply felt and expressed emotion as proof of a past life. People under hypnosis experience imagined events as real. They are totally convinced of the hypnotic life they are living, and the intensity of their emotions is such that it can persuade not only the subject but also the observer that a genuine experience is being remembered.

If one is looking for evidence of reincarnation, these cases don't provide enough to be conclusive. A mixture of fantasy and cryptomnesia is certainly a possible explanation for the memories of both Virginia Tighe and Jane Evans, though it doesn't give anything like a complete answer to the questions they raise. But for the moment let's keep an open mind and look at another case that might bring us nearer to the point of accepting that reincarnation is a real possibility.

SHANTI DEVI FINDS HER FAMILY

One of the most convincing of all past-life stories is that of Shanti Devi, and it began in Delhi in 1930, when Shanti was four years old. According to her father, Shanti, unusually for children who remember past lives, began to talk later than his other children. But, more typically, she seems to have been very mature for her age, the peacemaker among the children, often behaving more like a small adult than a child. At the age of four she began to talk about her previous life as Lugdi, a woman who had lived in Mathura, a town 80 miles (129 kilometres) away, and had died the previous year. Her memories were often sparked off when she was eating or being dressed. She would comment on the food she was given, saying that it was not what she used to eat in her house in Mathura. She talked about her husband and her children, described the dresses she used to wear and the house she had lived in: "yellow stucco with large arched doors and latticework windows. Our yard is large and filled with marigolds and jasmine. Great bowers of scarlet bougainvilleas climb over the house. We often sit on the veranda watching our little son play on the tile floor. Our sons are still there with their father."

At first Shanti's parents didn't take this seriously, but eventually they were worried enough about these "fantasies" to ask their doctor's advice. He concluded that she was simply a bright child seeking attention, and tried to get her to admit that she was fantasising. But Shanti not only stuck to her story but horrified the doctor and her parents by describing to them in some detail the circumstances of her death during her last difficult confinement. Everyone agreed that an only child of Shanti's age could not possibly have known or understood the obstetric details she had described. But no one could offer any explanation for or suggest how to eradicate these memories.

Eventually, when she was eight, people began to take Shanti's story seriously. Shanti had not previously named her husband, as it is a Hindu tradition that a woman should not speak the name of her husband without good cause. Finally, she was persuaded to write down his name (Kedarnath) and address, and enquiries were made at the address she gave. It transpired that a man named Kedarnath did indeed live there, and that his wife had died in 1925, a few days after the birth of their son.

Kedarnath, however, though a Hindu, was not altogether convinced of his wife's reincarnation. Prudently, he sent a cousin, Kanjimall, who lived in Delhi, to call on the family and meet Shanti, under pretext of doing business with her father. Shanti herself opened the door to Kanjimall and immediately recognised him. She asked about her son and spoke about the family home and business, so impressing him that he went straight back to Kedarnath to tell him that his wife had been reborn.

There followed a strange family reunion. Kanjimall returned to Shanti's home, bringing with him Kedarnath and his son—their son, a boy only a year older than Shanti—and Kedarnath's new wife. As a test, Shanti was told that Kedarnath was her husband's older brother. But as soon as she saw him she insisted that he was her husband, and her emotions at the sight of her 'son' struck everybody who saw them as truly maternal. She seemed overjoyed to see him, wept as she embraced him, and ran to get her toys to show him. She also noticed that "her" jewellery was being worn by Kedarnath's new wife and reproached him, reminding him that they had agreed he would not marry again. According to Shanti's father, Kedarnath hung his head and said nothing. After a private talk they had together, Kedarnath announced that he was convinced that Shanti was indeed his former wife.

By now the case of Shanti Devi had become a *cause célèbre* in Delhi. The story was published in the Indian press. Mahatma Gandhi himself came to see the girl, and a committee of enquiry was set up to investigate her claims. It was decided that she should be taken back to Mathura to see if she could indeed recognise the places she claimed to remember.

Together with a lawyer, a prominent local politician, and the managing director of a newspaper, Shanti travelled to Mathura. Crowds gathered at the station to see her and to watch as, in an open carriage, she directed the driver to Kedarnath's house, pointing out several landmarks on the way. She also recognised "Lugdi's" parents and other members of "Lugdi's" family and, in the house, showed the committee a corner of a room where she claimed she had once hidden 150 rupees under the floor for safekeeping. Nothing was found, but Kedarnath then admitted that he had discovered the money after Lugdi's death and removed it. Altogether it has been estimated that Shanti made 24 correct statements about Lugdi's life, and that she gave no incorrect information. The many witnesses who met Shanti on her visit to Mathura were convinced that she knew more about Lugdi's life than could possibly be explained except on the basis of past-life memories.

Shanti Devi died in 1987 aged 61. She never married, and to the end of her life she maintained her conviction that she had lived before as Lugdi. She remained in touch with Lugdi's family and was an honoured guest at family occasions.

There is an interesting postscript to this story. Four years after Shanti's initial reunion with her family, in 1939, the whole case was reexamined by Mr. Sushil Bose. He interviewed Shanti, and for the first time asked her detailed questions not just about her previous life as Lugdi but about her death. What she told him seemed at the time preposterous. Shanti described how just before death she felt a profound darkness and then saw a dazzling light. She knew then that she had come out of her body in a vaporous form. She described seeing four men in saffron robes who had come for her, a beautiful garden and a river. Now, half a century later, this is instantly recognisable as a typical near-death experience.

This is a remarkable story, for the quality and sophistication of the data given initially by a four-year-old child, then added to and maintained throughout her life. Although the amount of detail and the narrative quality of her memory are common enough in adults remembering past lives under hypnosis, children's memories usually consist of only a few statements. To have such good recall of a past life, especially a past life as an adult, is rare in children. Despite considerable public interest, nobody suggested a source of information that she could have been using.

The story can't easily be dismissed as a plot of a lower-caste Indian family claiming a relationship with a higher-caste family in the hope of some material reward. Shanti's parents were discouraging initially, and Lugdi's family seems to have been put under no pressure to substantiate her claim.

Finally, and perhaps most convincingly, this story links into the literature of near-death experience. Before the 1970s, when Raymond Moody wrote his first book on the subject, *Life After Life*, little was known about near-death experience. Shanti's description has many of the typical features of near-death experience—her awareness of her consciousness leaving her body, her meeting with a being of light and then entering a wonderful garden—and also has cultural features (being collected by men in saffron robes) which are more typical of an Indian experience. It is highly unlikely that a young child could have invented this, and at that time no way she could have been told about it or read it. She believed she had the experience at the time of her death in childbirth in her previous life: we don't, unfortunately, know whether she had ever been seriously ill in her present life, and perhaps had a near-death experience that later surfaced as an apparent memory from a previous life.

But without this evidence we are left with little alternative but to believe that somehow she had acquired extraordinarily accurate and extensive memories of Lugdi's life. Perhaps she had actually lived the life of Lugdi. At any rate, if we accept the facts as they are given (remember all this happened over 60 years ago), we have to take the story seriously. It provides at least the prima facie case that's needed to persuade us to look more seriously at other people who are convinced that they too have lived a previous life.

2

Glimpses of the Past

I have been here before,
But where or how I cannot tell;
I know the grass beyond the door,
The sweet, keen smell,
The sighing sound; the lights around the shore,
You have been mine before,
How long ago I may not know;
But just when at that swallow's soar
Your neck turned so,
Some veil did fall—I knew it all of yore.

Dante Gabriel Rossetti

TWO of the people whose stories are told in the previous chapter—Virginia Tighe and Jane Evans—remembered their past lives under hypnosis. This shouldn't surprise us. Anyone who is a good hypnotic subject can be almost guaranteed to produce at least one past life, and often a string of them, when given a past-life regression; the suggestion is heavily implanted by the hypnotherapist, and under hypnosis most people are very suggestible indeed (see Chapter Seven). But the past-life memories of Shanti Devi are far more interesting. Nobody, as far as we know, ever suggested to her that she had lived a previous life. Her memories emerged spontaneously.

What is it that makes ordinary people leading everyday lives decide that for them this is the second (or even the third or fourth) time around? We know that past-life memories occasionally emerge in illness or under the influence of psychoactive drugs such as LSD. Strong emotions such as grief may trigger them too. But we don't know how common they are in a healthy person in a normal mental state.

Most of the spontaneously remembered past lives that

have been studied have occurred, like Shanti Devi's, in cultures where reincarnation is accepted, even expected. Much less is known about past-life experiences in the West, and indeed it is usually assumed that if they occur at all they do so very rarely.

It was therefore with little sense of expectation that we wrote an article about reincarnation in the *Daily Mail* and asked people who believed they or their children had memories of apparent past lives to contact us. The response to this was overwhelming—well over 300 people wrote to us—and made it clear that spontaneous apparent past-life memories are remarkably common.

Many people told us they had had the feelings for as long as they could remember; others said that their memories first surfaced in adulthood. Some people reported just one remembered past life; for others one experience seemed to open the floodgates of past-life memory.

Sometimes memories emerged in dreams, or in "waking visions," usually when the person was relaxed or in a meditative state—a state very similar, in fact, to a self-induced trance. "Sometimes it feels like dreaming," one woman said; "other times like watching a TV programme but you are in the programme." Very often the memories were triggered by seeing something or meeting someone who seemed familiar. And often people said they "just know" that they have lived before without really being able to explain why.

What is it that convinces someone that he or she has lived before? The best way to get a flavour of what it feels like to believe that you are remembering a past life is to listen to the accounts of people who have actually had the experience. John Cornwall, for example, describes himself as a very stable and level-headed type, and in fact a bit of a sceptic when confronted with the paranormal. This is his past-life memory:

From around five years old into my middle thirties and up to my forties I perceived an image when I closed my eyes. I would "see" a large square created with broken lines (dashes). These were gold and would form a rectangular pattern. Soon this would be followed by a "picture." The picture gave me the impression that I was

facing a large crowd of people. All these people had
their mouths open as if expressing horror or shock.
These people surrounded a square, black entrance, similar to that of the mouth of the entrance where foot-
ballers emerge from their dressing-rooms. The whole
scene was well illuminated. As the picture emerged I
experienced the feeling of trying to chew on a huge
sweet which was so big that it hurt me. It was accompanied by the feeling that my mouth was unable to operate normally.

This picture appeared frequently, sometimes every
time I closed my eyes. As time passed I got so used to
it that it became part of my make-up and gave me no
reason for concern. I am now 66 and the image and sensation with it has gone.

Imagine my shock when I was confronted with this
exact picture in a book I was reading during my fifties.
The book was the illustrated and abridged version of
The Rise and Fall of the Third Reich by William L.
Shirer.

Through a bit of research I did find out that a National Socialist member was actually shot in the mouth
while appearing on a stage alongside Hitler at an early
rally of the Nazi Party, in the late 1920s or early 1930s.
I was born on 31 January 1932.

While I would be happy to admit to having been the
King of Siam or some such person in my previous life,
I am not very proud to admit that I am fairly certain that
I was nothing more than an early member of the Ger-
man National Socialist Party who came to a sudden
end.

"I HAVE BEEN HERE BEFORE"

Most of us at some time or another have probably experienced
déjà vu, the flash of familiarity in a strange place that Rossetti
describes, or had the related experience (*jamais vu*) of walking down a road that we have been down many times before
but which suddenly and momentarily seems strange and unfamiliar. These moments don't usually last long, and they are

seldom intense enough to persuade us that what we are feeling has any basis in reality.

But for some people the *déjà vu* experience is much more intense. The person has a feeling of familiarity amounting to an absolute conviction that he or she has been here before, or seen this person or lived in this place. Many people have described past-life feelings which have this intense quality of recognition or belonging. Alan Rushton (pseudonym) here describes just such an experience:

> Before I left the armed forces a resettlement course was arranged for me at Catterick Camp in Yorkshire and lodgings arranged in nearby Richmond. The billet was shared with another warrant officer, and after unpacking we left the house for a stroll down to the town. At the bottom of the street he made a left turn and I immediately said, "No, the town's up there on the right. All that is round the next corner are some gardens and the road to Catterick." A surprising statement considering the fact that I had not been to Richmond before at any time in the past. As things tamed out I described the gardens before we reached them, but they were slightly different.

About ten years ago Vera Schonberg went on holiday with her husband to Egypt. Their trip included a visit to Abu Simbel. "We walked down a path with high rocks to the side of the temples, discussing them. I walked around the corner and went into total shock. I burst into tears, I was shaking, my legs had turned to jelly, I was laughing, crying, I felt happy, afraid, overwhelmed. I knew I had come home." She continued:

> After I had calmed down a bit my husband made me tell him exactly what was in the temple. I told him every detail, including the room I worked in as a High Priestess, to the right behind the last enormous column.
> When I walked up to the temple my husband—a total non-believer—pulled behind as he said I looked different, walked differently. I felt totally different,

shorter, darker, with a very full mouth and very high cheekbones. I took much smaller steps.

We entered the temple and I went into shock again, mixed with anger that common people were allowed in there, unheard of 3,000 years ago. After the guide took us around the main part, which was exactly as I saw it, he said we had half an hour to wander around. My husband asked me where my room was. I told him exactly as I had seen it. We went to the last pillar on the right, walked behind it and there was my room. I had come home. I spent that time crying my eyes out, I was so happy. By the end of the day I had remembered everything: my name, even my pet monkey and the bedclothes and décor of my room.

When I returned home I contacted a hypnotherapist and asked her to disprove it. She spent over an hour asking me everything about Egyptian life. I never faltered once. My husband still can't believe it. He reckons it's inherited memory. We checked all our books on Egypt to see if I'd read it, but no.

What is fascinating about this experience is the wealth of detail that Vera remembered, which seems to have proved remarkably accurate—even convincing to her sceptical husband and told to him before she entered the temple. It would seem that a possible past life is the only explanation.

However, ancient places such as the tombs of the Egyptian pharaohs do seem to exude a kind of magic, an atmosphere so powerful that it is almost tangible to people who visit them. Most of us, whether or not we believe in reincarnation, find our imaginations stimulated by such places, aware of the myths and legends associated with them and the hundreds or thousands of years of history that have preceded us there. And although we have no idea what being "sensitive to atmosphere" really means, certainly some people respond much more strongly than others to the atmosphere of such places. Could it be that they are picking up feelings and—who knows?—possibly even memories of the distant past? In the panoply of non-scientific explanations for these feelings, this is as likely as reincarnation.

In the early 1980s Elizabeth Hadfield was on holiday in Crete, where she had many friends and returned to many times, always feeling that she was going home. She set off one afternoon to walk to an ancient Greek fort two and a half miles (four kilometres) away which she had never visited. "I set off to walk over a dried-up waterbed and into an enormous olive grove as far as you could see. As I walked, it suddenly came over me: 'You have walked this track many a time—it isn't strange to you and when you go around the next bend there is a church.' And as I had envisaged, there was a small ancient shrine about 30 feet by 15 feet. I opened the olive-wood door—a wooden peg kept it closed—and inside was just a shrine with a Byzantine frieze and candles, and it felt right that I should be there. I walked on trying to capture more memories, but nothing happened."

Such experiences are by no means unique. Nine years ago Pauline Carter was on holiday in Yugoslavia. On a day trip to Rovinj, near the Italian border, she too was amazed to find that she knew what she was going to see as she wended her way through the streets. The three-storey buildings next to the sea were familiar to her. She knew instinctively the way to the ancient church up the hill, and felt a sense of returning home as she stood by the water's edge. She believes that she was previously Italian and lived in Rovinj, which until 1948 was actually part of Italy, called Rovigna. Pauline has a natural flair for Italian; she taught herself the language, and at her oral O-level exam (before she had ever been to Italy) was asked by the examiner how long she had lived in the country.

Maureen Saltman and Davina Williams both describe similar feelings of recognition when visiting places they had never seen before. Maureen Saltman was ten years old when she visited Lichfield with her stepmother. "I had never visited there before, or in fact heard of the place. We were walking up an alley when I stopped. I explained everything that was round the corner—windows, houses, etc. I had the feeling of crinoline dresses: in fact, I could feel myself in one."

Davina Williams had a similar experience when she went with friends to visit the former home of Lord Byron, Newstead Abbey in Nottinghamshire. "As we approached the large iron gates, I had an uncanny feeling I'd been there before, although it was my first visit. The guide showed us around the house, and one room which we entered contained a large red and black lacquered chest of oriental make. This had been brought home by Byron from one of his visits abroad. On looking at this I felt I had seen it before, but of course I couldn't recollect how or where."

Tom Burgess describes what happened to him in 1944, when he had just returned from serving in the RAF in the Middle East:

> I was posted to an RAF Regiment Depot at Belton Park, Grantham. One evening I decided to go into Grantham to have a look at the town, and I suddenly realised I had run out of cigarettes. I thought, Well, I'll just pop into the little shop around the corner in the main road that I was coming to. I knew this little shop had an entrance down a few steps below pavement level. On turning the corner I walked down the steps into the shop, purchased my cigs and as I strolled along the road I was suddenly struck by a very strange feeling, and suddenly asked myself, However did I know that shop was there, for I had never, ever been to Grantham in my life, yet before seeing this shop I knew just where it was, and it was low-ceilinged and darkish, being below pavement level.

Déjà vu is a quite common experience, but possibly more common among psychiatric patients, especially those with anxiety states or a neurotic illness, and people with temporal lobe epilepsy. In some migraine-sufferers, too, the typical migraine headache is accompanied or even replaced by mental disturbance or confusion that can include *déjà vu* feelings. People who are very fantasy-prone are also more likely to experience *déjà vu*.

Can we write off all the experiences described above simply as *déjà vu*? In a true *déjà vu* experience there is a feeling of familiarity, a feeling that you know what is going to happen *as it occurs*, and, many apparent past-life memories (Davina Williams' for example) certainly do fall into this category. What *déjà vu* does not do is to predict the future before it unfolds. Vera Schonberg's and Tom Burgess's accounts are particularly interesting as they seem to show some fore-knowledge of the place as well as recognition of it. Tom Burgess's account shows clearly that he knew about the shop *before* he turned the corner and reached it.

Of course, if we can explain these experiences of reincarnation in terms of *déjà vu*, we can equally well explain *déjà vu* in terms of reincarnation, and indeed this has often been done. Aristotle and Pythagoras both believed that feelings of *déjà vu* derived from a previous existence. In the nineteenth century the writer Frederic Myers (1895) believed that *déjà vu* was the product of ancestral and antenatal memories recollected through hereditary transmission of mental phenomena or images, and the twentieth-century philosopher and mystic Peter Ouspensky (1931) explained *déjà vu* as repetitive reincarnation working through the same situations. More recently, Professor Ian Stevenson, Professor of Psychiatry at the University of Virginia, a world authority on reincarnation, has suggested that perhaps in people who don't have any conscious memories of a previous life the *déjà vu* experience may be the tip of an iceberg—flashes of a memory of a previous life that cannot be brought further into consciousness.

MOMENTS FROM THE PAST

Spontaneous past-life memories are nearly always just fragments of a life, scenes picked out in the spotlight of memory from a story that seems to have no beginning and no end, and which often seems to come from nowhere. Barbara Conduitt describes very well the first time she became aware of these fragments of memory about five years ago. It began on a tour of Norwich, when she was looking down a long passage with arches open to a courtyard on one side.

> As I looked down the passage (which was lit by sunlight pouring through the arches), I had such an overwhelming feeling of sadness and disorientation that I was almost ill. The feeling was not with the place, but with the sunlight and the pattern it made on the walls and floor of the passage. I went on about my business,

but couldn't put the incident out of my mind. I can't think when I've felt such strong emotions over what I considered nothing out of the ordinary.

Later, I just sat and gave myself over to my recollection of the incident, and the memory of a little girl, about seven or eight years old, just poured into my mind. I do not know where she lives, or when she lived. All I know is that she lived in or near a church and that she was killed in some sort of battle. It was as if a film were being played—and as clear and vivid as if it were actually happening right before me. My memory of her is very vivid, as I remember her at her time of death, and then only because she had an out-of-body experience, and I/she could see what was happening to her. She is being carried by a frightened man, running down a long vaulted passageway, with pillars opening on to a courtyard on one side. She is roughly dressed, and barefoot, as is the man who is carrying her. He is calling for help, and outside can be heard the sounds of screaming and battle of some sort. She/I, the girl dies as the man is running down the hall—I can see her head fall back and her eyes are half-open. Her hair, which is curly, long and tangled, gets into her mouth and eyes. Then the picture fades away. The picture is very vivid, as it is a lovely warm, bright day and sunlight is streaming down the hill.

I've never been able to remember any more about her, perhaps because there was nothing eventful in her life that preceded her death—but I know I was she because of her hair. It is just like mine was as a child, reddish, tinted in the sunlight, and always tangled, and I feel her hair on my head when I see her. I do not see her often—but I am always vividly reminded of her when I walk down that sort of passage when the sun is shining. Poor child died violently, and in pain, or I do not believe she would have had an out-of-body experience.

I think I must have laid her to rest, because I can think of her now without the terrible emotion I felt when I first became aware of her. I don't think of her often, but I will never forget her. I really wish I knew more of the details of the time, the place, and what was happening outside the building where she met her death, but I don't seem to have any recall of that. She was just a little girl who died some sort of violent death—me.

I myself had an out-of-body experience when I was about 11 years old. I was dreadfully ill with pneumonia and was running a dangerously high fever. My mother and grandmother filled a metal tub with ice and water, and dipped sheets into the water and wrapped me in them to break my fever. Believe me, it was horrible! I finally just left my body and retreated to a corner of the room, up by the ceiling, and watched them work over the body in the bed. When that body's fever broke and they stopped wrapping it in icy-cold sheets, I went back and joined it. It must have been at least 30 years before I could put a name to what had happened, but I do believe that was all that saved my life.

DEATHBED SCENES

Awareness of your own death, and often a vision of your own deathbed, seems to be a quite common element of past-life memories. Shanti Devi's account of her death in her past life (see page 14) describes her awareness that her consciousness had left her body. The out-of-body experience, in which someone finds that he is outside his own body, usually seeing it from above, is a common feature of the near-death experience (about which we have written in a previous book, *The Truth in the Light*) and is frequently mentioned by people who have "seen" their own deaths in a past life. Barbara Conduitt's memory of watching herself being carried is typical. Lynn Lowe, too, remembers looking down on herself, watching the end of her life (see page 267).

Rex Caddick also watched himself die. During a self-induced hypnotic trance, Rex found himself in what seemed to be twelfth- or thirteenth-century France, where he felt that he was involved with the Templars, though he was not a Templar himself. He had been charged with taking a package to England for safekeeping, and managed eventually to cross to

Bristol in a tiny boat. "I went up a hill to a church and gave thanks for a safe crossing. I was stabbed to death while praying. I left my body and looked down on it and on my killer, and then as a bodiless entity I observed the church from above, the town, the earth and went out into an endless space where I seemed to 'hover' for a while before being whisked back to earth. It was an incredibly vivid experience and one which I found emotionally moving. Relating it here makes me aware how absurd it all sounds now, but that is what I experienced!"

Paul Clark (pseudonym) has memories of out-of-body experiences as a very young child and of experiencing a sense of fear at what he might remember. He also has a strong conviction that he once drowned. Despite knowing that some people who recover from a near-drowning say that it is a painless experience, he remembers it as being incredibly painful. It felt, he says:

> . . . as though I had been literally fighting for my life, perhaps in wartime, and this may have aroused me to desperate underwater struggles and tortured efforts to fill my lungs with air. The combination of pain and hopeless panic was about the worst thing I have ever experienced. In the midst of all this I had a "flashback" that the whole dread experience had happened before, perhaps more than once, and I knew how unspeakably bad it would become. Then, just as the anguish grew intolerable, my consciousness separated from my body and I thought, with profound relief, Thank God that's all over! I am sure that this was the moment of physical death. There seems nothing in my present life to inspire such a memory. I was always careful to stay within my depth while bathing, because the sensation of water in my nostrils always caused uncontrollable panic.

The near-death experience is now so widely reported that its characteristics have become part of our culture. When someone describes it now it is difficult to know how accurately they are describing their subjective experience and how much they have been influenced by what they have heard and read about what "ought" to happen. However, Paul's experience, like Shanti Devi's, occurred when he was a child, at a time when he would have known nothing about out-of-body or near-death experiences.

People can experience apparent memories of a past life whether or not they hold any belief in reincarnation. Mr. D. E. Rhodes, too, saw what seemed to be his own death in another life and considers himself to be a very logical and stable person—reluctant for this reason to consider the idea of reincarnation. He has no religious beliefs and isn't seeking confirmation of life after death or proof of reincarnation. It is life as it is today that holds his attention. He finds what happened to him interesting and puzzling, but nothing more than that.

From a very early age I have had an incredibly strong "vision" accompanied by an equally strong emotion. Both occasionally come over me and are as clear and vivid now as they have ever been. As a child I was unable to understand what I "witnessed," but as I got older the picture became clearer. I have no idea who I was or where I was, but the event is split into two parts.

Imagine the first part if you can. I know that I am male and that I am lying in bed in a heavily furnished bedroom; no bright colours, maroons and dark browns appear to be the norm. The room has one large window. It is daylight outside. I hear no sounds at all.

I can close my eyes now and see it all so clearly. The bed is of a very heavy ornate wooden type. The window is to my left. I cannot see a door at all. Also on my left sits a woman in a chair dressed all in black from head to foot. In heavy Victorian garb. She is looking at me and her hands are folded on her lap. I cannot see her face clearly; I think that she wears a veil. I have no idea who she is, but I "know her"!

The second part of the vision remains essentially the same, but now I am no longer lying in bed but viewing the scene from above the foot of the bed, looking down on myself and the lady. She has not moved. I get a great feeling of sadness and also one of "freedom," of having no more cares.

The images used to fascinate me as a child, and the only "connection" that I could make with what I saw in my mind's eye and everyday things was some of the very heavy ornate headstones in a local cemetery. I knew that certain of these had something to do with what I saw. I've always known that I was "alive" then when the events took place and that what I remember is my own death. I have no other memories or recollections prior to these events.

What is intriguing is how closely these glimpses of death in a past life resonate with reports of near-death experiences. The sense of freedom, of having no more cares, that Mr. Rhodes describes are very similar to the feelings often described in the near-death experience—almost always one is given the impression that the shackles of the body are cast off with no regrets. Both phenomena, reincarnation and the near-death experience, carry the implication that consciousness can continue after death.

In the following account it seems to have been a near-death experience in this life that triggered off apparent memories of death in a past life. Nineteen years ago Christina Edmonds had a near-death experience when she saw herself on a hospital bed surrounded by doctors and her husband. Since that happened she has had amazing and bizarre visions of what could have been a past life. While staying with an aunt in Yorkshire, she and her husband one day came across a ruin of a tower. "When I first saw this building I became very distressed but could not stop myself rushing up the steps in an effort to reach the inside of this place. Already in my mind I had envisaged how it was meant to be . . . I seemed to have no control whatsoever in this urgent quest to enter this building. Once inside it, the unbearable pain and torment which I started to feel made me afraid that I might be losing touch with reality. I raced up the stairs leading to the tower when fate intervened. I could not move, either up or down . . . My husband managed to get me down, and once outside I calmed down almost at once."

Later, her aunt told her that the building, Clifford's Tower, had been home to a large Jewish community who had lived within the tower and cut themselves off from the outside world. Rather than surrender to their enemies, they made a pact to commit suicide by throwing themselves from the tower.

Images of a past life very seldom offer a continual narrative with the story unfolding scene by scene. Instead, they are usually a series of flashbacks triggered by some event, and are often described as being like a "waking vision." Often they occur when the person is resting and relaxed, and yet the people who experience them are quite certain that they are not asleep or even on the borders of sleep. Beatrice Poulter describes an experience she had about twenty-five years ago which, she says, has stuck in her mind as vividly as the day she experienced it.

I was sitting in the garden, not asleep, not doing anything, just thinking I should be gardening, when I found myself walking out of what appeared to be a cave. I felt the heat of the sun strike me as I came out of the cool interior. I was wearing a long garment, loose and light coloured (sari/toga-like), and when I turned round I saw several people hesitantly following me. There was a tall, bearded man with a staff, other adults and some children—about eight or nine people. All were dressed in similar clothes to me. I felt that I was a woman, although I cannot be sure about this, however. I knew that it was because of me that all these people had survived "something" (?winter, siege?), and we could now emerge safely into the sunshine again. It seemed that it had been a long time since we had dared to venture out. I had a feeling of satisfaction and knew that all the others were grateful to me for "saving" them.

I don't remember anyone actually speaking, but I know we all smiled at one another in relief. It all took place in a moment, and all the feelings I had were just something I *knew* as if I were that person.

I don't know if it is evidence of reincarnation, or perhaps I was travelling in time—or was it my imagi-

nation? Anyway, it seemed very real at the time, and
still does seem like genuine memory.

People who have these experiences very often have genuine
difficulty in knowing whether or not they are the product of
imagination. One forty-two-year-old woman who describes
herself as "down to earth, pragmatic and rather a sceptic" told
us what happened one day when she was giving a massage to
a friend. The tape she had put on as background music was
playing an Eastern/Arabian-sounding passage. During the
massage she looked down and saw her friend "as a man in a
white turban, with a black moustache and black eyes, sitting
on a horse in a souk and laughing. I am there, too, also a man
in a turban, with black eyes, moustache and goatee beard, and
sitting on horseback." At the time she put this down to her
vivid imagination. But a fortnight later, when she was again
giving her friend a massage, "I felt her suddenly go limp and
when I looked up her eyes were closed and she appeared
asleep. For some moments I found I could not move my hands
and then suddenly felt a release of energy from her hips, and
I said 'Here it comes.' With that she opened her eyes and said
that she had just had a strange dream. She said she had
dreamed of a citadel up on a dusty, dry plateau which had a
big round dome. The dome had collapsed and all these men
had come running out of the gate." She continued:

> I interrupted her and then described what the men were
> wearing (turbans and red waistcoats), their weapons
> (scimitars and round shields), the vantage-point where
> Gail was standing (high up and on a level with the
> plateau but looking across a valley at it) and the sur-
> rounding countryside (low mountains, very dry and
> dusty and very hot). She told me that I had described
> exactly what she had seen in her dream.
>   This could all be the result of my wacky imagina-
> tion, but I truly doubt it.

Suzanne Mancey's flashback of memory also occurred when
she was resting and relaxed. She had just put her two-year-old

son to bed for his afternoon nap and had sat down to relax
with a cup of coffee and read the paper.

> I remember this so clearly. I'd started reading a piece
> on some political issue or other, when this very, very
> strange thing happened—I was standing on the running
> board of an old vintage car, except that to me it wasn't
> vintage. I could see the leather seats, a. deep maroon,
> the wooden dash of the car, and on the floor there were
> wooden slats. I reached down and picked up a leather
> football. All I could see of myself was my sweater,
> which had a red band around the jumper's edge. I was
> tall, male, and I sensed in my twenties. As long as it
> would take you to reach into a car and pick up a foot-
> ball was all it lasted. And there I was still clutching the
> paper. I thought, Oh my God, I'm going bats. I hadn't
> dreamed, I was wide awake. Then I thought I'd read
> something about vintage cars, so read through every ar-
> ticle in the *Guardian* to make sure—*nothing*.

Mrs. M. Williams describes how some years ago she was
meditating with a group of people in a church. The object of
meditation was to learn how to relax, and not to explore past
lives. However, after a few minutes of relaxation she had
seven flashbacks of what seemed to be past-life experiences.
Most of these were brief visual images, but very vivid: for example, kneeling at the end of a bed with a white counterpane
in which a person lay dying, praying for their recovery; pa-
trolling a square in Russia in freezing fog, on horseback,
dressed in military uniform; taking part in a religious ceremony in a large cathedral.

It is extraordinarily difficult to empty the mind. When we
are relaxed, thinking of nothing in particular, even trying to still
the mind through meditation, visual imagery tends to arise.
Some techniques of meditation are especially likely to facilitate
visual imagery, but the meditator is always told to ignore any
distracting and intrusive imagery that arises and to continue
with the focusing of attention, which is the object of the meditation. It is interesting, then, that Mrs. Williams did not see

the scenes as simply intrusive visual imagery, but as meaningful flashbacks of her own past lives.

Children who talk about what seems to be a previous life usually stop doing so when they are around six or seven years old (see Chapters Thirteen and Fourteen), and it is always assumed that they stop because they eventually forget. But many adults have told us that feelings about a past life are something they first experienced in childhood and have remembered ever since.

Mrs. V. English is now 46 years old, but in her early childhood, at around the age of five or six, she kept having dreams or flashbacks of being in a cave or stone tunnel with what she felt to be her family. "I say felt, because I cannot remember faces, just feelings . . . There were a couple of 'grown-ups,' and I remember feeling just small but safe. We all wore grubby, smelly animal skins, and the area was lit by a massive fire. The feeling of safety was quite clear. It was also very dark once I was away from the glow of the fire. It was only in my late teens and twenties and early thirties that it was very clear. As I've got older, I've hardly ever thought about it again. But to have such clear thoughts so early in life—we had no TV then, and as far as I know I hadn't seen cavemen or women in books (baby books didn't have such things, did they?)"

The feeling that this lifetime is only part of a much greater picture seems to be a natural part of many people's consciousness, so much so that often they say they cannot remember when they *didn't* have this certain knowledge. Olive King (pseudonym) says that she was born believing in reincarnation, although it certainly wasn't part of the family's belief system (her father was a Baptist, her mother orthodox C of E). She says: "I just accepted it but never talked about it to anyone. One of my first memories is being taken through a very poor area in winter. Some of the children were not wearing shoes, and I can remember thinking, When their parents are born again, I hope they haven't got any shoes."

Paul Clark (pseudonym), too, had similar feelings as a child. "I have always had the feeling, even in early childhood, that there was 'something before' my birth—some radically different previous experience of existence, sometimes joyful, sometimes traumatic or awe-inspiring, which I had no language to express."

Occasionally, someone's memories, and their belief in a past life, remain so strong that they can dramatically affect the course of their present life. Jenny Cockell, whose story is described more fully on page 121, retained her memories, and much of her adult life has been devoted to finding her "lost" family. Ronald James Pafford is someone else whose past-life memories have, he says, "been the mainspring of my life." He said:

My earliest memory as a tiny child was of complete frustration at finding myself in a heavy unresponsive body again. I had been sent back from a place where I was completely happy, because I had failed in my previous life. I was going to have to live through the same life again and get it right this time. I think that this was mainly due to the fact that I always saw the future quite clearly, so that when something happened it was as though I was living through the event for a second time.

I am certain that this belief did not originate from my parents. They were entirely orthodox in their beliefs and had probably never heard of reincarnation. I was in no doubt about why I had failed in my previous life. It was due to total fear. As a child I used this fact to my own advantage, and on being told to carry out some task always replied: "I couldn't do it last time that I was alive and won't be able to do it now." I expect my parents just hoped that I would grow out of it, which I eventually did do.

However, this memory has been the mainspring of my life. As a child, if I saw drunken men fighting on the other side of the street I had to cross over and, quaking, walk through them. It was the cause of my leaving a comfortable happy home to go to sea when I had just left school. It was the cause of my volunteering for the armed forces at the outbreak of war, when I was in a reserved occupation. It was also the reason why I volunteered for service on an active front when I was in a comfortable station in England. It was also the reason

why I joined the Sussex police at the end of the war. I
hated the idea of pushing myself forward and knew that
as a policeman I would be forced to do so.

It is interesting to compare Ronald Pafford's feeling of frustration at finding himself in a heavy unresponsive body again
with this extract from *Autobiography of a Yogi* by Paramahansa Yogananda, one of the great spiritual figures of the
twentieth century: "I still remember the helpless humiliations
of infancy. I was resentfully conscious of being unable to
walk and to express myself freely. Prayerful surges arose
within me as I realised my bodily impotence."

Other people, too, describe very early memories which are
extraordinarily similar to Ronald Pafford's. David Hird
strongly believes he was in the First World War and can remember as a child "being totally devastated about being back
here again. On more than one occasion there has been an internal voice screaming at me, 'Not again'."

Simon Wallace (pseudonym) also has memories that have
convinced him that birth is not the beginning and death is not
the end. "I'm sure I can remember travelling at great speed
and then being profoundly disappointed—I'm sure this was
being born. I remember thinking, what happened to the light?
In the ward I was nicknamed 'the dormouse' because I was always asleep or at least had my eyes shut—what they didn't realise was that this was because I was so disappointed to be
here. I also had very clear notions of right and wrong. Kept
thinking I must hang on to the knowledge that this life is not
what 'they' think it is!" For him, too, this feeling of having
been born with knowledge of the way life should be lived has
been a guiding force in his life.

For these people and many others, knowledge of reincarnation is just that—something that they *know*, not part of a belief system they have been taught or brought up with. They
know it just as they know that they are living and breathing in
this life. Susan Locke says:

Those who believe in reincarnation have usually done
so all of their lives, and like myself thought everybody
else thought the same way. It was not until I was well

into my twenties that I discovered that not everybody had the same feelings. I personally am aware of at least four other lifetimes, and all I can say to you is that when you have a past-life experience the memory is a different experience. I will often go quite cold and have goose pimples on my arms or my hair will stand up. I could for instance be doing something and remember I had done it before. One of my first jobs was working at the Briglin pottery, where one of my responsibilities was kneading the clay. You get into a rhythm kneading clay, and with that rhythm came the memory that I had made bread before. I was a baker in the sixteenth century in this country. Smell is another trigger. Quite recently I was standing in a village supermarket queue and in front of me was a man (a baker) with an apron covered in flour. He had a distinct smell about him, rather sweet and yeasty, and it made me have a very strong reaction. I went cold and my hair stood on end. I knew it was a past-life recollection from my days as rather a fat male baker.

Explaining something doesn't always help us understand it. In purely physiological terms, Susan Locke's experience can be quite easily explained. The temporal lobe is the area of the brain which creates a sense of meaning and adds the tag of familiarity to experiences. It is closely connected to the part of the brain which mediates the sense of smell and also to the structures that mediate emotion. Susan Locke's description is a very clear and precise one; almost everything she describes which leads her to think that she has remembered a past life takes place in that particular area of the brain—the temporal lobe. She describes the emotional arousal—goose pimples, hair standing on end—which occurred simultaneously with the familiarity tag—knowing that this had happened before. She mentions that the rhythm of kneading clay triggered the memory of kneading bread, and that on another occasion it was a "sweet, yeasty smell" that triggered the same memory. Both rhythm and smell are potent activators of temporal-lobe functioning.

But while we can certainly say that Susan's apparent past-life memories may be due entirely to an abnormally sensitive temporal lobe, functioning in a semi-deviant way, how much further does this really take us? Does the explanation necessarily invalidate the memories themselves? We could equally well argue that it is just because she has this abnormally sensitive temporal lobe that she is able to gain access to past-life memories that elude those of us with less sensitive temporal lobes.

Very often what seems to be a memory of a past life is triggered by something the person sees or hears. Ronald J. Buzzard:

> Some years ago I was watching the TV when a news item came on concerning some frozen bodies of a Norwegian exploration party that had been found. They then showed on the screen the preserved bodies of two members of the expedition that had been found frozen in the ice. I immediately knew that one of the bodies was mine, and that parts of the body had been removed at the time of my death to feed the still-living members of the expedition.
>
> It was reported in a later news bulletin that the thighs and buttocks of "my" body had been removed postmortem, presumably as a cannibal act to preserve the lives of those remaining alive. I have no further instances of this happening since then of this or any similar event.

Albert Crow describes how, when he came home from the war in 1947 (he is now seventy-four) his father took him to Sandwich. "As we walked through the old churchyard, without prior thought or reason I suddenly pointed to a grave, turned to my father and said: 'Dad, that's me down there!' I was shocked at saying such a thing, but convinced that I was right. My father looked serious and told me that all our relations had lived in this village, the family name was Payne, and the gravestone bore that name."

INVOKING THE PAST TO EXPLAIN THE PRESENT

For many people, belief in a past life seems to make sense of feelings they have about their present existence. It seems to explain why they feel particularly drawn to a place, or have an interest no one else in their family shares. John Gallagher's conviction that he has lived before, for example, seems to be based more on elements of his present life than on any memory of a past one:

> I am convinced that I have lived before and had a seagoing existence. The pull of the sea has been so strong all of this life. I long for it and, what's more, I can take a trip on a ship where everyone around me is as sick as a dog . . . Also what convinces me more of this previous seagoing existence, I can eat the same menu for many days, as did old mariners, and, I may say, without getting tired of the same old menu.

Mrs. D. Beecham, a thirty-seven-year-old mother of four and a childcare lecturer, believes she lived a previous life as a male consultant surgeon. This life was, she says "probably in the 1940s some time. I sort of remember me as a middle-aged man in a fawn suit helping others. Since my adulthood I have had numerous experiences whereby I have been at a scene where individuals have needed medical help. At these times I seem to know exactly what to do and do it. I want to take over and organise so the patient can get the best possible care."

Alan Waddington:

> Since a very early age I have had a deep interest in Roman Britain and have visited many sites in the UK. There have been times when I have travelled down a road and felt that it was Roman in origin. I am also fascinated by the sea and things nautical. I enjoy travelling by sea when able to do so. I also imagine living in a cottage in a coastal area such as Devon and Cornwall, and for some reason tend to be drawn towards Teignmouth. I know that there are some family connections with both Cornwall and Somerset. Could these feelings have

more to do with inherited DNA through the generations?

Belief in a past life can often provide a satisfying explanation for a present-day phobia, especially when the victim can think of nothing in his present life to account for it. As far back as he can remember, Martin Houghton has had a phobia of flying, and specifically of falling out of an aeroplane. Even the noise of low-flying aircraft instils terror in him. He believes that this was because he was in the RAF during the Second World War, was shot down, and died when falling out of the aircraft. He says: "This all sounds very dramatic, and I feel slightly embarrassed about discussing it, but my feelings and emotions are very real to me."

ICONS AND IMAGES

Certain themes recur over and over again in the imagery of past-life memories. Countless early settlers trek in covered wagons across the plains of North America. Tribes of American Indians pursue them. Squadrons of pilots from both world wars hurtle to their certain deaths from blazing aircraft. A surprising number of early Egyptians, too, figure in twentieth-century Western past-life recollections. Martin Houghton has almost a full house of previous incarnations not only as a Second World War pilot but also as a "very wealthy but cruel Egyptian man who lived in a huge house with sandy floors and painted interiors." He also remembers living as an American Indian before the years of colonialism. "I lived surrounded by mountain ranges in a huge tepee/wigwam with a wife, small children and two elderly people. My companion was a wolf, with whom I hunted, and I feel that the bond I had with him was very deep and spiritual."

In her childhood, Jeanne Jones used to dream of a long, narrow underground room with wall-paintings. Then, on her fortieth birthday, in 1981, she had the "vision" that convinced her that she has had a previous life as a queen of ancient Egypt. She was watching television with her husband, and was in a relaxed state of mind, when:

Suddenly I became aware of something heavy and
tight-fitting upon my head and simultaneously the vision of myself, wearing the crown and seated upon a
dais within a temple, appeared, seemingly superim-
posed upon the television screen. I recall being able to
see the river through the open spaces between the pillars on two sides of the temple (indicating that the temple was situated on a bend in the river) and being
surprised that these pillars were rectangular rather than
round, as I would have imagined. But what I remember
most vividly was that the whole peaceful scene was
bathed in the most beautiful golden light. Viewing the
scene from above, I wanted to go down into it in order
to see more and made a conscious mental effort to do
so, but, as I did, the vision faded, leaving me feeling
highly emotional.

   Aware of the criticism often levelled at people like
me that they nearly always claim to have been someone
famous or important, I can only repeat what I saw. I do
not know *who* I was, only that I lived in Upper Egypt,
since I was wearing the white crown of that region—an
unglamorous affair which does not appeal to my aes-
thetic sense. Had I *imagined* myself as a queen of
Egypt, I should certainly have opted for more elegant
headwear!

   That experience is as vivid to me now as it was then,
and I feel that there are many people "out there" who
have had similar experiences but hesitate to tell any but
their closest confidants for fear of being thought over-
imaginative or worse! But I know that my vision was
not the product of an overactive mind but a spiritual experience which was given to me for a purpose.

Some time later Jeanne saw a picture of an artist's impression
of the inner sanctum of the temple at Dendera in Upper Egypt
which corresponded exactly to the vision she had seen, except
that it was viewed from ground level. Finally, in 1989, she
was able to see the temple itself on a visit to Egypt with her
husband. The inner pillars of this Ptolemaic temple were rectangular, and the temple had been situated on a bend in the

River Nile (though through centuries of silting, the temple was now some distance from the river). Moreover, the temple proved to be the only existing temple in Egypt to have a crypt, which corresponded to the underground room which she remembered from her childhood dreams.

The sinking of the *Titanic* is one of the icons of disaster for this century, a story told and retold, which has captured and recaptured the imaginations of every succeeding generation. Several people who wrote to us described memories of having gone down with the *Titanic*, and all were spontaneous memories, not produced under hypnosis.

Anne Sharpe was reluctant to tell her story just because of the high media profile of the *Titanic*. She can't give place-names or dates or any other "proofs" except that she has *always* known the date the *Titanic* went down. As she says, it is a story so well known that had she wanted to manufacture "proof" it would have been easy.

> I can remember starting to watch the film *A Night to Remember* again about 20 years ago and feeling really ill. I was happily watching until the drowning scenes, when I began to experience a panic attack—sweating palms, palpitations, shortness of breath, dizziness, etc.—and was unable to watch any further. I have since had these feelings, but only when involved in discussing or watching things about the actual sinking of the ship. I also feel sick and slightly hysterical. I am not, however, frightened of water or boats or the sea, am a good swimmer and enjoy it (again, if I felt I was making it up it would be more effective to say I'm frightened of water!). I am very drawn to any information on the *Titanic* but I am aware that thousands of people share this interest. But I only developed this interest *after* I had the feeling I was on the ship, not the other way around. I have read the passenger list looking for some feeling of recognition, but other than feeling sure I was not Captain Smith or any of the rich or famous passengers I could not pick out a name.

Annette Adaway, too, believes that she was aboard the *Titanic*. It is, she says, something she has known ever since she was little. She has collected memorabilia from the ship to enable her to feel close to it. She cannot remember dying but can remember the cold. Miss J. Fermor believes she has lived many times and feels "an absolute horror" over anything connected with the *Titanic*. Tessa Grimmer is now 19 and describes how even as a child she had an obsession with the *Titanic*.

Dr. J. Davis has a similar feeling:

> Probably my feeling, like most people's, is fantasy, but I do often wonder whether I picked up a soul on that February 14, 1912, when my mother would have been about two and a half to three months pregnant with me. The reason for my supposition (or suspicion) is that my early abiding memories are that I was lying face-downwards on a small plank, which was going up and down all the time, and I had to hold on in fear of falling into a rough sea. These memories went on for some years in my childhood. Perhaps these suppositions are all fantasy, but the rocking on the plank is still very real in my mind.

Why the *Titanic*? Since the *Titanic* sank, tens of thousands of sailors have drowned in the First and Second World Wars and there have been many peacetime disasters at sea. If these memories were truly representative of drownings at sea, then one would predict that many other maritime disasters would figure in past-life memory recall. But it seems that the *Titanic* captured the public imagination in a way that few other shipwrecks have done and so stimulates a disproportionate number of past-life memories. Of the approximately three hundred people who told us about their past-life memories, eight had memories of dying in the *Titanic*. None had memories of any other maritime disaster. This does suggest that *Titanic* memories are over-represented in our sample and that, on a worldwide scale, the number of *Titanic* reincarnees is probably greater than the 1,500 who actually went down with the ship.

The Holocaust is one of the most shameful chapters in

twentieth-century history, and for Westerners it is probably the one that throws up the most powerful visual images and most haunts our memories. For this reason alone it is perhaps not surprising that it is a source of past-life memory for many people. Rabbi Yonassan Gershom suggests in his book *Beyond the Ashes: Cases of Reincarnation from the Holocaust* that Nazi victims have been reborn *en masse* since 1945. Rabbi Gershom says that when he acts as spiritual adviser to the people who have told him about their Holocaust memories, he tries not to judge the experience as either true or false. He doesn't claim that every case he is told about is actually reincarnated from the Holocaust, but some stories do strike him as being more probable than others. What convinces him? He lists several criteria, including dreams containing specific details the child could not be expected to know, non-Jews who, despite having had no contact with Jews or Judaism, show habits or behaviour which indicate knowledge of Jewish customs and rituals, and Jews who, even though they come from a non-religious background, seem to have an innate grasp of Jewish mysticism.

This vivid account of apparent past-life memory of a Holocaust victim was told to us by David Strickland.

For most of his life David, who is not Jewish, has had an intense fascination with Judaism. He has studied the cabbala and learned enough Hebrew to be able to read it. From the age of about 13 he began to show what he himself describes as a morbid fascination with anything to do with the horrors of the concentration camps. "I just had to out-stare the horror photos of tortured, mangled bodies, and it extended to nightmares. I could not let it go, as though I were a masochist, and it took over my life and took away my carefree childhood completely. I had to face down and spiritually confront this evil, whereas any other person would quickly avert his attention away. At eighteen I was so depressed I joined a religious cult, which ended up devastating my life."

In 1991 David had a spontaneous flash of a past life of his own great-great-grandfather, which seemed to make sense of many things in his present life—an obsession with trains and railways, for example, which is something he has had for as long as he can remember. He became interested in the whole topic of past-life regression, learned to meditate and go deep within himself. In this state of self-induced trance, he started to have visions of a rocky and wooded landscape containing an American Indian settlement and saw scenes of an Indian brave and his wife. Although he was looking at both figures from a vantage-point outside them, he knew the brave was himself. David stresses that the importance of both these lives for him was not the physical memories but the attitude of mind and the perceptions he had. They seemed to show him things about himself, and lessons he had learned.

Some time later David was shown another life, and for him this was even more remarkable because it seemed to explain his obsession with concentration camps and Judaism, and also the feelings of depression which had troubled him most of his life.

My present life has been mostly one of sorrow and torment, and now I know why. In bed one day I had vivid flashbacks of being inside a prison camp with rows of barracks. I was a thirteen-year-old girl in a ragged grey frock, barefooted on a muddy ground, my left hand holding the right hand of a little brother. The two rows of barracks on the left and right ended at a T-junction, with a building going across my vision. The year was 1944, and I knew I was going to die and that I would never see my brother again. I had another vision where I was ill and being carried on a stretcher at an obscene pace to my place of death. Lying on my back, the roofs of buildings swept past my vision, and the last thing I saw was a tall chimney with black smoke escaping from it.

A few days later, without my mentioning this disturbing vision to anyone, a friend wrote to me from Oklahoma in the USA to say that he had come to the knowledge that he and I had been victims of the Holocaust in World War Two. This was totally out of the blue; our deep and prolonged correspondence up to that point had touched on many spiritual issues which showed me that he and I had lives which closely paralleled each other.

So was it a past life as a Nazi victim who died at the age of thirteen that caused David's interest in Judaism, his morbid fascination with concentration camps? Or was it that an impressionable and sensitive thirteen-year-old, reading for the first time about the Holocaust with its dreadful, unforgettable images, was so affected and obsessed that (by his own account) it coloured his whole life and precipitated a severe depression? In these circumstances it seems almost inevitable that, once his interest in past-life regression had been sparked, flashbacks should re-create these scenes and convince him of a previous life as a Nazi victim.

How valid are these sudden feelings that a past-life experience is a reality? The easy answer is to say they are just tricks of the brain, experiences that occur in altered states of consciousness, such as in deep relaxation or on the borders of sleep, or in meditation, or in response to a specific stimulus, the meaning of which has been forgotten. One can almost always find a brain mechanism to account for any particular experience, and, using a current scientific framework, a trick of the brain is the only permissible explanation.

What is more difficult is to decide whether these experiences have a meaning and validity over and beyond this "scientific" explanation. If we want to employ this wider interpretation, we have to regard consciousness as something that extends beyond the brain. We have to use an entirely new explanatory framework and employ entirely nonscientific concepts.

For example, Ian Stevenson and others have suggested that violent death in a previous life is one of the most common features of past-life memory, something we will return to in the next chapter. It's quite true that violent death figures very prominently in many of the accounts that we have received. But does this then mean that the images seen are literal visions of a previous violent death? Or that the present-day memory bank of your brain has presented knowledge it has somehow acquired of a previous violent death in symbolic, almost archetypal, twentieth-century images? Or that these are simply random memories, not personal ones, plucked from a universal, cosmic memory bank? You can see that abandoning a scientific framework doesn't necessarily make explanations any easier—simply more plentiful.

Our current neuroscience says that the mind is only elaborated by neuronal processes within the brain and does not extend beyond it. So any other explanation but an entirely brain-based one has, in scientific terms, to be wrong. Where we are likely to run into trouble is if we try to "prove" (or, indeed, disprove) reincarnation in a scientific manner, within the old scientific framework. But there is no harm in trying—and, indeed, trying to prove it in this way is a very interesting exercise.

There are plenty of cultures throughout the world where reincarnation is widely accepted and is part of the religious and cultural belief system. But all the accounts in this chapter were given by ordinary men and women living in a Western culture that doesn't hold with such things at all. One thing we can be sure of is that whatever science can prove or disprove, past-life feelings occur independently of culture or of belief; they are part of normal human experience.

3
Culture and Reincarnation

The best definition of Europe is that it is that part of the world that does not believe in reincarnation.

Albert Schopenhauer

CLAIMS of reincarnation are certainly easier to find and investigate within a culture that accepts and even expects them. Whether they actually occur more frequently within such a culture is less certain. It seems more likely that past-life memories are part of the normal spectrum of human experience, so that a similar proportion of people in every culture will have them. There may also be racial or personal characteristics quite separate from cultural expectations which make some people more likely to have these memories than others. There is a strong link, for example, between psychic experiences and past-life feelings. Some experts suggest that in Thailand (where reincarnation is part of the culture) children are less outgoing, less impulsive and more contemplative than Western children. Might these differences facilitate remembrance of past lives? Are the children who have these experiences more imaginative, more given to fantasy than others?

Professor Ian Stevenson, of the University of Virginia, has studied possible cases of reincarnation for over twenty years and has collected an enormous body of data—over 2,600 case studies, far more than any other researcher. Most of his cases are from cultures in which reincarnation is accepted, and most of his data comes from studies of children who remember past lives.

One of the conclusions he has reached is that it is difficult to find much of a pattern in terms of consistency of culture, time and place from one incarnation to another. He has found that the death-to-rebirth time interval, for example, varies from thirteen months to nineteen years. Some people migrate hundreds of miles between one life and the next; others may be reborn into the same family, in the same place. Almost all Tlingit Alaskan Indian cases are reborn within the same family, almost all Asian Indian cases are of rebirth outside the family.

However, Stevenson believes that one can lay down some sort of a blueprint about reincarnation. Most of the cases of apparent reincarnation which he has studied have three or four of the following features in common.

1. PREDICTION OF REBIRTH

Occasionally an old person may predict his own rebirth. This sometimes occurs in North American Indians, and less often in India, Tibet and Burma. The person who makes the prediction may also select the parents for his next incarnation.

2. ANNOUNCING DREAMS

Sometimes a prediction of reincarnation is made in a dream. "Announcing dreams" occur often in North American Indians, in Burma, Thailand, Turkey and occasionally elsewhere. Usually it is a woman who is pregnant or shortly to become pregnant who has the dream; occasionally it may be a close relative of hers—a mother or grandmother, for example. The person who is to be reborn appears in the dream and announces his intention. In Western society, announcing dreams and predictions of rebirth are rare.

3. BIRTHMARKS AND BIRTH DEFECTS

In many of the cultures Stevenson has studied, the parents or relatives of an infant born with a birthmark or birth defect will attribute this to an injury or some other event that took place in the person's previous life. The mark is often in a similar place, and it may even look similar. Usually, but not always, the person who is the reincarnation claims to remember some events in that life. Stevenson maintains that he has found such birthmarks or defects in about a third of all the cases of possible reincarnation he has studied.

Parents are much more likely to look for and notice birthmarks in cultures where reincarnation is not just accepted but is expected to occur within the family. Among the Tlingit of south-eastern Alaska and the Igbo of Nigeria, for example, a birthmark may help to identify the baby's previous personality or be a sign that some notable person has reincarnated; in Burma it may confirm expectations of a reincarnation that has been predicted by an announcing dream. Indian Hindus and Sinhalese Buddhists, while they believe in reincarnation, do not expect a baby to be a reincarnation of anyone they knew. They therefore tend not to pay any particular attention to birthmarks or defects, or at any rate do not see them as being important in establishing a baby's previous identity.

4. MEMORIES THE PERSON SEEMS TO HAVE ABOUT THE PAST LIFE

Memory of a past life would seem to be a *sine qua non* for any possible case of reincarnation. However, where a strongly held belief in reincarnation is part of the culture, a family may persist in believing that they have evidence that a child is the reincarnation of someone they have known, even if the child never talks about a past life and seems to have no memory of one.

More often, though, a child will start talking about his or her previous life between the ages of two and four, and go on doing so until between the ages of five and eight, occasionally later. Most mention the mode of death of the person whose life they claim to remember. Usually they talk with great intensity about their past life, sometimes speaking of it in the present tense, even when they are old enough to have some concept of time. Sometimes they show confusion about their own identity, especially if they remember a past life in which they were of a different sex, or have memories of themselves in an adult body. The children may feel conflicting loyalties towards their past and present families.

5. RECOGNITION BY THE PERSON OF PEOPLE, PLACES OR OBJECTS WHICH THEY HAVE KNOWN IN THEIR PREVIOUS LIFE

Parents of a child whom they believe is a reincarnation often deliberately seek out the family or community where the child previously lived to see if he or she shows any recognition. In Western cases the child is more likely to show spontaneous recognition and say things like "I lived there once" when passing a particular house or "My mother had a dress like that" when looking at a picture or a model in a museum.

6. FREQUENT OCCURRENCE OF VIOLENT DEATH IN THE PREVIOUS LIFE REMEMBERED

This is a common feature in many of Ian Stevenson's cases, and he acknowledges first that the proportion of violent deaths in past lives is much higher than in the general population, and also that in the cultures he has studied the incidence of violent death is in any case much higher than in, for example, a general Western population. He does not claim that violent death is a necessary condition for a memory of a past life, only that it appears to be a common one.

The belief that a violent death in a past life is more likely to be remembered is, on the face of it, an odd one. It can be argued that violent deaths are usually swift and that the brain will therefore have no chance to register and record the event. People who have been knocked unconscious in a violent accident, for example, seldom have any memory of the actual event when they recover. One might expect the slow, lingering traumatic death of an illness such as pneumonia to be more likely to be remembered, and yet this seems not to be the case. But perhaps the effects of the violent death are due not directly to memory but to the strong emotional impact of being wrenched from life.

Probably this is because for all of us death is surrounded

by rituals. Even people who have no particular religious belief usually believe that the dead should have a decent funeral. In many cultures there is a belief that if your death is violent you won't make the normal transition from life to death. In Western culture you are likely to hang around as a ghost, either troubled or troublesome, returning to haunt your murderer or the place in which you died. In Eastern cultures you will probably return as a reincarnation. Some cultures even have special rituals for people who have met a violent death to ensure that they are properly laid to rest and do not return.

7. UNUSUAL BEHAVIOUR ON THE PART OF THE SUBJECTS

Often the person shows behaviour or personality traits that seem to correspond much more closely to the previous personality than to anyone in the present, living family. These behaviours tend to persist, in the case of children, long after the memory of the past life itself may have faded. They may show phobias related to the previous personality's death (as in the case of a child said to have died in an air crash in a past life who developed a flying phobia), or a particular liking for the people, food or clothes enjoyed by the previous personality. A craving for alcohol or tobacco may be attributed to a similar addiction by the previous personality. There may be a nostalgic longing for the previous family and insistent demands to be taken to see them. Children may play out their previous life or work as a teacher or doctor or car mechanic, for example.

Children may also show odd or inappropriate sexual behaviour. If they come into contact with their previous sexual partner, or someone who resembles him or her, they may show precocious sexual attention towards them, and if their "spouse" has remarried, they may seem jealous or resentful of the new partner. A child who remembers a past life as a member of the opposite sex may show a desire to cross-dress, or a preference for the games usually played by the opposite sex.

Finally, and much more rarely, they may exhibit a skill or talent which they have apparently never been taught, but which seems to be innate within them—the ability to speak a foreign language, for example, or to play the piano fluently.

CULTURAL DIFFERENCES

Even among those cultures that accept reincarnation as a fact, beliefs about it differ. The Tlingit of Alaska, for example, have a matrilineal society and think it important to be reborn in the family of one's mother, whereas the Igbo of Nigeria, who have a patrilineal society, think it important to be reborn in the family of one's father. Not surprisingly, when cases of supposed reincarnation do occur, they reflect those differing beliefs.

INDIA

Most Indians are Hindus, who believe in reincarnation, as do the much less numerous Jains, Buddhists and Sikhs. Most Muslims and Christians do not believe in reincarnation. Hinduism emphasises the doctrine of karma—that your conduct in one life will have an effect on your circumstances in your next life. If you are seriously wicked you may reincarnate in an animal body. Claims of sex change from one life to another are uncommon.

BURMA (MYANMAR)

Most Burmese are Theravadan Buddhists who believe that if there is misconduct in one life this may lead to "payback" in the next, or even, as Hindus believe, to rebirth as an animal. A sex change from one life to the next is quite common. Usually the past life is someone from the same family or someone who was at least known to the family. Announcing dreams occur frequently and birthmarks and birth defects are widely regarded as evidence of reincarnation. People often claim to have some memory of an existence between death and rebirth.

THAILAND

The Thais are mostly Theravadan Buddhists. Their beliefs are similar to those of the Burmese Theravadan Buddhists, but the Thais have fewer same-family cases and claims of sex change are less common, though more frequent than in other countries. Many claim some memory of experience between death and rebirth.

In both Burma and Thailand there are strong regional expectations about rebirth. Although the doctrine of "no soul" in Theravadan Buddhism would seem to preclude any idea that memories can be carried from one life to a subsequent one, Buddhism accepts the idea of some kind of link between lives. There is, in Buddhism, a gradual accumulation of merit through deeds, and this can be carried over to a subsequent life. In Thailand there is a strong cultural expectation of a conscious out-of-body intermission between two successive lives, which makes memory of a previous life possible.

SRI LANKA
Tamils are mostly Hindus; otherwise most Sinhalese are Theravadan Buddhists with beliefs similar to Burmese and Thais. But there are few same-family cases, and announcing dreams almost never occur.

TURKEY
Most cases of reincarnation occur among Arabic-speaking Alevis, a sect of the Shiite branch of Islam. They hold a belief in reincarnation but without supposing that conduct in one life influences circumstances in a later one—conduct in Islam is assessed at the Day of Judgement. Sex changes almost never occur.

LEBANON, SYRIA, ISRAEL AND JORDAN
Most cases occur among the Druse, whose religion derives from the Shiite branch of Islam but has separated from it almost completely. Reincarnation plays a greater part in the life of the Druse than in any other religion. Druse parents nearly always encourage their children to tell them what they can remember about their previous lives, and a large proportion of Druse children are born with past-life memories. The Druse believe reincarnation as a newborn baby occurs immediately after death, and always with the same sex as in the previous life. Conduct in one life does not affect the circumstances of a later one, but is rewarded or punished at the Day of Judgement.

TLINGIT OF ALASKA
Most are formally Christians, but their traditional religion includes belief in reincarnation. They do not believe in sex

change from one life to the next, or in animal reincarnation. Many believe that you can influence the circumstances of your next life before death: for example, by wishing for particular parents in the next life. The Tlingit also regard birthmarks and birth defects as identification marks of a previous incarnation. Announcing dreams are fairly frequent.

HAIDA OF ALASKA AND BRITISH COLUMBIA

The Haida are formally Christians, but their traditional religion persists and includes a belief in reincarnation. Most don't believe that sex change can occur. Neither do they believe that humans can reincarnate as animals, although they do believe that reincarnation is possible in two or more later physical bodies ("soul-splitting"). Announcing dreams are common, but attempts to identify a previous incarnation through birth defects and birthmarks are less common than among the Tlingit.

IGBO OF NIGERIA

Although most are formally Christians, they still adhere to their traditional religion, which includes a strong belief in reincarnation. When a new baby is born, they believe it is important to identify the person of whom the baby is a reincarnation, and for this birthmarks and birth defects that correspond to wounds or other marks on a deceased person are important. Sex change is accepted and common. The Igbo, as well as some other groups of West African people, believe a baby who dies may be reborn in the same family, die again as an infant, only to be reborn yet again into the same family. These are called "repeater children"—the Igbo have developed strategies for thwarting the intention, as they see it, of the baby to die young.

Overall, in Stevenson's cases there is an unequal balance between the reincarnated sexes. A sex change is claimed in 12 percent of the cases Stevenson has collected. Three times as many girls say that they were boys in previous lives as boys who say they were girls. Only in Burma were there more cases of reincarnated women than men. In most other cultures boys outnumbered girls by about three to one and by two to one in cases where the previous life ended in a violent death.

Stevenson suggests that there may be cultural reasons for this preponderance of male past lives. In many Asian countries, for example, women are expected to take a low profile; publicity resulting from a claim to reincarnation might damage a woman's chances of marriage. Among the West African Igbo, a male-dominated society, more interest is likely to be shown in and more attention paid to a boy's previous incarnation than a girl's. Finally, he suggests that in these cultures men's lives are more eventful, and therefore more memorable, than the lives of women.

There seems to be no hard-and-fast rule governing change in socioeconomic status from one life to the next. Princes may reincarnate as paupers and vice versa. Ian Stevenson has pointed out that of his Indian cases, two-thirds were better off in their previous life, one-third worse off. Some critics of his research have suggested that this is because fantasy or wishful thinking plays a large part in the recovered memories. In Stevenson's view this is unlikely: in India there is no moral or social high ground to be gained by claiming a past life that is markedly better than your present one; all it suggests is that you may have done something pretty dreadful in it to deserve such demotion. Moreover, people who have been "demoted" in their present life tend to alienate the rest of their family either by boasting of their previous circumstances or complaining about their present ones.

REINCARNATION IN THE WEST

Mainstream Christianity believes in the immortality of the soul but not in reincarnation. Instead, the belief is that at death souls go to some kind of intermediate state where they await the resurrection of the body—a prospect that seems a good deal more improbable and less desirable than any notion of reincarnation.

But even though reincarnation is not an accepted part of either the Jewish or the Christian tradition, it is a belief which is probably much more widespread than is generally acknowledged. An article on reincarnation in the *Daily Mail* in

March 1998 elicited over 300 letters from people who had either had memories of a past life or at least held a belief in reincarnation. A *Sunday Telegraph* Gallup Poll in April 1979 reported that 28 percent of all British adults believed in reincarnation, as opposed to 18 percent in 1969. And despite the fact that reincarnation is a belief incompatible with Roman Catholicism, an official survey on attitudes among Britain's Roman Catholics, prepared by Michael Hornsby-Smith and Dr. Raymond Lee of the Sociology Department of the University of Surrey, found that 27 percent admitted to a belief in reincarnation. The apparent strengthening of belief in reincarnation may well be a reflection of a general weakening of conventional religious faith and the encroachment of New Age beliefs. Surveys have also shown that people whose religion is important to them are less likely to believe in reincarnation (or, incidentally, in the devil, astrology or ESP).

However, a belief in reincarnation is still not generally accepted within Western culture, and so people tend to keep quiet about it if they or their children have memories of a past life. Children who talk about their "other family" are often discouraged by their parents, and such cases seem to be quite independent of any family belief in reincarnation. The parents are highly unlikely to try to identify a previous incarnation. In any case, memories are seldom specific enough for an identification to be made. Predictions of rebirth and announcing dreams are rare. Birthmarks and birth defects are not regarded as having any link with a previous life (unless, as in the case of the Pollock twins [see page 229], they are used to confirm an existing belief). Past-life memories, recognition of people or, more commonly, places, and odd behaviours, phobias or skills are the most common "markers" of an apparent past life in the West. Quite often, too, there is a suggestion of a violent end to the previous incarnation.

America is the only other Western society in which there has been a serious study of people who claim to remember past lives. Ian Stevenson has compared a sample of 79 American children (43 boys and 36 girls) with cases in Indian children and found some interesting differences.

Most Americans do not believe in reincarnation. Stevenson found that many of the parents he talked to were distinctly uncomfortable with the idea. The statements their children made about a previous life often conflicted with the families' religious beliefs, and when the children made them they were frequently scoffed at, scolded or even punished.

In about a third of Stevenson's cases he was not able to find out whether the family had any particular interest or belief in or knowledge of reincarnation. Of the remainder, about 16 percent occurred among children whose parents did believe in reincarnation, and 37 percent had heard of reincarnation and had at least some interest in it. In 20 percent the family had a general interest mi parapsychology, but in the remaining 27 percent they had little or no knowledge about reincarnation. The families Stevenson studied tended to be Christians, to be residents of small towns and villages, and to have had little education beyond high school.

The most obvious difference Stevenson found between these American children and those he had studied in India was that the American children made far fewer specific statements. They seldom mentioned names, for example. Of 266 Indian cases, 75 percent mentioned the name of the person whose life they remembered; only 34 percent of the American children did so. Overwhelmingly, the person whose life the American children felt they remembered was a member of their own family, such as a grandparent or a sibling who had died before the child was born. The single exception was a child whose past-life memories indicated that he was someone who had been a close friend of his mother. This has to raise the possibility that these children may have elaborated a fantasy about a past life based on what they had learned in a normal way about some family member.

On the other hand, only 16 percent of the Indian children believed that they were a reincarnation of a relative. In some cases the two families concerned had known each other, but in almost half the cases the families lived far apart, had never met and had no knowledge of each other.

Both groups of children began speaking about their past life at around the age of three, but the American children tended to stop speaking about it at around five, about twenty months earlier than the Indian children—perhaps because they got no positive feedback or encouragement from parents, and no attempt was made to verify what they said. The two groups made about the same number of different statements about their lives—usually around fourteen. The Indian children were much more likely to mention the way they died: 78 percent of them did so, and of these 56 percent had died a violent death. Only 43 perent of the Americans mentioned their mode of death, but of these 80 percent remembered dying violently. In both cultures, many of the children who remembered a violent death had phobias about the instrument or mode of death.

More American children (15 percent) remembered life as someone of the opposite sex, and nearly all of these were girls who remembered life as a man; only one boy remembered life as a girl. Of the Indian group, only three percent claimed to remember a previous life as someone of the opposite sex; a third of these were boys, two-thirds were girls. In both groups the life remembered was usually a very ordinary one. None of the children claimed to have been a famous person or to have performed extraordinary or heroic deeds—in stark contrast to many of the past lives remembered by adults under hypnosis.

Both Hindus and Buddhists believe that animals as well as human beings reincarnate. But even in southern Asia, despite this wide belief, claims that humans have reincarnated as animals, or animals have reincarnated as humans, are extremely rare. Professor Ian Stevenson has collected only about thirty such cases. Most are humans who claim to remember an incarnation as an animal; occasionally a human will identify an animal as the reincarnation of a human being. In the West such claims are rarer still. So the following story of Ruff the spaniel, told to us by Dr. June Alexander, is unusual, particularly as it describes the apparent reincarnation of a dog as another dog—an event that most people would agree fits far more comfortably into the natural order of things than any trans-species reincarnation.

One of my dogs—a springer spaniel called Ruff who died age sixteen in March 1988—always travelled in the car with me, slept by my bed and was very close. The hour he died Tuff and Rufus were born, two liver and white spaniels with nine black and white siblings of

black and white parents. Tuff came to live with me
when he was about fourteen weeks. I took him in the
car to visit a residential home where Ruff had visited
weekly all his life, seen the old ladies, then went upstairs to the matron's sitting-room, where I had tea and
Ruff a chocolate biscuit. To my amazement, having
seen the residents, I noticed this puppy clambering upstairs and going along the corridor to matron's sitting-
room, then pawing at the cupboard where the chocolate
biscuits were kept! Two weeks later we went to visit my
mother, who lived in a block of seventy-two flats at
Blundellsands near Liverpool. The puppy jumped out
of the car and ran to the correct block of flats, up on to
the first floor and into the correct flat. More than that,
Ruff always used to find a mirror in the dining-room
which went down to the floor and always enjoyed sitting down and "laughing" at himself. To my amazement, when I went into the flat this puppy was sitting
by the mirror with his lips curled up "laughing." I have
no explanation.

Dr. Alexander adds that as he grew older, Tuff behaved like all
the usual wayward springers; just as seems to happen in the
case of children, Tuff's apparent past-life memories seemed
to fade.

"SOLVING" A PAST LIFE

In the many cases he has studied, Professor Ian Stevenson has
made meticulous attempts to check every statement made by
someone claiming to have memories of a previous life, and to
discover the identity of the previous incarnation. If a memory
of a past life contains a great deal of detail which can be
proved to be correct *and* it can be proved that there is no way
the present personality could have known it, then Ian Stevenson regards the case as "solved."

When a society believes in reincarnation there are usually
well-recognised links between one incarnation and the next—
reincarnation is expected to occur (and may even be predicted) within the family, for example, or at any rate in the

same neighbourhood, and usually within a limited time-frame. Identification within this framework is feasible.

However, very few Western cases are solvable in this way. The statements that children give seldom contain enough specific, verifiable information to enable their stories to be checked out. Many of the past-life memories of adults, particularly those that are remembered under hypnosis, seem to be more romantic, less culture bound, and usually contain very few specific, verifiable statements. The scenarios that appear most frequently—the tales of Indian braves and intrepid settlers, visions of ancient Egyptian temples and of death in battle—are an accurate reflection of the cultural icons and preoccupations of our age. They are also, surely, an indication of a natural sense of drama and love of romance common to us all.

Westerners are much more likely to remember a previous incarnation in another culture. It seems that in our past lives we can go anywhere, do anything. We can cross boundaries of time, culture, even sex. When there are literally no limits on our past-life experiences, when we are as likely to be the reincarnation of a sixteenth-century European peasant, an African slave girl, an American Plains Indian, or a passenger on the *Titanic*, the chances of verification are virtually zero. Ian Stevenson, too, has found that the most striking difference between children he has investigated who apparently reincarnate within their own culture, and those who claim to have had a previous life in a country or culture quite different from their own is that in cross-cultural cases the child is never able to give enough information for any of his or her claims to be verified.

Most of us are ordinary people leading unremarkable lives, and the chances are that if we *have* had a past life it will have been equally unremarkable and ordinary. It will also be difficult to verify. There is no argument, for example, about whether Florence Nightingale or Genghis Khan were real people or not. But someone who claims to be the reincarnation of Florence Nightingale or Genghis Khan is a mite less convincing than someone whose claims to a past life are more modest—an estate agent called John somewhere in the south of England whose surname you can't quite remember, for example. However, the more obscure a personality, the more difficult it is to find proof that he or she ever existed, though of course if such proof *is* found, it is all the more convincing. Names, place-names, dates, all need to be reasonably accurate if anything like proof is to be found.

What seem to emerge most strongly in Western past-life memories are visual and emotional impressions. Hard data such as names and dates are seldom produced. Perhaps this should not surprise us. Visual and emotional impressions, rather than names and dates, are the stuff of which most of our memories are made in this life. We may remember the torment of being bullied, for example, long after we have forgotten the name of the child who bullied us. There is no reason to suppose that memories of a past life should be any different.

But this does, of course, make it very difficult to check out the facts of a past life. The most easily verifiable facts—names, addresses, dates, etc.—may not loom as large in the past-life memory as incidents that made a great visual or emotional impact but which cannot be checked.

It is very, very seldom that a past life can be "solved" in the way that Ian Stevenson attempts to solve it. What happens much more often is first of all that correct statements are mixed with incorrect ones, in variable proportions, and that there are usually a lot of near misses. In one particular case of Ian Stevenson's, for example, the parents of a boy called Imad Elawar believed he was claiming to have been one Mahmoud Bouhamzy, who had a wife called Jamilah and who had been fatally injured by a truck after a quarrel with its driver. When the Bouhamzy family were traced, it was discovered that he was called Ibrahim, not Mahmoud, that he had a mistress, not a wife, called Jamilah, that he had not died in an accident at all but had witnessed his cousin Said who had indeed been killed in such an accident . . . Those who are so disposed will say that these inaccuracies invalidate the whole story; those who are more sympathetic will be inclined to take the view that it is impressive that the boy was so near the mark so often and that one should not expect him to have perfect recall.

LOOKING FOR EXPLANATIONS

Reincarnation is one way of explaining a host of phenomena—the feeling of familiarity with places or people, the fact that you seem to have information or skills or talents that you know you have not acquired in this life, or even memories of what seem to be other people's lives or experiences. It can also give an explanation for the inequalities of this world which seem so unfair. But there are other ways of explaining these phenomena, some rational and scientific, others irrational and entirely outside the current domain of science.

We have to start with the rational. Past-life experiences may be the product of fantasy or imagination, for example, motivated by the unconscious needs of the person and sometimes unconsciously generated. They may be dramatic examples of the quite common *déjà vu* experience. They may simply be self-deception or a fanciful kind of fraud. Dissociated states (including the so-called multiple personality) are another possible explanation. Or it may just be that memory is playing tricks on us.

If none of these seems to provide an adequate explanation, then we have to abandon the scientific and the rational and look elsewhere. Often a child may have not only the looks but also the gestures, habits, predilections or personality of some other family member. We know that some tendencies—criminality or alcoholism, for example—are inherited. "He's his grandfather all over again," people who have not the slightest belief in reincarnation may say, whether they are talking about the way a child's ears stick out or his or her sweet smile or foul temper, or tendency to steamroller anything that might obstruct a desire to get his or her own way.

All these are indeed characteristics that can be inherited and don't require any other explanation than currently accepted genetic mechanisms and family cultural influences. One of the most intuitively appealing alternatives to the theory of reincarnation is that we inherit not only the physical characteristics of our ancestors but something of their memories too. It is popularly supposed that memories of experiences might leave physical traces within the genes, which could then be transferred to the next generation when they can be re-experienced. In several cultures—the Igbo of Nigeria, the tribes of north-western North America, for example— when someone remembers a past life it is nearly always as a member of their own family or extended family. So if memories could indeed be passed on through the genes, these cases of reincarnation could easily be explained.

Unfortunately, the theory of genetic memory does not stand up. The only kind of genetic memory that science recognises is the memory that is already encoded in the genes at birth. The genes determine the protein structures that go to make up the next individual. Some of these proteins determine the structure of the brain and, in simple animals, also determine certain instinctual behaviours. Even if memories left physical traces in the cells of the brain, for these to be transferred to the next generation these complex and widespread memory traces would have to be transferred to the egg or sperm which contains the genetic material for transfer to the next generation. There is no known mechanism by which this could be done.

So it is difficult to see how the genes could acquire memory of a lifetime's events and, even if this were possible, how these could be passed on using the normal mechanism of inheritance, from parent to child. Neither could it explain how someone born into a different family, a few months or even years after a previous personality's death, could have inherited these memories through the normal genetic mechanism. Even if memories *could* be transmitted via the genes, and reincarnation occurred within the same family, a child could still only receive genetic memories of events that had occurred before he or she was conceived. Many people who remember a past life say they remember their previous death. It is difficult to see how they could pass on this particular memory to their descendants.

Some interesting non-scientific theories are often advanced to account for the phenomenon of past-life memories. One set of theories makes use of parapsychology. The point about parapsychology is that some parapsychological processes are thought not to exist in linear time. Thus, it is possible to know what is in the past and what is in the future, and to become aware of other people's previous life experiences through retrospective telepathy. We may then interpret these experiences as our own past lives. Parapsychology does not necessarily say that these lives are our own, simply that we resonate with past experiences, though we may of course interpret them as our own. (See chapter 16, page 300.)

Another non-scientific theory is that there is a common memory pool—something akin to Jung's collective unconscious or the morphic resonance theory of Rupert Sheldrake (see page 300)—that certain people under certain conditions can "tune in" to. Yet another suggests that the experience is the result of a shift in time, a step back into the past.

These are all quite logical and interesting alternatives to the theory of reincarnation, but they don't actually solve anything as they are outside our current scientific structure—they simply raise more questions that have to be answered. So perhaps we should start by looking at the rational. And because the best evidence for reincarnation lies in the memories of past lives, we should start by looking at memory.

4

The Tricks That Memory Plays

The richness of life lies in memories we have forgotten.
Cesare Pavese, *This Business of Living: Diaries 1935–50*

MEMORY is that most paradoxical of the senses—at the same time so powerful that even fleeting impressions can be stored, forgotten completely, and then reproduced in perfect detail years later, and yet so unreliable that it can play us utterly false.

Elizabeth Loftus, professor of psychology and adjunct professor of law at the University of Washington, has demonstrated just how easily the memory of an event can be distorted by giving new and misleading information about it. She devised an experiment in which subjects were asked to view a simulated car accident at an intersection with a stop sign. After the viewing, half the subjects received a suggestion that the traffic sign was a yield sign. Later, when all the subjects were asked what traffic sign they had seen at the intersection, those who had been given this false information tended to claim that they had actually seen a yield sign and not a stop sign. Those who hadn't been fed this misinformation were much more accurate in their recollection of what sign they had seen. Professor Loftus suggests that misinformation can invade our memories when we talk to other people, when we are suggestively interrogated, or when we read or view media coverage about some event that we have experienced ourselves. The more the original memory has faded through the passage of time, the more easily it can be distorted.

It is even more disturbing to discover how easy it is to implant false memories of events that never happened at all, and how difficult it is to distinguish false memories from true ones. A recent report by the Royal College of Psychiatrists indicates that there are numerous cases of women who have, in therapy, developed memories of sexual abuse in childhood which have later proved to be false. Some of these memories are in direct conflict with physical evidence—a woman may have memories of rape or abortion, for example, which she is convinced are genuine, even though medical examination confirms that she is still a virgin.

False memories are often created by combining actual memories with suggestions received from others. Just how easy this is to do has been convincingly shown by Professor Loftus and her colleagues. They wanted to find a way to plant a "pseudo-memory" that would have been mildly traumatic had it actually occurred but wouldn't cause too much emotional distress either when it was "remembered" or when the subject discovered that it was, in fact, only a "plant." They decided to implant a memory of having been lost in a shopping mall or large department store at about the age of five. For each subject they prepared a booklet that contained three short accounts of events that had actually happened in the person's childhood (from information gleaned from close family members) and one that had not—the mythical lost-in-the-mall incident. (They also sought confirmation from relatives that the subject had never, to their knowledge, actually been lost in a shopping mall as a child.) The account included being lost for some considerable time, crying and being helped and comforted by an elderly woman before finally being reunited with the family.

Twenty-four subjects were each asked to read the four accounts in their booklet and then write what they themselves remembered about each event. If they didn't remember it, they were asked to write "I do not remember this." At two later interviews they were reminded of the events, though these were not read to them verbatim, and again asked to try to recall the four events in as much detail as they could.

All the participants recalled about 68 percent of the true events immediately after reading the booklet, and again at each of the follow-up interviews. Seven of them, however, remembered all or most of the false event as well, and in the two follow-up interviews six subjects (twenty-five percent) continued to claim that they remembered the false event. There were differences between the true memories and the false ones—more words were used to describe the true memories, and they were felt to be more clear. But an onlooker hearing the events being described would have had difficulty telling whether the account was a true memory or a false one.

Other, similar experiments have shown that imagining an event can increase someone's belief that it actually happened. Having imagined it makes the event seem more familiar, but eventually the source of the feeling is forgotten, so that it may be thought to be a real memory and not an imaginary one. False memories can also be induced when someone is encouraged to imagine experiencing specific events, whether they really happened or not.

When people try to recall a new experience, they usually remember much of what they actually experienced. But, when questioned, they also usually claim to remember things that were not truly part of what they experienced. Research workers in America who have been able to test split-brain patients (people whose left and right hemispheres have been partially surgically separated—an operation sometimes performed to relieve very severe epilepsy) have found that this kind of creative rewriting of an event is performed by the left hemisphere. The right hemisphere produces a much more veridical account.

Exactly how and when such false memories are laid down we don't yet know. Some researchers think that they are recorded in the brain at the time of the event; others believe that people develop a schema about what happened and retrospectively fit other events that are untrue, although consistent with their schema, into their memory of the original experience. Research at Dartmouth College by Dr. Margaret Funnel and her colleagues suggests that it is indeed this interpretive mechanism of the left hemisphere that is responsible. The left hemisphere is constantly seeking the meaning of events, looking for order and reason, even when there is none, and this continually leads it to make mistakes. It tends to overgeneralise, often constructing a past that *might* have been true, rather than remembering one that *was*. The right hemisphere presents a truthful, literal account, but it does not seek to go beyond the facts presented to it or to find explanations for why events occur.

One can speculate that this capacity of the left hemisphere is more highly developed in some people than in others. If so, then this might provide us with an explanation of why some people remember past lives and others don't. These people may "believe" what their left brain presents more readily than the right.

The ease with which memories can be implanted is shown by the age-regression techniques used by some hypnotherapists. It is highly unlikely that any adult can recall genuine narrative memories from the first year of life, because the hippocampus, which plays an important role in the forming and storing of long-term memories, is not yet fully mature. (You might not remember, for example, being stung by a bee at this age, but you might well have a feeling that bees are nasty.) Workers at Carleton University devised a technique for implanting "impossible" memories about events that happened soon after birth. They told their subjects that they had particularly well-coordinated eye movements and visual exploration skills, and that this was probably because they were born in hospitals that hung swinging, coloured mobiles over the infants' cots. To confirm whether they had indeed had this (purely fictitious) experience, two methods of age-regressing the subjects were used. Half the subjects were hypnotised, age-regressed to the day after their birth and asked what they remembered. The other half of the group were not hypnotised, but were also age-regressed using a guided imagination technique. About half of both groups reported "remembering" seeing the coloured mobiles over their cots, and even more reported other infant memories such as doctors, nurses or bright lights. Of those who reported these memories, 49 percent believed that they were genuine memories; only 16 percent said they were merely fantasies.

One of the problems about investigating past-life memories, then, is that distortions and inaccuracies in informants' memories are particularly likely to happen in societies in which reincarnation is accepted—indeed, expected. In some societies, such as among the Druse, it is important to know a dead loved one's next incarnation and equally important to learn the previous incarnation of your newborn baby. It is easy to see how families may unintentionally deceive themselves by weaving very slender evidence into a myth that pleases both families. Parents trying to make sense of a few comments their child may have made which seem to suggest that he is talking about a previous life may unconsciously elaborate them and build up a picture of the kind of person he is talking about. They may then start to search for someone who seems to fit this picture. If someone in the family has had an announcing dream, the unwitting baby may be forced into a role almost as soon as he is born. Parents may treat him as if he were the reincarnation they'd been led by the dream to expect. They may encourage and reinforce characteristics that remind them of the dead person without even realising they are doing so.

FORGOTTEN MEMORIES

The past is a source of endless fascination and innumerable story lines. There is hardly a period of history which has not been re-created for us as a film or play or novel, a television costume drama or an informed and informative documentary. Memoirs, biographies, the reminiscences of an older generation can all hold us spellbound for a while in another age. Usually we forget most of the information we are exposed to, often so completely that, if through some faint trigger of memory it suddenly surfaces again years later, we feel sure that although we know it we have never learned it, at least not in this life.

The emergence of these "forgotten memories" is called cryptomnesia, and the capacity of the mind to reproduce events that have been so completely forgotten that the surfacing memory seems to have come from nowhere is truly astonishing. The case of Blanche Poynings is essential reading for anyone interested in reincarnation because it shows so clearly the wealth of detailed information that can be hidden from the conscious mind, how deeply it can be buried, and how genuinely unaware the person may be that they have ever acquired it. The case shows how greatly most of us underestimate the capacity of the human brain to absorb information, whether or not a conscious effort is made to retain it.

This case was investigated, and ingeniously solved, by Dr. G. Lowes Dickinson for the Society for Psychical Research and published in the Proceedings of the Society for Psychical Research in 1911.

Miss C. (we are not told her real name) was the daughter of a clergyman, and Dr. Lowes Dickinson described her as a simple, straightforward character with a strong sense of humour. She had a good general education and a strong interest in psychical matters. One day in 1906 she agreed to be hypnotised by a doctor for a series of experiments. The results were a surprise to them both. Miss C. found herself "going up" into "the blue," a strange world with no time and no space, where, if she thought of anything, she immediately saw it: "If I want to see anything, it is there at once, just as real as if I hadn't made it up. . . ."

At the beginning of one of these sittings, Miss C. began to speak: "Standing beside myself. Can't stop here now. Got to a different place. Lots of people. Real people. They have been alive. I don't know where it is. Never been there before. Perhaps 100 years ago."

It was in this place that she met and fell into conversation with a woman who gave her name as Blanche Poynings. Blanche seems to have been the Tara Palmer-Tompkinson of her day, good company, a great gossip, and a name-dropper with a large circle of distinguished friends.

Blanche told Miss C. in staggering detail about her life, her connections with the court of Richard II, and her great friend Maud, Countess of Salisbury. She talked about members of her own family and of Maud's, giving their names and the names of members of their households, describing their family affairs, activities and fortunes. Blanche herself seems to have been no intellectual. She was impressed that the countess could write her own name, and although she described the earl, Maud's husband, as a cultivated man and a poet, she could not quote any of his poems because "she never remembered that sort of thing."

She was, however, full of information about the clothes that were worn. "She used to wear brocaded velvet, trimmed with ermine, and a high-peaked cap of miniver. She wore blue velvet, embroidered with gold. Men wore shoes with long points which were chained to their knees. They had long hair cut straight across the forehead." She described the food that was eaten: "three kinds of bread, simmel, wastel and cotchet, eaten by different classes," and her favourite dish, lampreys stewed in oil. She described the medical treatments of the day (the doctor "used to bleed them for everything") and talked about the time she had spent at court and the royal figures she had met.

But perhaps the most intriguing thing about these conversations is that they could not really be described as conversations at all. When, in the trance, Miss C. was asked what language Blanche talked, she said that she didn't talk but only communicated thoughts. When asked what Blanche looked like, she said first "she wears only her blue mist" and then that "She has white hair, is tall, with dark eyes. But she looks like that because she was like that when she died. She can look any age." Asked what Blanche looked like at the age of eight, she said she had "long brown hair, long dress and sleeves with grey fur round the edge . . . [she was carrying] what she thinks is a doll. But really it's only a block of wood. They hadn't got any proper toys then. They made their own."

When Lowes Dickinson checked the details of these conversations he found that the historical information relayed by Blanche was astonishingly accurate. Time after time he found that what she had apparently told Miss C. about the Earl and Countess of Salisbury proved to have been true. However, of Blanche Poynings herself he was able to discover very little, except that she had indeed been one of the ladies-in-waiting at Richard II's court.

Miss C. was genuinely at a loss to account for her apparent knowledge of the period. She had never studied it, and when the only historical novel she remembered reading about the period, *John Standish*, was examined, it was clear that this could not have provided her with the facts and framework for her story. And yet Lowes Dickinson was convinced that there must be some rational explanation. Then one day he went to tea with Miss C. and her aunt—a woman who shared her niece's interest in spiritualism. They began to talk about planchettes. A planchette is a small board (supported by castors) and a vertical pencil which, when fingers are placed lightly on the board, will draw or write messages without any apparent guidance by the people using it. Like a Ouija board, it can be used for spirit communication. Miss C. showed Lowes Dickinson how she had learned to use a planchette to draw faces that could be seen as faces whichever way up they were viewed—something she could not do by conscious effort. Lowes Dickinson was not particularly impressed by the faces. But the demonstration did give him an idea. He suggested that Miss C. should try to communicate again with Blanche Poynings, this time through the medium of the planchette, and she agreed to do so.

Contact with Blanche was made almost immediately. Lowes Dickinson first questioned her about things to which he already knew the answers. Her responses were accurate. Then he began his real objective, to try to discover the source of Miss C.'s information about Blanche.

Q: How can we confirm what you are telling us?
A: Read his will.
Q: Whose will?
A: Wilshire's [Blanche's fourth husband]. He died first.
Q: Where is it?
A: Museum.
Q: What part?
A: On a parchment
Q: How can we get it?
A: Ask the man.
Q: Any particular man?
A: No. Ask E. Holt.
Q: Who is E. Holt?
A: An antiquarian.
Q: Where is he?
A: Dead. There is a book.
Q: Where is it?

A: I don't know where it is. Mrs. Holt.

Q: What has she to do with it?

A: Ask her.

Q: Do you know where she lives?

A: No. Wrote a book.

Q: What about?

A: About all of them. All the people are in it.

Q: What else?

A: I am there.

Q: What else is it about?

A: Maud.

Q: Is what it says about you good?

A: Not interesting enough. *Countess Maud* by Emily Holt.

Q: Why didn't you tell me that before?

A: I would have told you but you went away.

The planchette session evidently struck the chord in Miss C.'s memory that previous questioning had failed to do. Both she and her aunt had, she thought, read a book called *Countess Maud* some years earlier, though she had completely forgotten about it and couldn't even remember whether it had mentioned Blanche Poynings. Once a copy of the book, a historical novel written in 1892, had been acquired, it was easily established that this must have been the source of Blanche's memories. Emily Holt was a novelist who paid particular attention to the historical accuracy of her books; in an appendix she had listed everything known about the Earl of Salisbury's family, including a mention of Blanche Poynings and her four husbands. Blanche herself played only a small part in the story, but otherwise the people and events she had described were all accurately portrayed in the novel.

As his own final chapter in the story, Lowes Dickinson decided to see if he could help Miss C. recover, again under hypnosis, the memory of when she first read the book. This time the hypnotist deliberately regressed her to this particular point in her childhood. This is what followed:

Q: Can you see yourself young?

A: Yes.

Q: Can you see your aunt reading a book, *Countess Maud*?

A: Yes, blue book with gold line across name of it. *Lowes Dickinson comments that his own copy is red.*

Q: What is it about?

A: Ellen Turval [one of the countess's attendants] and the Earl and Countess of Salisbury.

Q: How old were you?

A: Twelve.

Q: Did you read it yourself?

A: I looked at it, and painted a picture in the beginning.

Q: Did you read the appendix?

A: No.

Q: Did your aunt?

A: No.

Q: What was it about?

A: The people in the book. I used to turn over the pages. I didn't read it, because it was dull. Blanche Poynings was in the book; not much about her.

Q: How much did you get from Blanche Poynings—how much from the book?

A: Nearly all the events from the book, but not her character . . . There was a real person called Blanche Poynings that I met, and I think her name started the memory, and I got the two mixed up.

Twelve is an impressionable age, and if Miss C. had been particularly interested in the novel it wouldn't have been surprising that she would have remembered it in the detail she recounted under hypnosis. However, under hypnosis she also maintained that she "looked at it" but didn't read it because it was dull. It's possible that Miss C. had a photographic, or eidetic, memory. Only a few people have this kind of memory, which enables them to look at a page of a book and later recall and read the image of the page from memory. It is a capacity which is strongest in childhood and usually fades with age, but Miss C. was only twelve when she read *Countless Maud* and may still have had the ability. At any rate, she clearly remembered enough of the events in the book to create a background for Blanche Poynings. She had, however, imposed some personality changes on the character of Blanche, who is described as pious and discreet in the book, but is portrayed by Miss C., according to Lowes Dickinson, as "a garrulous and flippant gossip."

This case is interesting, too, because it occurred long before hypnosis for the purpose of past-life regression became fashionable. This may indeed be why "Miss C." experienced the memories not as if they were her own but as if she had been told about them by someone else. But although she felt that she was reporting someone else's life rather than remembering her own, the mechanism by which the memories were accessed is presumably the same. Only the subjective interpretation of them differs.

To the layman, cryptomnesia may seem as difficult an explanation to swallow as reincarnation. How can such detailed memory be stored, and then accessed, without the conscious mind being aware of it at all? And if it is, surely the recovered memories would then stir such a chord in the conscious mind that their source would be remembered? Even if you have genuinely forgotten someone or something, when your memory is jogged, memory of the person or event usually comes flooding back.

Experiments with memory have shown that we are more successful at recognising things than remembering them. Often we try unsuccessfully to remember a name, for example, but if we see it in a list of names we'll immediately recognise it. Miss C. herself describes how something very like this seems to have occurred: "There was a real person called Blanche Poynings that I met, and I think her name started the memory, and I got the two mixed up." In this case, the meeting stimulated one particular memory—the memory of Blanche Poynings—and could have led by association to other memories from the book, though not in a logical or coherent order.

However, what is just as fascinating is the skilful way in which Miss C. wove the information stored somewhere in her memory into a convincing story. Although the facts came from the book, she, the narrator, made up a different setting, and a different central character—not Countess Maud, the heroine, but Blanche Poynings, a very subsidiary and unimportant character in the book. Moreover, the facts were introduced not in the order or with the connections seen in the book but quite naturally, as they might come out haphazardly in conversation. If Miss C. skimmed the book but didn't actually read it, then connections between the characters would not have been clear in her memory. And in characteristic fashion, the left hemisphere created its schema and manipulated the available data to fit it and to form a coherent and logical story. This is a characteristic that past-life memories seem to share with dreams, which show equally inventive and skilful use of data, the dream-mind making its own connections, so that different elements are woven into a new, and at first sight unrecognisable, whole.

It's clear, then, that we can't rely on memory as an infallible guide to experience. And the less we can understand an experience, the more we have to try to interpret it to make sense of it, the less reliable our memory of it is likely to be. Past-life memories may seem absolutely real, and the story they tell very convincing, but we have to bear in mind that they may simply arise because the creative, interpretive brain is trying to make sense of something that doesn't fit into its logical, coherent view of the world.

HOW MEMORY WORKS

What do we know about the way memories are stored and recalled? The current view is that the laying down and recall of memory is essentially a modification of cellular processes within the brain. Simplified, the theory suggests that if a cell is repeatedly stimulated, a cascade of reactions occurs within the cell which result in the cleavage of a protein fragment. This fragment enters the central cell genetic mechanism and stimulates the production of a protein, nerve-growth factor. This protein does three things: it breaks the linkages between the cell's processes and those of its neighbours; it instructs the cell membrane to grow, which it can do as it is no longer constrained by its surrounding linkages; and it increases the number of vesicles within the cell which are involved in the transmission of impulses from one cell to another. Thus, at the end of this process the stimulated cell is larger, has made more connections, and is more active. This means that the activities that use this cell pathway are enhanced.

The right and left hippocampus are the brain structures that appear to be especially involved in the recall and filing of memories. In righthanded people, the left hippocampus deals with memory for words, whereas the right hippocampus deals with memory for space and form. Thus, if you think of a dog, when you recall its name (Rover) you use the left hippocampus; when you recall the white patch on its nose or the way it bounds through the fields, you use the right hippocampus.

If memory is, as our present knowledge suggests, entirely a brain function, then there is *no* possibility that memories of personal experiences might exist beyond death of the brain, as there would be no structure to store or recall them. By locating memory fair and square in the brain, science removes at a stroke the possibility of reincarnation. Is any non-scientific evidence sufficiently persuasive to suggest that memories can in some way be held and mediated outside the brain?

There are certainly theories which would allow for the storage of memory outside the brain. The first group depends on different metaphysical assumptions about the nature of science, suggesting that consciousness is the fundamental property of the universe. Then there are the "field" theories, such as Jung's theory of the collective unconscious and the morphic resonance theory of Rupert Sheldrake (see page 300), which suggest that memories might become part of some universal field to which individual minds have access. Finally, the theories of quantum mechanics (see page 315) suggest the presence of multiple universes. These, too, allow for the possibility for the storage and personal continuation of memory.

But is there any convincing evidence that these theories are any more than just theories? It depends on how much you want to be convinced and how prepared you are to search beyond the limitations of our current science. This is something we will return to in later chapters.

5

Taken Over by the Past

Do you know who you are?

Dostoevsky

FEELINGS about a past life are usually little more than an echo of the past, a scene that flashes before the mind's eye. But sometimes a previous personality can emerge so strongly that it takes over an individual completely, replacing his (or her) present-day personality so that he does indeed seem literally to be living again the life that he remembers.

This happens most easily and most often under hypnosis, when the personalities that emerge can take over, dominating the ordinary personality so powerfully that it is completely suppressed. But for this to happen spontaneously, so that a secondary personality takes over whole periods of a person's daily life, is extremely rare. The best-known example is probably that of Chris Sizemore, whose life formed the basis of the film *The Three Faces of Eve*.

The phenomenon is popularly known as multiple personality. Multiple personality became a fashionable diagnosis in the last half of the nineteenth century. Before 1850, most such cases would probably have been diagnosed as demonic possession. It has been pointed out by experimental psychologist Richard Gregory that the great majority of the physicians reporting cases of multiple personality have been men, and the cases they have reported have been women younger than themselves. Certainly, Dr. Morton Prince of Boston, Massachusetts, fits this picture very well.

It was Dr. Prince who in 1905 wrote the classic textbook on multiple personality, *The Dissociation of a Personality*. It was a subject on which he had already published papers, and in which he was well known to be interested. The book developed from his meeting with Miss Beauchamp, a young woman twenty years his junior, who suffered from various nervous disorders. Miss Beauchamp pleaded with him to hypnotise her, and when he agreed she produced not just one but four distinct personalities. "There was," Dr. Prince recounts, in all pre-Freudian innocence, "over her spine a 'hypnogenetic point,' pressure upon which always caused a thrill to run through her that weakened her will and induced hypnotic sleep." One of Miss Beauchamp's manifestations was as "Sally," a flighty minx who liked to play practical jokes, on one occasion evidently persuading Miss Beachamp herself (a high-minded young lady who neither smoked nor drank and would naturally never have thought of such a thing herself) to pose stark-naked on a pile of furniture.

Dr. Prince's explanation of the phenomenon was that the self was a fusion of several simultaneous psychological entities, and that multiple, or dissociated, personalities emerged when these entities failed to integrate. A more plausible explanation, given the nudity and the hypnogenetic thrills, was that some erotic *frisson* had developed between doctor and patient, and that in producing these multiple personalities, which she knew would arouse his interest, Miss Beauchamp was aiming to please.

In any case, most modern psychiatrists would give a different name and offer a rather different explanation of multiple personality. They would describe it as hysterical dissociation and explain that it was not a failure of the personality to integrate, but rather that it is psychological in origin, an escape or defence mechanism, a manifestation of the ability of the mind to dissociate—to split off and suppress various mental processes, either partially or completely, perhaps because they are particularly painful. The dissociation may take the form of a fugue state in which the person wanders off not knowing who or where they are, or by a total loss of memory for the event. Fugue states are relatively common and can occur in many forms of psychological distress.

A tendency to dissociate in this way is known to be related to a variety of childhood traumas, in particular to childhood sexual abuse, and also to be linked to damage to a particular area of the brain, the hippocampus. One theory to account for this association is that traumatic events, particularly traumatic events early in life, such as sexual abuse, may damage the hippocampus through the action of a hormone, cortisol, which is secreted by the adrenal gland in response to stress. It is the hippocampus, together with other neighbouring structures, which switches on the production of cortisol. Normally, once the stress has passed, cortisol secretion is switched off via receptors in the hippocampus. Unfortunately, these receptors themselves can be damaged by high levels of cortisol: this then interferes with the feedback mechanism so that cortisol secretion continues, causing further damage. High levels of cortisol are also linked to depression, and so people whose hippocampus has been damaged in this way also tend to suffer from depression.

With these links in mind—an unhappy childhood, a tendency to depression, and a tendency to dissociate and develop an apparent alternative personality—let us look at the case of A. J. Stewart, a woman who for the last thirty years has believed herself to be the reincarnation of James IV of Scotland.

A. J. Stewart was born Ada F. Kay in Lancashire in March 1929. She is certainly very knowledgeable about the historical facts of the time of James IV and has even written an "autobiography" of herself as James "presented by A. J. Stewart," composed of her own fragments of "James's" memories. She gives interviews and lectures as James and often wears an approximation of sixteenth-century costume. She even bears a certain facial resemblance to at least one portrait of the real James IV.

From early childhood and throughout her teens she had flashbacks of historical scenes involving images of "men in steel" and battles, and of riding out through a gateway at the head of a small band of horsemen. She also had a longing to visit Scotland.

None of this at first prevented her from leading a normal

and productive life. In 1949 she began a successful career as a television playwright, and in 1957 she married Peter Stewart, an architect. But gradually her obsession with Scotland became more powerful and her flashbacks more frequent and intrusive. She moved to Edinburgh and began to research and to write a play about James IV. As she retreated further and further into a private world, her career began to suffer and so did her marriage. She suffered bouts of depression and self-neglect.

Gradually, her feeling that she might be the reincarnation of the Scottish king grew stronger. For her, the conclusive proof that this was so came one night in 1967, while she was staying in a house at Jedburgh, in the Borders region between England and Scotland. The next day she had planned to visit Flodden Field, a place she had always tried to avoid without understanding why. In bed that night she had a waking vision of a sixteenth-century battlefield. "I could see the flash of blades before me . . . I was fighting. Through the slits in my visor grille I could see the English standard-bearer before me on his white horse. I looked downwards at its hooves. There is great difficulty in looking through a visor grille. It is like tunnel vision . . . At that point I felt a mighty explosion in my face and must have been rendered unconscious. I awoke lying on my back looking up at a circle of blades and staves driving into my body, and I remember howling."

A. J. Stewart's vision that night was of James's death at the Battle of Flodden Field. And it was with that vision that the twentieth-century A. J. Stewart seems finally to have been submerged in the reborn personality of James IV.

How and, more important, why did this takeover of one personality by another occur? Ian Wilson examined the case of A. J. Stewart in some detail for his book *Mind Out of Time* and has documented a childhood that was, in her pre-school years, very lonely and isolated, and later, in her pre-teen years, what she herself has described as "hideously unhappy," though she does not make explicit the reasons for this, Ian Wilson also mentions one other significant fact: A. J. Stewart suffered from migraine.

Alterations of consciousness and mental confusion are common accompaniments of migraine. There may be disturbances of speech or memory, hallucinations, or odd dreamy mental states in which the person may have feelings of *déjà vu*, depersonalisation and derealisation (uncertainty about whether they or things around them are real or not), timelessness, or forced reminiscence (memories of the past which come back into the mind unbidden), and all or any of these may appear in the absence of the typical migraine headache as what is called a "mental migraine equivalent."

It seems to be during adolescence, the time at which migraine attacks typically start, that A. J. Stewart's identification with James IV began in earnest. Just how easily migraine-induced mental disturbances might be interpreted as scenes from a past life is shown by the following case history, given by Oliver Sacks in *Organic Psychiatry*:

> A forty-four-year-old man suffered very occasional attacks of migraine from adolescence . . . In one attack a profound dream-like state followed the visual phenomena thus: "First I couldn't think where I was, and then I suddenly realised that I was back in California . . . It was a hot summer day. I saw my wife moving about on the verandah, and I called her to bring me a Coke. She turned to me with an odd look on her face, and said: "Are you sick or something?" I suddenly seemed to wake-up, and realised that it was a winter's day in New York, and there was no verandah and that it wasn't my wife but my secretary who was standing in the office looking strangely at me.

One more incident from her adolescence forms yet another link between A. J. Stewart's migraine and her identification with James. Ian Wilson describes how, in her late teens, A. J. Stewart looked into a mirror in the WC compartment of a train and "saw herself with a masculine-looking face, longer and older than her real face, and with points of sapphire around the head." This inability to recognise something very familiar—agnosia—is also a characteristic of migraine, and almost certainly accounts for this distorted perception of her own image. But for A. J. Stewart it may have been all that was

needed to consolidate her growing conviction that she was not
Ada Kay but James IV of Scotland.

There are other clues to the genesis of James in Ada's adolescence. When she was twelve her class was set Sir Walter
Scott's narrative poem *Marmion* to read. *Marmion* is set in
Scotland in the reign of James IV and is particularly concerned with the events leading to the Battle of Flodden Field.
But although it is an obvious source both for Ada's historical
knowledge of the period, and also as a trigger for her personal
fascination with James, she insists in her autobiography not
only that she never discovered what the book was about because she missed the relevant lessons because of migraine but
that she could not even bear the sight of it. It brought her out
in goose pimples so that she was forced to bury it in her desk
beneath every other book she could lay her hands on.

Any of these incidents alone would probably not have
been enough to create this alternative and convincing personality. But the flashbacks and change of body image which
were almost certainly migraine-induced, combined with the
need of a lonely child and an unhappy adolescent to find a
more fulfilling fantasy life, all these made fertile ground for
the dream that triggered the final metamorphosis.

THE CASE OF SHARADA

Psychiatric diagnosis sometimes depends on a particular patient meeting a particular doctor at a particular time. If Uttara
Haddur had met Dr. Morton Prince in the 1870s she would almost certainly have gone down in psychiatric history as a
classic case of multiple personality. If she had visited a British
psychiatric clinic in the 1990s she would probably have been
diagnosed as having a hysterical dissociation. As it happened,
she met Dr. Ian Stevenson and, separately, Dr. V. V. Akolkar
in the 1970s. Both of them were interested in cases of apparent reincarnation, both of them examined her case very
painstakingly and in great detail. And both of them concluded
that her experiences were best accounted for by supposing
that she had memories of a previous life as a Bengali woman,
Sharada, who died in about 1830.

They based their conclusions, quite logically, on her behaviour as Sharada, her memories of Sharada's life, and above all on the fact that she seemed to speak Sharada's language. But it may be that if they had started in the present, if the focus of their attentions had been primarily Uttara herself, and not Sharada, her alter ego, they might have come to a different conclusion.

Uttara Haddur was born in Nagpur, India, in March 1941. She grew into an intelligent young woman with a flair for languages. She took MA degrees in English and in Public Administration in 1969 and 1971 respectively, and was on the teaching staff of Nagpur University from 1973 to 1975.

Until she was thirty-two years old, Uttara's life was unremarkable. But then, in March 1974, she began to undergo alterations of personality during which she claimed to be a young married Bengali lady named Sharada. "Sharada" emerged at regular intervals, usually on the same day of each month. She claimed to be from Burdwan, about 590 miles (950 kilometres) north-east of Nagpur, and to be the wife of a physician and the daughter of a Sanskrit pundit, both of whose names she gave. She said that when she twenty-four and pregnant, her husband had taken her to her maternal aunt's house in Saptagram. Here, in the seventh month of her pregnancy, she received a fatal snakebite while picking flowers in the garden, and died on the same day of the month as Sharada habitually appeared.

To begin with, Sharada manifested frequently—more than twenty-eight times between March 1974 and August 1981. At first the episodes were relatively brief, lasting less than half an hour. But as the Sharada personality became more established, she emerged for longer. Between 1974 and 1983 Sharada manifested almost twice a month and often remained in control for several days—the longest spell lasting for 41 days. Thereafter her influence started to fade, and she would appear only occasionally, around the time of the religious festival of the goddess Durga.

When Sharada retreated, Uttara would have no memory at all of this other life. Sometimes Uttara would go to bed as her normal self and wake up as Sharada. But usually Uttara had a premonitory sign a few hours before Sharada emerged—a feeling as though ants were crawling on the top of her head.

The most likely explanation of this feeling is that it was due to anxiety: "funny feelings" or a feeling of bands around the head are all common features of anxiety. Feelings like this can also signal the onset of some epileptic event, but this is unlikely simply because there is no evidence that Uttara suffered any loss of consciousness. However, we can't discount this possibility entirely because there is some evidence that at these times she did become confused. One observer described Sharada's emergence on 8 February 1976 thus:

> Visiting the toilet, returning from it in a state of exhaustion and disorientation with pallor in the face; lying on the bed for quite some time, as though in a strange house and among strangers; taking a head bath with cold water; then putting vermilion in the parting of her hair; dressing up in a Bengali way, draping only a sari and covering her head with the sari.

What can be said is that in epilepsy a personality change of the degree shown by Sharada would be extremely rare, so unusual that we can probably discount epilepsy as a factor in the emergence of Sharada.

Sharada was devout, and spent almost all her time in prayer, the worship of the Bengali goddess Durga and the singing of devotional songs. She always spoke as though she was living in the Bengal ruled by the East India Company, and used to refer to fights between the natives and the English soldiers. She displayed a wide knowledge of Bengal and Bengali customs, and her social behaviour and the type of Bengali she spoke were both consistent with this time-frame. She seemed fearful and suspicious of modern electrical appliances, referring, for example, to a tape recorder as a witch. She wore a sari but no undergarments. When she was menstruating she asked for plantain leaves and cotton wool. She bathed and washed her hair with cold water, rubbing herself dry with one end of her wet sari instead of using a towel. At meals she would watch the way Uttara's family ate and copy them.

Sharada claimed to be a daughter of the Chattopadhyaya family, a family of pundits, and mentioned the names of several members of her family. Such a family did indeed live in

Bengal during the first quarter of the nineteenth century, and much (though not all) of the information Sharada gave about them was found to be correct. So completely did the "Sharada" personality take over that she did not seem to recognise Uttara's family and friends and behaved as though her house was unfamiliar.

Uttara's native language was Marathi, and she is known to have read Bengali novels in Marathi translation, including novels by Sharad Chandra Chattopadhyaya, who not only shared the same surname as Sharada's presumed family but also came from the same general region of the country. Stevenson and Akolkar asked authorities on Bengali literature whether any of the elements of Sharada's claimed life—family and place-names, the locations and descriptions of temples, for example—might have any fictional basis in these novels. But despite an extensive search, no evidence seems to have been found that this was so. Although Uttara adopted the name Chattopadhyaya, for example, this is a very common Bengali name: other names of Sharada's relatives and ancestors don't appear in the novels at all. The names that do crop up in both Sharada's life and in the novels are again such common Bengali names that no particular significance can be attached to them.

But the feature of the case which has aroused the most interest is that although Uttara and her family spoke Marathi, one of the northern Indian languages, during those periods when Uttara seemed to be completely taken over by Sharada's personality, she spoke Bengali, a language she claimed never to have learned. And not only did she speak it when she was awake, but she muttered it in her sleep and when she was suddenly awakened by a splash of cold water on her face. When family or friends spoke to her in Marathi, Hindi or English, "Sharada" did not seem to understand.

As a young girl Uttara had shown a great interest in Bengal and Bengali, and we know that she had expressed a strong desire to learn the language. She had even had at least some Bengali lessons with a classmate, F., in her matriculation year at school. But she seems to have been much more fluent in the language than these rudimentary lessons would explain. What is more, she spoke Bengali much as it would have been spo-

ken in the early nineteenth century, the period she claimed to
have lived in.

This is the aspect of the case which, if one is to believe the
language experts who have studied it, is very difficult to explain by rational hypothesis, and it is discussed in more detail
on pages 211–213. In fact, interest has always focused so
strongly on Uttara's apparent ability to speak Bengali that little attention has been paid to the personality of Uttara herself,
to why the Sharada personality emerged when it did and in the
form it did.

It has always been accepted that thirty-two is an odd age
for the spontaneous emergence of a past life. Past-life memories that emerge spontaneously, not under the influence of a
hypnotic regression, nearly always do so in very early childhood, and have usually disappeared by the age of seven or
eight. So what happened to Uttara around the time that her
past-life memories began to emerge?

To understand this we need first to go back to Uttara's adolescence. When she was a young child, Uttara had lived
mainly with her grandparents and had seen little of her father.
Not until she was 14 did they become closer and develop what
has been described by Dr. Akolkar as more of an intellectual
friendship than a father–daughter relationship. Uttara's father
was a strongly spiritual man who would have liked to become
a yogi, but he was too involved with political and other activities to be able to fulfil this ambition. Perhaps in compensa-
tion, he did his best to put his daughter on a spiritual path. The
two of them discussed philosophical and spiritual matters, and
he introduced her to meditation in 1965.

At around this time, when she was twenty-four, Uttara suffered an emotional blow that seems to have been powerful
enough to change the course of her life. She met again F., the
young man with whom she had shared those adolescent Bengali lessons. This time she felt drawn not only to F., but to his
father, Bhau. The two seem to have developed a close emotional relationship, and Bhau told her: "Like a straw to a
drowning man, your support is like that of a little goddess."

Gradually, she began to dream of marriage to F., but her
dreams were not simply of becoming F.'s wife but of being
Bhau's daughter-in-law. However, when she made her feel-

ings clear to F., she was devastated to find that they were not returned. Some years later, describing the experience to Akolkar, she wrote:

> I simply could not believe him. But at the same time I resolved, and even expressed it, that if I could not marry him, I would not marry at all. The fear, however, that I would lose my life's pillar made me very restless. But I kept on hoping. During this period I began to experience mental exhaustion.

She begged Bhau to get his son married, if not to her then to the girl he preferred, so that her misery might end. But he did nothing. In November 1972, a few months before her thirty-second birthday, and the first manifestation of Sharada, Bhau died. To Uttara, this was the final blow, the end of her hopes of marriage to F. She also seems to have been tormented with guilt:

> The thought that Bhau did not favour the marriage was already pricking me; now it began to torment me. I began to feel terribly exhausted, perhaps because the pillar of my life had begun to shake. I was at a point of transition in my life . . . I began to feel that I had sinned against the girl to whom F. rightfully belonged.

One wonders, though this is speculation, just which of the two, father or son, she regarded as her "life's pillar" whose loss she dreaded.

It was while she was in the state of emotional turmoil which followed Bhau's death and the death of her hopes of marriage to his son that another male father figure entered Uttara's life. This relationship was to prove crucial to her future and to the emergence of Sharada.

Uttara's spiritual life was already important to her, and so, like many a young woman disappointed in love, she sought solace in religion. In 1970 she consulted a homoeopathic doctor, Dr. Z., a man in his fiffies. He, too, had strong spiritual leanings and had established an ashram-cum-nursing home near Nagpur. At Dr. Z's first touch, Uttara felt drawn to

him "like an iron particle to a magnet." She felt a strong desire to meet him again and again. Soon after his treatments
began, her agony of mind was calmed, and she started to
sleep soundly, for the first time in months. Uttara decided to
go to stay in the ashram, giving herself entirely over to the
meditative life. Once the decision was made, it was liberat-
ing, as is evident from the description of her feelings at this
time when she wrote in an autobiographical note of 14 October 1974:

> A hurricane-like force swept me off and liberated me
> completely from the attraction towards my young
> friend F. . . . I was now rid of everything that had so far
> stood in the way of spiritual search . . . Knowledge and
> ignorance, good and evil, happiness and suffering of
> the entire world had now reached up to my heart, and I
> myself became that which I so much had wanted to
> be . . . In my mind now there was no opposition; there
> was no past behind me and no eagerly awaited future
> ahead. I had no caste, no name, no clan, no country,
> nothing . . . It was as if a new happiness was sprouting.
> I began to feel that I must now allow my life stream to
> stagnate. I must move towards a new life regardless of
> the sacrifice it might entail. I experienced a strong urge
> within me to give myself fully for the sake of whatever
> I thought proper in this transition to a new life. I had to
> keep my psychic stream flowing. It was impossible to
> arrest it and allow it to stagnate.

This is the background, and the state of mind, against which
Sharada made her first appearance.

Uttara joined Dr. Z's ashram in December 1973. Almost
immediately, "a strange idea began to take shape" in her
mind. She became convinced that she was to embark on a
spiritual pilgrimage and that she needed a companion to help
her on this spiritual journey. Needless to say, it was Dr. Z.
whom she had cast in this role. She envisaged their relationship as a purely spiritual one, but marriage would, she believed, be necessary to make it socially acceptable.
Unfortunately, Dr. Z. failed to share her belief that their mar-

riage was necessary for Uttara's spiritual development. Once again, she was rejected.

Early in 1974 she began to experience spells of blankness and an inability to recall. Sometimes she would see, in her mind's eye, images of places, people and situations which bore no relationship to her own life and which would interrupt her prayers and meditations. Uttara would also "sort of see" in the mirror another image behind her own, which she felt was her own image but slightly different.

In February she began to "see" Bengali alphabets before her mind's eye and "hear" Bengali sentences. Occasionally, she would mutter in Bengali. Dr. Z. and a woman friend of his kept notes of what she said, and Dr. Z. told Uttara's father that she referred to having had a relationship with him (Dr. Z.) in a previous life.

Uttara's feelings about Dr. Z. were made clear when, two years later, Dr. Akolkar interviewed her during one of Sharada's manifestations. He read her a list of names and asked her to write down next to each what came into her mind. Some were the names of the relations Sharada had named, and her response was to write down "grandfather" or "brother" or whatever was appropriate. But when the name of a woman friend of Dr. Z.'s was read out, her face became visibly tense and she refused to speak. When she was pressed, the following conversation took place, in Bengali:

Sharada: I shall not speak about her.
Q: Why not?
A: She is a *bhogadi* [woman of bad character].
Q: Why don't you wish to speak about her?
A: It is *guja katha* [a secret tale].
Q: But where did it take place?
A: In this *masi-ma's* town [Nagpur].
Q: How old is that lady?
A: Thirty-five years.
Q: Is she married?
A: She does not wear ornaments. She has a husband.
Q: What language does she speak?
A: This *masi-ma's* language [that is, Marathi].
Q: Does she have a male friend?

A: *No answer.*

Q: About the name S. [the woman friend].

A: *A vigorous shake of the head indicated her refusal to speak.*

Here is the evidence that however hard she tried, Uttara was not able to separate herself completely from Sharada. Sometimes during dissociation there is not a total suppression of normal personality, some awareness is maintained, separation of the two streams of consciousness is not complete. Dr. Z. and his woman friend were part of Uttara's life, not Sharada's. And yet it is quite evident that Sharada was not only very well aware of this relationship but was very deeply affected by it. Sharada is Uttara; Uttara is Sharada.

Uttara was thirty-two, the age at which a single, childless woman starts to become increasingly aware that her biological clock is running down and her chances of finding a mate are decreasing every year. Her emotional life had been highly unsatisfactory. Now, in Dr. Z., she seemed to have found the perfect focus for both her emotional and her spiritual needs; he was the older man, the spiritual adviser, the lover. But when she suggested marriage he failed to understand how she felt.

Sharada provided a solution. By displacing her love into a past life, Uttara could both arouse Dr. Z.'s interest and keep his attention. As Sharada, she could declare her love in perfect safety—because it was in the past it was a *fait accompli* and allowed of no rejection. As Sharada, she could make her sexuality very clear: she wears her sari without undergarments; she draws attention to her menstruation by demanding plantain leaves and cotton wool.

And yet in the end—and this is why hers is such a tragic tale—Sharada was not quite enough. When there is a dissociation of personality, it is because there is some gain to the individual. To begin with the Sharada personality was so strong and so much in evidence that it has to be assumed that it was working for Uttara, influencing those around her as she wished them to be influenced. Sharada was shy and especially reluctant to meet men—with one exception. She was eager to meet Dr. Z., who, she claimed, was her husband in her previous Bengali life, again. But even then, even when she had made the bond between them clear, he would not acknowledge it or reciprocate her interest; he made it clear that he himself had no memories of a past life with or without Sharada.

Sharada appeared regularly until 1983, and then gradually her influence started to fade. When Dr. Akolkar met her in 1989, Uttara told him that in 1988 Sharada had emerged only once, on the eighth and ninth days of the festival of the goddess Durga. The Sharada personality had no more to offer Uttara; it had run its course.

6

Dreams of Forgotten Lives

Dreaming is akin to the bardo of becoming, the intermediate
state where you have a clairvoyant and highly mobile "mental
body" that goes through all kinds of experiences.
   Sogyal Rinpoche, *The Tibetan Book of Living and Dying*

ANYTHING can happen in our dreams. It is through some
of the stranger phenomena of sleep and dreams that many
myths and legends have arisen—astral travel, abductions by
aliens, night-time visitations by the legendary "Old Hag."
Often such bizarre adventures can be explained as the by-
products of sleep and dreams.

Nearly all the dreams we have relate in some way, however tenuous the link, to our ordinary, everyday life. They
may rerun the past, or embellish the present, or even occasionally show glimpses of what seems to be the future. Very
occasionally, though, they may present us with scenes from
what looks to be another life entirely, in a different time and
a different place. Davina Williams, for example, wrote to us
describing a vivid, unpleasant and disturbing dream in which
she was back in the late seventeenth or early eighteenth century, a woman in a crowd of people awaiting the hanging of a
man, whose crime was stealing a sheep. The man was, she
knew in the dream, her husband. Karen Byfield's five-year-
old son has had two nightmares in which, she says, "I am not
the mummy he is looking for to comfort him." At these times
Karen's little boy calls out for "Mamma"—not a word he ever
normally uses; she has no idea where he got it from.

Paul King, now forty-one, describes two connecting

dreams remembered from childhood. Although these dreams occurred so many years ago, they remain the same in his memory and so vivid he believes he would recognise the places in the dream if he were to see them. In one he is walking down a wood-panelled Tudor-style gallery, conscious of people seated on window seats to his right. He feels a sense of unease, almost as though these people are looking at him. He makes himself look down (the feeling here is similar to a lucid dream, a dream in which you know you are dreaming but feel you are awake) and sees that he is wearing tights. In the second section of this dream he feels he is with his sister (actually he is an only child) in a room with a servant; the servant is very friendly and takes a very large key to open a door. He is taking them into a herb garden surrounded by a high red-brick wall. In the second dream Paul recalls climbing on to a "dumb waiter," trying to ride on it. It crashes, and he feels he may have been killed.

Such dreams certainly have a reincarnation "feel" about them, but what makes people who have them believe that they are anything more than ordinary dreams? Is there in fact anything different about them at all? People who have these dreams describe them as being more vivid and real than their ordinary dreams. They lack the bizarre quality of an ordinary dream, and they are often recurrent, so that each time the same scene is replayed, and each time the person wakes from it at the same point in the dream. Often these dreams start in childhood and become less frequent as the person grows older, sometimes ceasing altogether.

It's understandable that when a dream recurs, when the same place is visited, the same scene replayed each time the dream occurs, it may seem to have a special significance and carry a special message. Recurrent dreams are quite common, and they tend to follow this same pattern, being common in childhood and then weakening until eventually they cease altogether. Despite this, these people feel there are special factors in their dreams which convince them that they are not in the ordinary run of recurrent dreams but have a definite reincarnation feel.

V.L. of Gloucester says that she and other members of her family have all experienced spontaneous past-life recall, mainly in dreams. But, she says, those dreams are markedly different from a normal dream. "I could *feel* the tight silk skirt of my dress restricting my length of stride as I tried to run down a slope—felt the painfal throbbing of a boil on my cheek, the swaying of a horse-drawn coach as we drove along a rutted, muddy lane." She adds: "I have had a couple of lucid dreams, and they have a different quality entirely to past-life dreams—and both are markedly different from ordinary dreams."

The "real-life" quality of V.L.'s dream certainly sounds very much like a lucid dream—a dream in which the dreamer is aware that he is dreaming. Lucid dreams mimic almost every aspect of waking experience—the visual imagery is always vivid, and the dreamer seems able to hear and feel, think and reason, make decisions and act on them. However, the lucid dreamer can to some extent "guide" their dream, make things happen and force dream-events to take a particular turn, and there is no suggestion that this is happening in V.L.'s or, indeed, any of the other reincarnation dreams described. The "painful throbbing of a boil" would be unusual in a lucid dream too—pain is seldom experienced in lucid dreams. V.L.'s account is especially valuable because she has experienced both types of dreams and feels able to distinguish between them.

Several other people describe what seemed to them to be knowledge of a past life which came to them in dreams. Mrs. B. Hunter believes that she has had two previous lives, one as a children's nanny and one as a man. Her knowledge came in dreams when she was a small child. Judith Anderton describes a reincarnation dream that regularly recurred between the ages of seven and twelve, in which she was walking along an avenue of stones which got bigger until they formed a circle. This dream was so vivid that even now, forty years later, she can close her eyes and remember every detail. Grace Morse describes a recurring nightmare that her two-and-a-half-year-old daughter used to have of "crowds of angry people pushing against the house, pushing heads on sticks through the window. Of course, my daughter was terrified. I had an old grandmother who years later in life told me her grandmother's people had died during the French Revolution. It has always crossed my mind that my daughter could have had a flashback of a previous life."

Ian Stevenson (in *Children Who Remember Previous Lives*) has observed that some children who claim to remember previous lives have vivid and recurrent dreams that are very similar to their spontaneous, apparent past-life waking memories. He describes the case of an American girl, Alice Robertson (pseudonym), who had a recurrent childhood nightmare in which she was an adult woman dressed in an ankle-length garment walking along a road in the evening with a young girl whom she knew to be her daughter. Suddenly there was a deafening roar, and the earth seemed to give way beneath her. At this point she would wake up, screaming in terror. The dream seemed so real to Alice that each time she would try to explain to her mother that she had really lived through the scene of her nightmare. But each time her mother had insisted that it was "only a dream." The nightmares persisted, though they happened less often as Alice grew older.

When Alice grew up, she recognised that the garment she wore in her dream was a sari—something that seemed to resonate with her because she felt a powerful attraction for India. As a young woman she saw a film about Darjeeling, which aroused in her a strong sense of *déjà vu*. She also discovered that a series of disastrous landslides had occurred in Darjeeling between 1890 and 1920, and she became convinced that it was here that she had lived, and that this was the manner of her death. Attempts to regress Alice under hypnosis to see whether she could recall any more details of her Darjeeling life failed—she merely relived the terrifying death she experienced in her nightmare but remembered nothing further about a previous life.

Anthropologist Antonia Mills has described another, similar case, a fascinating story which is difficult to explain in current scientific terms, and is particularly interesting because it was so well recorded. The mother of the little boy concerned, Thomas Mather (pseudonym), kept a diary, and when Thomas started talking about a previous life she wrote down everything he said.

Thomas was born in Canada in British Columbia, in 1982. He began to talk when he was eighteen months old and was a very verbal child. When he was about two years old he started having recurrent nightmares. He seldom said much about the content of the dreams, but they often seemed to be about Africa and San Francisco. After the age of four he started to have these dreams less often, and by the time he was seven he had only the occasional nightmare, usually related to something he had seen on television.

From the time he was just over two, Thomas started saying things that puzzled his parents because they seemed to bear no relationship to anything he had experienced.

The first time this happened was when the family had been watching the British royal family on television. Thomas remarked: "I know Diana, another Diana. Diana and I were running and there was fire all around. Diana got a fire on her foot. She didn't stop running. That was a long time ago, when I was big."

Fires were a recurrent theme in Thomas's apparent memories, as were other kinds of accidents (including a car accident and a plane crashing into his house). He also talked a lot about airports, aeroplanes, bridges, moving, and "being big like Daddy." Although the family had never even been to California, Thomas often mentioned San Francisco, Richmond, near San Francisco, where he said he had lived in a big house near the airport, and a place called "Disco," where he said there was an airport that was not as big as San Francisco's.

When he was three and a half, Thomas heard his mother describing a car accident she had been in some years before. He commented that he had been in a car accident once, "when I was big." A few days later he mentioned this again, saying, "I was in a car accident when I was big, big like Daddy." Asked when this was, he answered: "When I lived in San Francisco and was big like Daddy. I lived by a bridge over a big river." He also said that there were two little ones in the back of the car at the time of the accident.

At around the same age, Thomas also started talking about a plane crash. He mentioned a jet plane crashing into his house and said: "When I was driving at the airport all the people waiting for planes saw me crash." He also mentioned that he lived in Disco with his uncle, and that there were "jets with big tired mouths that opened so that cars can go inside." As he grew older he showed considerable fear of flying, and also of fires, which he would refuse to go near.

His mother describes how, when Thomas was just four, she was showing him a book that asked if the child had seen certain kinds of trees. She asked if Thomas had ever seen palm trees and he replied that he hadn't seen them in San Francisco but he had in Richmond, a neighbouring city where they do indeed thrive. Thomas's preschool teacher was struck by the fact that the boy reported that the mail deposit boxes were "the wrong colour" (they are blue in the United States, red in Canada).

Soon after he was four Thomas stopped talking about Disco, Richmond and San Francisco. But he continued to feel, and often to act, as though he were older than his chronological age. Thomas's parents and his teacher both noticed that he seemed to feel that he was older than he actually was. He resented being treated as a little boy, consistently had friends who were a few years older than himself, and could not understand why he was not allowed to do things that adults did, such as staying up late or going out on his own.

What struck his parents was the matter-of-fact way in which he talked about the places and people he mentioned— as if they were events that had really happened. They realised that most children have fantastic imaginations, but this seemed to them to be more than normal childish imagination. They had read about Ian Stevenson's work on reincarnation, and although they didn't have any personal belief in the idea, because nothing Thomas described seemed to have any connection with his everyday life, they began to wonder gradually if memories of some past life might be interwoven with normal childhood fantasies and formed the basis of his dreams.

Even the most vivid dream produces only flimsy evidence for establishing a previous identity. Ian Stevenson describes a correspondent of his who had a vivid dream in which she was an elegantly dressed woman some time in the early nineteenth century, being paid court to by a similarly well-turned-out aristocratic man. She became convinced that she had had a previous life as Lola Montez, the notorious *femme fatale* who cost King Ludwig I of Bavaria his throne. Stevenson comments: "Another of my correspondents also thinks, for different reasons, that *she* was Lola Montez. Perhaps I should introduce these two correspondents to each other."

But although there is very seldom anything like convincing evidence for these dream past lives, occasionally dream evidence can be very persuasive. This account is given by Joan Pidgeon.

> In 1977 my husband and I bought an old cottage in Belper, Derbyshire. It was over 350 years old and in need of much restoration. One night there, I had a startlingly vivid dream in which I was sitting beside my coachman (I was quite affluent) as we drove down the lane where the cottage was. It was only a rough track in my dream. As we travelled along, I noted a huge blaze on the far hilltop and said to my coachman: "That looks to me like Ward's bakery is on fire." He replied: "Maybe it has been done by the daughter. She has to marry an old man." He mentioned a name which I cannot recall, but I remember thinking, What a horrible old man, mean and rich. I replied to the coachman: "That must be a fate worse than death!" We both laughed and the dream was gone.
>
> Later, during the next few days, I mulled over the dream, still vivid and real, myself as a young lady in Puritan garb (I am convinced I was the young woman in the coach). So real that I looked up a book on the history of the old mill town of Belper and found there had been a Ward's bakery in that same spot, which had burned down in the early 1800s. After my dream everything settled to normality, with no more happenings.

Especially interesting is the following dream, dreamed by Heather Charles when she was a fourteen-year-old schoolgirl:

> In the dream I was a man, a soldier on a battlefield at night. We were moving forward, the earth was wet, very muddy; there were strands of barbed wire everywhere snagging at clothing. The night sky was periodi-

cally illuminated by flares and explosions. In the dream I was aware of a burning sensation at the back of my throat and a strange smell in the air (a little like the smell from fireworks). As I moved forward I sensed something coming at me. It was all so very quick there was no time to react. I sensed it was a missile like a shell that passed extremely close to the left side of my head. In its wake was a vacuum of hot air. In that split second, a part of the left side of my head was torn off, my right arm instinctively came up to support the injury, and I was for a brief moment aware that my hand could feel my gaping head wound, but the wound in my head could not feel my hand. I then fell forward to the earth.

Since then I have found out that battlefields are full of cordite and other substances which could cause a burning sensation at the back of the throat. Missiles travelling very fast through the air do create a vacuum of hot air behind them, and if a piece of the skull is removed, the surface of the brain has no touch sensors, but the hand, does. I wouldn't have known these facts as a schoolgirl of fourteen, and I do not come from a military family.

I have lived and worked for a short period of time in Germany and have visited the country on a number of occasions. I have always felt "at home" there. I have never had formal German lessons, and yet I managed to pick up an understanding and use of the language quite quickly, so that I could easily find my way around and take care of myself. When I have spoken German, German people say that my pronunciation is like that of a native German.

What is particularly interesting about this dream is the smell of cordite Miss Charles noticed. Smells are very evocative, and a particular smell can conjure up a host of vivid memories or emotions. But both taste and smell are very difficult to conjure up spontaneously from memory, even when they are familiar. Smell imagery rarely occurs spontaneously in dreams, although smells can be incorporated into dreams relatively easily—in one experiment to investigate this, sixteen different smells, including coffee, roses and onions, were put under subjects' noses while they were in dreaming sleep. The smells were incorporated into almost a quarter of their dreams. But presumably no one was sticking cordite underneath Miss Charles's nose while she slept. The smell and the burning in the back of her throat are very unusual dream images indeed.

It is also interesting that if the shell had indeed damaged the left side of the brain, and not just removed the left side of the skull, then the motor supply to the right hand and sensation from the right hand would both have been affected and the arm would have been paralysed and numb.

Miss Charles recounts another odd experience. One morning she was lying awake thinking about getting up. "I brought my hand up to my face with the thought I'd better get shaved. In the next instant reality kicked in, and I was astounded to have had that brief experience of thinking and feeling as if I were a man. It has never happened again."

Anne Jones (pseudonym) was born in 1944, two months after her father was killed during an air raid. Even as a child she had felt there was somebody with her, never more so than when she started holidaying in Spain as a teenager. Since 1964 she has had recurring dreams in which she is always a child. "In the happy dreams I am laughing and dancing around the campfires, always with soldiers dressed as I imagine Roman soldiers were dressed. I'm in the camp with my father, who is not a soldier but always wears a white robe tied in the middle. In the bad dreams he puts me in a basket and lowers me over huge high walls, and I'm so frightened I can hardly breathe. He tells me to run away and save myself."

A friend put the obvious interpretation of this dream to Anne—that she was looking for the father she had never seen. And she agreed with him until the following incident:

In 1989 I again went to Spain for three months. I was staying near Málaga. I went for breakfast early one morning, and the waiter was being stroppy about understanding my Spanish (it's strange that though I adore Spain and in spite of lessons galore I find the language difficult to grasp) when a voice behind me ordered just what I wanted. I turned to thank him and there was the dad from my dreams. I was so shocked I couldn't speak, and he apologised for offending me and was gone.

A few days later I saw this man again having coffee, and I asked if I could join him and explain. I just felt I knew him, and he didn't seem a bit surprised as I rambled on about my dreams.

In fact, we became friends, as he was taking time out as well. We did a lot of exploring in the mountains during the next few months, and when we finally had to part he explained that though I was much younger he felt me to be his mother in a previous life.

Unintelligible jargon is a quite common feature of dreams. One lucid dreamer described how he switched on a radio to listen to the shipping forecast, and, although to begin with it sounded to him just as the shipping forecast usually sounds, as he listened more carefully he realised that instead of the familiar sea areas—Rockall, Shannon, German Bight, North and South Uitsera, etc.—he was hearing the weather in nonexistent places such as Wolf and Sofa. Unintelligible dream-language quite often leads people to believe that they are glimpsing a past life in some foreign country, but could it be that this is just simple dream-jargon? K. Holsman describes such a dream, which he felt may have reflected some past-life memory:

I dreamed on five separate occasions I was helping two workmates manhandle a large wooden boat down towards the water's edge using wooden rollers as a slipway. The weather was very cold and the shoreline made up from fist-sized pebbles. Our feet and lower part of our legs were shrouded with soft leather and kept in place with leather strapping crisscrossed from our feet and tied just below our knees. It was extremely hard work, but from my own experiences manual workers usually laugh, joke and horseplay around, which seems to assist in these heavy manual chores. By the witty and spontaneous comments voiced between us as we laboured, it was obvious we knew one another very well, and every comment uttered, but the uncanny thing is that I didn't understand the language. It sounds positively contradictory to make such a comment—but can you possibly grasp my meaning of the situation?

The following dream, described by Christina G., also gives a very convincing picture of a past-life memory. Christina G. says she has always considered herself to be a level-headed middle-aged mum with no definite views one way or the other regarding reincarnation. Then,

One night late last summer I had a dream, or rather three dreams in succession. They were very vivid, and even now I can still recall them clearly. It was as if I was moving from early times to what I presume were, judging by the clothing worn by myself and others in the dream, the 1930s or 1940s (around the time I was born). Obviously, I have had dreams before and remembered them but never with such clarity.

In the first part of the dream I was standing on an apron or entrance to an extremely tall building. It was very hot, but the interior of the building was dark with tall narrow columns/pillars or even statues on the left going out into the dark interior (I could only see the left-hand side from where I was standing). I stood slightly apart from the group of people on my right, and as I entered the dream I heard myself speaking a language I didn't understand. The people were listening to me respectfully, and I felt I was someone of importance. As I glanced down I saw I was wearing a white/cream robe or gown.

The dream then changed, and I was standing on a cobbled street leading up through the town. I had a feeling we were near the sea. The woman with me wore a green skirt and some sort of mobcap on her head. I was wearing a rust-brown skirt. We watched some soldiers come round the corner wearing metal helmets and carrying pikes or staffs. It suddenly became very important to rush to get some papers before the soldiers found them, and we ran up the steep street to a house. The papers were hidden between the wall and the floorboards in a room. The floorboards were polished a lovely golden colour. As I picked up the papers the dream changed again.

This time I was walking with a man down a country lane in front of a large house. It looked very gloomy and neglected. I noticed the man had an old-fashioned double-breasted suit and trilby, and although I couldn't see it I knew I was wearing a black swagger-backed coat. As we turned up the side of the house, a woman came out of the house across the field next to the garden. She was either fair or grey-haired, wearing a blue floral old-fashioned wraparound pinny. She carried a wicker shopping basket and had a black labrador-type dog running around. She smiled and said it was a shame they had let the garden go—indicating the overgrown garden. We then carried on to the rear of the house and saw a large wooden cross lying on the ground. It was about eight feet long, one foot square, and had a crossbar close to the top. On the crossbar was a metal plate with the inscription "In loving memory of Heidi." The man and I then turned towards the house and walked towards some french windows. As we walked forward I had the most terrible feeling of dread and reluctance to enter the house. I then woke up.

Even now I still feel curious about the language I was speaking in the first part of the dream, the urgency to find the papers in the second part, the feeling of unhappiness and dread in the third.

The fact that Christina G. was able to recall her dream in such detail does suggest that there was something special about it. But this degree of clarity and intensity of feeling do occur in ordinary dreams. Neither can we take her ability to speak a language she didn't understand as an absolute indication of reincarnation. Just as in the earlier dream described, the appearance of dream-jargon masquerading as an unknown language suggests that, after all, it could be just a dream, an interesting and very vivid dream, but nevertheless felt by the dreamer to be indicative of reincarnation.

Mrs. N. R. Thomas is now seventy-five years old and says that for approximately twenty years she has lived secure in the knowledge that she died in the Great Fire of London. Since the sudden realisation of that, she has no longer been subjected to the terrifying nightmares that plagued her since she was a child.

> I am unaware of my age when the waking nightmares began, but I must have been seven or eight when I recognised them as being exactly the same as I had experienced before, and began to fear the next. These were that I was an adult woman in a street; there was an unseen presence beside me, on the left, and in front were another woman and a man. We were all reaching the top of a slight incline and could see the way ahead in this street of tall houses. All the time the fearful roaring noise became worse, and the buildings on either side continued to fall upon us. I always tried to scream, but no sound ever emerged, then there was complete and suffocating darkness, Then I was again awake, with a great sense of relief. These nightmares seemed to begin while I was awake, and knowing what would follow I tried to escape them but never could. I remember that I wore some sort of black woollen dress that impeded my movements, although it seemed pretty shapeless, but ankle-length. For what it is worth, that is it. I know of nothing before this "death," and I ask myself no questions about it. It has slotted into place and I fully accept it, finding some comfort in the acceptance of this in a way I cannot explain.

During dreaming sleep, although the cortex of the brain is aroused, providing the rich imagery of our dreams, the muscles are paralysed. This is the reason we cannot act out our dreams—and why when we see a dog dreaming in front of thefire he snuffles and whimpers and twitches, as if dreaming of chasing rabbits, but he does not—cannot—actually get to his feet and chase a dream rabbit around the room.

Usually, when we awake these two processes stop together; the paralysis goes, dream imagery vanishes, and waking consciousness returns. Sometimes, though, the wakening process doesn't go through to completion. Then, although the person is partially awake, either the dream imagery, or the feeling of paralysis, or both, are still maintained. This is called "sleep paralysis," and it can produce frightening feelings, such as the classic "incubus attack" when the sleeper wakes to feel a crushing weight on his chest, or sees some terrifying creature in the room and is unable to scream or to run away. The dreamer appears to waken, and, indeed, feels that he is fully awake, but in reality he has only partially aroused into a hallucinatory world.

Mrs. Thomas describes what happened to her very clearly. She mentions the "suffocating darkness," the "fearful roaring noise" and buildings falling on her, the fact that she "tried to escape but never could" and the "woollen dress that impeded my movements," and that she "tried to scream but no sound ever emerged." Most significantly, she says that the nightmare episode seemed to begin when she was awake. All these point to the probability that what she was experiencing was an episode of sleep paralysis rather than a memory of death in the Great Fire of London. But what is more interesting is that the nightmares stopped when Mrs. Thomas had the sudden realisation that they were about a terrifying event in a previous life. This is perhaps an indication of how well past-life therapy can sometimes work—one wonders whether telling Mrs. Thomas that her nightmare experiences were merely the result of sleep paralysis would have had the same curative effect.

This interpretation comes from our current science, where experience is generated by the brain and when the brain dies so does the conscious life of the individual. There is now evidence that mind is not confined to just the brain, and the current scientific work on telepathy indicates that mind is extended through space and through time. In our book *The Hidden Door* we looked in some detail at precognitive and telepathic dreams. If these do occur (and there is persuasive evidence that sometimes they do), it leaves open the possibility that dreams of a past life are possible within that frame-work.

Sharon Bond is twenty-eight, married with three children. Her flashbacks to a previous life started about five years ago, around the time her stepmother, to whom she was very close, died. She says they are not dreams but "scenes" that she sees when she closes her eyes and tries to go to sleep, like a film being played in her mind. "I can see an old black and white photo of a boy around two years old dressed in satin shorts and top. He has got dark hair and eyes. I hear a voice in my head which tells me to speak to him. Then I see him as a man dressed in a First World War uniform, and he asks me if I know what it felt like to be shot in the belly. He calls me Sarah and says I'm his sister and that we were very close in my last life. He also says that he was killed in the First World War."

Recently she has been finding these flashbacks very frightening, almost as though she is being haunted. Several times she has felt she can sense his presence in her room.

> In my mind I can see my father, who was a Doctor of Zoology at the Natural History Museum in London. I can also see my brother, who was about six years older than me. I often have flashbacks to the house where I lived and to the museum. I feel I lived as a child around the turn of this century. I've also come up with the surname Forsyth. I rang the museum and asked if there was a Doctor of Zoology named Forsyth working there at around the turn of the century, and they told me that there was—a Lord Charles Forsyth Major.

Sharon described some of these flashbacks in more detail. In one, she is walking down a street behind her father, who is dressed in a black suit and top hat. He is holding a walking-stick, which he taps to hurry her up. In another, she is again with her father going into the Natural History Museum. As she looks up she can see a skeleton of a dinosaur. She feels scared but doesn't tell her father. It seems a dark, cold place, and she doesn't like it very much. A third flashback has a def-inite nightmare quality—she is being chased by her brother and his friend. As she gets to a wooden door, her brother opens it and pushes her into the room, which is dark apart from the light from the door. As she looks up she can see a stuffed grizzly bear staring back at her. With this she panics and runs from the room.

She is sitting on the staircase in the house where she lives and has three dolls with her. One is on her lap. In the hallway is a group of men dressed in black suits. One comes over to her and admires her doll. Then a maid comes along and takes her upstairs so that she is out of the way. She also sees herself in a room sitting at a piano, her brother standing beside her teaching her the keys. In another scene she is in the kitchen standing at a huge wooden table, helping the cook make some pastry. The cook tells her: "Don't tell your father you've been helping me in the kitchen or he will be angry with me." The cook calls her "my lovely."

The final flashback is at a railway station. She is with her father seeing her brother off as he goes to war. On the door of the train is a number one in gold. There are people everywhere, some crying. As the train starts she runs to the door where her brother is by the window and kisses him and tells him to "keep safe."

The twilight zone that you enter just as you are dropping off to sleep or in the first moments of waking can give rise to weird, dream-like visions (called hypnagogia if they occur as you are falling asleep, hypnopompia if they occur on waking). These visions are usually fragments of experience, although they can occasionally have a story running through them. They have a hallucinatory quality about them, and often there is no logic linking the scenes. Science can describe these only as pictures being drawn from the memory banks of the brain and having no meaning beyond this. If a wider view of mind is taken, they might easily be interpreted as flashbacks of memory from another life.

Peter Thompson (pseudonym) is a well-balanced, capable and rational man, well educated and holding a position as a senior engineer in local government. Ever since he had this experience he has been searching for an explanation for it:

One Saturday evening my wife and I were sitting in the lounge watching TV, and probably I had been sitting there for perhaps fifteen minutes before the experience occurred. While it happened there was clarity of thought, but the way it started is strange. While looking at the TV the surrounds around disappeared, everything went black because some senses, for example sight and sound, apparently stopped working. The manner in which this happened was as if an image disappeared, as when an older TV shuts down, my vision withdrew to a centre circle point and went out, everything around just went.

At first it was a shock, and while still sitting I thought I had gone blind and deaf or suffered a stroke, but then the next event was that my body went horizontal. There was an incredible force upon me which pushed me down to a horizontal position. This was definitely confusing and frightening, because it meant that I had gone straight down into or through the back of the chair. [At this point Philip thought he must be dying, but then his vision suddenly returned.] I became aware that I was leaning against a wooden post in a hall and looked down to find I was holding a drink and wearing corduroy trousers with a waistcoat. Looking around, it was apparent I was in a music hall, but the people were wearing older, possibly Victorian-style clothing. There weren't many people in the audience, and there was a lady dressed in black holding her hat, with a friend. The lady turned and looked at me. My gaze then diverted forward to the stage, upon which an overly made-up and chubby red-faced man was singing and dancing. He wore a garish checked suit, while his female assistant wore a sort of thick whitish Basque costume with thick woollen tights. Smoke from lighting lamps was rising. I looked down at the front of the stage, where a row of shells could be seen which presumably housed oil or candle lamps which lit the stage and performers.

Next I looked to my left and saw people who may have been friends standing talking. There was a noise above me; looking up, I could see the dark wood floorboards of a mezzanine floor on which someone was moving a chair about. The post against which I was leaning supported this floor. Again I looked at the performers and suddenly the experience changed and reversed and the vision stopped. Again I was horizontal and the strong force suddenly returned me to the vertical sitting position into the chair and normal surroundings returned.

At this point I did not know what had happened and leaped out of the chair in fright, asking my wife what had happened. Mary did not know what I was going on about: apparently, she had not seen anything happen. The experience probably only lasted two or three minutes.

Perhaps I fell asleep, but I do not fall asleep easily and certainly have never dozed in a chair. Nothing similar has happened since.

Because Peter Thompson's account is so accurate and detailed we can say that this was almost certainly a hypnagogic experience. It happened when he was on the borders of sleep, and the experience was ushered in by loss of vision and sound. This is exactly what happens when you start to drop off to sleep: if you have ever nearly nodded off on a motorway, you will have noticed that your hearing changes and your vision becomes partially dominated by internal imagery before something fortunately alerts you and you call in at the next motorway station for a coffee. Changes in physical sensation are also very common in hypnagogia; feelings of falling, spinning and flying all occur, as does the sensation of a sudden forcible change in body position.

Peter Thompson's experience fits very neatly into this category. And if we accept that this was indeed a hypnagogic experience, there is no need to consider a previous life as an explanation. There is probably nothing in the visual imagery that couldn't easily have been recalled from his present-day memory. Science can certainly explain the mechanism of this dream. It's impossible for anyone to explain the content of a dream unless he knows everything about the dreamer. Only the dreamer himself or herself is truly in a position to be able to do this.

Dream memory is quite capable of playing the same tricks

on us as waking memory. Mrs. Kathleen Cliff had this recurring dream as a child: "I dreamed I was a girl of about seventeen with long, straight red hair. I was wearing a long dress that reached my feet, and I was stood on cliffs looking out to sea with a man who was my father. We were waiting for my brother Michael, who had gone out on a fishing-boat and hadn't returned. There was a feeling of loss and that he didn't return. The place was Ireland: how I knew this I don't know." The dream recurred until she was seven, then stopped. It wasn't until she was about ten and her parents had a TV for the first time that she saw a holiday programme about Ireland. Watching this, she turned to her mother and said: "I've been there."

From the information she gives, Kathleen's dream—cliffs looking out over the sea—does not sound specific enough to enable it to be identified as any particular place. But if a similar cliff and a sea scene were shown in the film about Ireland, they might well have triggered off a feeling of recognition, though without more detail we can't be sure. Kathleen does, however, add that "I also feel strangely drawn to Catholicism. I am not a Catholic, nor are any members of my family, but I feel that I was once, and sometimes if I pass a Catholic church I have an urge to go in. But being a sensible, logical person, I try and shrug it off."

Terry Courtnadge had a dream in 1980 which convinced him that he had lived before. He saw himself very clearly standing at the bow of a wooden ship entering a harbour which he did not recognise. Two years later he saw TV pictures of the city of Boston, USA, celebrating its 350-year-old history, and the harbour appeared exactly as it had done in his dream. Could he, after two years, have remembered the harbour he visited in his dream accurately enough to identify it as Boston Harbour? It does seem equally likely that he may have seen and forgotten pictures of Boston Harbour before, and that is why they appeared in his dream and later triggered feelings of recognition when he saw them on television.

When we are thinking about explanations for any of these experiences, we must be aware that we are looking at them through the filters of our current world-view, which limits the range of explanations possible. Sometimes, though, we have to decide whether the scientific explanation for one of these past-life dreams is less persuasive than the non-scientific alternative. In the following account, Stan Bailey describes how he found a place he had visited often in his dreams. Remember that although his description of the place—a village green where three roads met—might fit any number of English villages, Stan, a town boy, hadn't actually seen any such village greens, though he may, of course, have seen pictures of them in books.

I was born and brought up in Gravesend, north Kent. From the age of about three for about twelve years I had a recurring dream. It was of a place in the country where three roads met, forming a sort of small village green. On the green were a few small trees and a number of seats, and alongside the road on one side was a large brick barn. Nothing ever happened in the dream; I just stood there looking. Then in 1932, at the age of fifteen, I was out cycling with friends one day when we passed through this site. I nearly fell off my bike looking back, I was so surprised. Arriving home, I questioned my mother as to whether I had ever been taken there in childhood. She was quite adamant that I had not. She had no friends or relatives living there, and few people had cars in the 1920s: we certainly did not.

The place was Longfield, and everything was exactly as I had seen it in my dreams, which I had had three or four times a year over twelve years. I can remember telling my mother many times on waking that I had dreamed of "that place in the country again" (I was a town boy).

Needless to say I didn't dream of it again. For me it raises interesting questions. What happened on that green? Did I live near it, or play on it, or did it have some connection with my death?

It is interesting to note that once he had identified the "place in the country" the dream stopped, as though finding the source of the dream had finally laid a ghost. Others have commented on this: Elizabeth Paradise (see page 237), for example, reported that her young brother's memories of his "other house" seemed to vanish once he had satisfied himself that he had found it.

We are so locked into our scientific world-view that we prefer explanations of cryptomnesia or random dream imagery. But supposing we were to take a wider view and consider the possibility that dreams such as Stan Bailey's might be due to remote viewing (getting an image of a distant place by focusing the attention on it) or precognition? Not an explanation orthodox science could accept (though there is now good scientific evidence that both precognition and remote viewing occur) but not necessarily a past-life one. It would seem that using a past-life explanation adds another layer of complexity.

As a child, and throughout the early years of her life, Jean Wall used to have "dreams," or so she thought, of a large white house with a balcony around the first floor and balustrades on the front. She had all sort of memories of childhood in that house:

> Being scolded for going out on to the balcony because I could fall. The feel of my clothes on my body. Fastening boots up with a buttonhook, and lots more. Then in 1985 my husband and I had a holiday on the *QEII* that took us to New York. We booked a coach-trip to enable us to see more in the three days we were there. On the second day we went to see the oldest house in Manhattan. I couldn't believe it. There was my house. I always knew I would recognise it when I saw it but never thought I would have to travel 3,000 miles to find it. As we were waiting to go in, I was busy describing the inside to my husband. I told him that when we go up the stairs, offset to the right of a corridor was the balcony where I was scolded.
>
> Immediately opposite to that was a similar portion of balcony, but I never went out at that point because the bedroom of the person who scolded me overlooked it. When we went into the nursery on the second floor, my husband commented that the floor had sunk to the front, and I said: "Oh no, it's always had a slope on it."

None of the furniture was right, apart from one room, and it all looked so neglected; the gardens looked dreadful. But of course they don't have a National Trust or Heritage to take care of such things. It took me completely by surprise. The only way I could have known that house was by living in it, and believe me I did, from the age of eight to thirteen.

Cryptomnesia really does not seem to fit the facts in this case. And yet if we accept that this really was a past-life memory, we also have to acknowledge a very hefty coincidence—that Mrs. Wall's previous incarnation took place in the oldest house in New York and that this particular house has been preserved. Given this, the fact that she visited it is not so surprising. Another explanation, and in some ways one that is easier to believe, is that Mrs. Wall had a precognitive dream. As already mentioned, many people do have such dreams and sometimes subsequent events seem to confirm the dream prediction. However, precognition is not entirely satisfactory as an explanation, because in her dream she saw herself as a young child—there is an element of past as well as future time in the dream.

We are so used to the idea of linear time, progressing from past to future, that it is difficult to think of time in any other way. But the evidence now is that in parapsychological experiments time is not like this, and non-linear time is a concept that is now widely accepted in physics. Even within our present scientific framework, we can't dismiss apparent shifts in time as easily as we could have done twenty years ago. Who knows whether in another twenty years' time we will even have a mechanism for past-life experiences?

Perhaps the most intriguing dream-recognition experience is described by Philip Pratley. All his life Philip has had a recurring dream in which he is walking up a spiral staircase that gets smaller and smaller as he ascends. Eventually, he gets stuck, can go no further and wakes up. One day, on holiday in Normandy with his wife Terry, they visited a small château, Gratot, where legend had it that 600 years ago the lord of Gratot had been married to a fairy. As soon as Philip started to walk up the spiral staircase leading to the fairy's tower, he re-

alised that this was the staircase of his dream. "I stopped.
Terry bumped into me. Not really believing myself in what I
was saying, I told her of my dream. With some alarm she
asked what happens when I get stuck. The answer was nothing, nothing at all. I just wake up. We continued climbing, my
hands inexplicably cold, an odd sensation at the back of my
neck. The staircase was some four feet wide, the access clear
and unobstructed. Two more complete spirals and it was a different matter. The staircase finished, and a small, narrower
one commenced. With some trepidation . . . I stepped on to
the first tread. Ten steps later, I was stuck. The walls closed in,
the spiral tightened. I backed off, took off my coat and went
up again. This time, with much effort, I pushed my seventeen-
stone frame through to the top." Since this incident, Philip
says, the dream has stopped.

Was it simply coincidence that the tower corresponded so
closely to Philip's dream? Probably. But if we want a more romantic answer, there are two available. We can see it as a precognitive dream, a shift forwards out of time. Or we can
interpret it as a past-life memory. Philip adds what he considers to be a piece of corroborative evidence. On the landing at
the top of the tower, names were carved into the soft sand-
stone surrounding the door of the fairy's chamber. Most were
dated between 1820 and 1840, when the castle was still occu-
pied. It must, he suggests, have been the done thing for guests
at Gratot to carve their names on the entrance to the fairy
chamber. The names were written out in full, the Christian
name followed by the surname. All except one, where just the
initials were carved, with no date. The initials were Philip's
own: PP!

7

Searching for a Past Life

Seldom any splendid story is wholly true.

Dr. Johnson

MOST of the best past-life stories have emerged under hypnosis. And unfortunately a good story is just what one would expect from a hypnotic subject. Suggestibility is stock in trade for the hypnotist. Under hypnosis people become much more suggestible, or at least more inclined to accept suggestions uncritically. People vary in their hypnotisability, but regressions are easy to induce in those who will allow themselves to be put into a trance state. Moreover, people under hypnosis show very specific characteristics, all of which contribute to the creation of very convincing alternate personalities.

Hypnosis can induce a loss of inhibition and an enhanced capacity for imagery and role enactment, which means that subjects can play out their roles very convincingly. Under hypnosis, too, sources of memory are confused, and imagined events are experienced as real; the subjects may be totally convinced of the hypnotic life they are living, and because they are totally convinced themselves it's easy for them to convince others. It is the sheer vividness of the regression experience, the intensity of the emotions the subjects shows, that is so compelling. It often persuades not only the subject but also the observer that a genuine experience is being remembered.

Under hypnosis people seem to have easier access to child-hood memories, though they do not literally regress to an ear-lier stage of development. They are also less inclined to test reality, and to show a greater tolerance of logical incon-gruities—this is the so-called "trance logic."

If you are a good hypnotic subject you will probably ex-perience a past life (or even several past lives) if you undergo a hypnotic regression. The more hypnotisable you are, the more intense the experience will seem. But hypnotisability has nothing to do with how *credible* the experience seems. This is determined much more by your own previous beliefs and attitudes towards reincarnation, and also to your expecta-tions—and the expectations that may be transmitted to you by the hypnotherapist.

What must also be taken into account is that the person under hypnosis may develop a rapport with the hypnotist, with a consequent willingness to please him or her. If a hyp-notist suggests to a good hypnotic subject that he is going to regress to another life in another age, it is a virtual certainty that he is going to oblige, even if he has never before consid-ered the possibility of a past life. This is how Morey Bern-stein, having already regressed Virginia Tighe to the age of one, persuaded her to take the further steps into the past which were to lead her to her life as Bridey Murphy:

> Oddly enough, you can go even farther back. I want you to keep on going back and back and back in your mind. And, surprising as it may seem, strange as it may seem, you will find that there are other scenes in your memory. There are other scenes from faraway lands and distant places in your memory . . . I will talk to you again in a little while. Meanwhile your mind will be going back, back, back and back until it picks up a scene, until, oddly enough, you find yourself in some other scene, in some other place, in some other time, and when I talk to you again you will tell me about it.

Many past-life hypnotists take advantage of this suggestibil-ity to "lead" their clients in a way that would be considered outrageous in a court of law, and yet still claim that the accounts they are given are evidence of reincarnation. Dr. Helen Warnbach, for example, used to hypnotise her subjects and then suggest to them that they were regressing to a particular time, or a particular place. When they obligingly produced a personality for her, she would question them further: "I decided to ask my subjects to go to a market to get supplies and to describe the market and the supplies that they bought. Money is also a clue to a place and time in the past, so I asked them to visualise the money they might have exchanged for goods."

One young woman was regressed to AD 25 and discovered herself to be a carpenter in northern Italy. She found herself purchasing supplies with a very odd coin:

Subject: [It] was dark grey and had a hole in the middle. It seemed to be shaped like a square with the corners pounded to try to make it look round. I've never seen anything like it.

Dr. Wambach: Did it seem to be crude around the edges?

Subject: Yes, as though it had been hammered rather than moulded.

Dr. Wambach: I've had that coin described to me at least 20 times before. It was used around the Mediterranean Sea in the time-period 500 BC to AD 25.

Hypnosis seems to enhance our capacity for imagery and role enactment, so that imagined events are experienced as "real." Many hypnotists use imagination when they are inducing a trance state—the subject is invited to create a scene, step into it and experience it. For the hypnotic subject to create a fantasised character and act out a role is a natural extension of this. Many past-life memories produced under hypnosis probably fall into this category—they are simply fantasies, created, as dreams are created, by our own minds.

Self-induced hypnotic-trance states, deep relaxation or meditation all seem to create a similar state of consciousness which facilitates the emergence of apparent past-life memories. Rex Caddick told us about the experience he had under self-hypnosis about ten years ago. Rex is now sixty-four and is a linguist who has taught art and photography, writes short stories and paints a little. None of his immediate family showed similar interests or abilities; he was brought up in a poor working-class family and educated at a secondary modern school. Whether his experience was a genuine past life he doesn't know, but it does seem to him to explain many things about himself which had previously puzzled him.

Rex found himself in the 1790s, an elderly "pedant" living not far from Covent Garden in a small square of Georgian town houses. Here he had a room over a milliner's shop and earned his living by teaching young ladies to draw and paint. He also taught English grammar and French and occasionally translated German documents. "I can still see my 'rooms,' the milliner's shop, the street itself—a sloping lane about 16½ feet [5 metres] wide, mainly unpaved but with a sort of cobbled gutter in the centre. The lane was muddy, with pools of water in the ruts made by carts, both hand- and horse-drawn." He continued:

There was an exhibition of paintings by some new artist in one of the houses in the square and I went to see it. Again I felt a tremendous emotional turmoil as I looked at the paintings of this young upstart who had succeeded in doing what I had studied and had been trying to do all my life. In the current life I recognised one of the paintings—a painting of St. Paul's—and it was by Turner. I "knew" then that it was all imagination. I felt sure that Turner had not been painting that early. I checked in the *Oxford Dictionary of Art and Artists* and I was wrong. He had been painting at that time.

I have never liked Turner's paintings, which was something my son could never understand when he was studying art, design and photography.

I don't know if this is proof of reincarnation, but I am sure in my own mind that I "lived" these events. I could smell the stink of the river and know that my shoes let in water. The teaching, love of painting and art, even some little facility in art all seem to stem from this time. To argue against the episode being a genuine past-life experience, in the 1970s I had seen a televised programme about Turner's life, although I can remember little of it. And I had later spent a day looking at the paintings held in the Tate (and thinking similar daubs by another artist would have been consigned to the waste basket!).

Was Mr. Caddick recognising elements of his past life in his present one? Or was he simply creating a past life that incorporated many of the feelings experienced in his present one (including his views on Turner), in much the same way as dreams are created?

It has certainly been suggested that at least some reincarnation experiences, like dreams, are just an expression of conscious or unconscious desires or hopes or fears. Every hypnotherapist who offers past-life regressions has a sprinkling of emperors and queens and courtesans among their case histories. But the late Helen Wambach, who had recorded 1,100 past lives in her casebook, believed that fantasy and wish fulfilment were not the explanation because, she claimed, the lives most of her subjects regressed to were very ordinary lives. They included a crippled beggar who starved to death, an infant born into a Seminole Indian tribe and a peasant dying of disease in ninth-century northern Italy. In her view these kinds of lives did not seem to be wish-fulfilling fantasies.

Perhaps they show no signs of wish fulfilment, but they were by no means "ordinary lives" from a present-day perspective, and the element of fantasy is certainly much more evident than it would be in, say, a past life of a solicitor in East Grinstead in the 1950s. One of the uses of fantasy is to give ourselves the freedom to explore situations we are curious about but don't particularly want to experience in real life.

Most people who want to undergo a past-life regression probably do so simply out of curiosity or because they think it might provide them with evidence of survival. Often, though, people want to be regressed to confirm some spontaneous glimpse they have already had of a past life. Spontaneous past-life feelings are always tantalisingly incomplete. To be given a mere glimpse of a life that seems so personal and so real is like reading a page or two of a book over someone's shoulder in a train, becoming instantly fascinated by the

plot but being unable to see the development or denouement
before they get off. It's not surprising that people who feel
strongly that they have had a past life should want to know
more, to explore their past and find out who they were, what
happened to them—in fact, to complete the story.

For such people the obvious next step is to follow up their
experience through hypnotic regression. The results are often
disappointing. It is seldom that the life they are regressed to is
the life they experienced spontaneously. The regression experiences are usually described as interesting but not convincing. Many people say that however vivid the hypnotic
regression seems, it has a different quality from the spontaneous experience. Robert, the violinist whose past-life memories are described in Chapter Twelve has also had a past-life
regression, but this produced a quite different incarnation, as
a victim of the Holocaust. It, too, felt utterly real, and was in
its way just as powerful. And yet, he says, it did not have quite
the ring of truth of his earlier, spontaneous childhood experience. The hypnotic regression, he feels, could easily have
been the product of fantasy and imagination, but he remains
convinced that as a schoolboy he was truly remembering himself in an earlier life.

Rachel J. (pseudonym), whose story is told in Chapter Ten
also experienced both a spontaneous past memory and a later
hypnotic regression and had much the same reaction. "In the
first experience I was that person, I was *in* that body. The hypnotic regression was an equally powerful experience in many
ways, and a very valuable one in what it showed me about
problems I was having to deal with in my current life. But it
wasn't quite the same—in the regression I was an observer,
watching my physical body but not in it."

R. Donald told us that he has been regressed a number of
times but has never been entirely convinced by the experiences. But, he says, he was quite gripped by an occurrence
that happened spontaneously:

> The first intimation came when I was walking near
> woods with very tall trees, and the call of the rooks trig-
> gered a feeling of pleasure—one could almost say
> joy—in that it was associated with me "being" a sol-

dier—an early Norman sergeant to be precise—accustomed to walking through such surroundings behind
two mounted officers. I noticed that "I" was a bit
shorter than my present height of six feet [1.8 metres]
and was of a thicker build. I did not resent the fact that
I had no horse: I had great stamina and did not suffer
from sore feet. Previously, I have always been "anti"
the Normans as I felt they came and took over England
and so were "baddies." Therefore I had certainly never
fantasised about being one.

Occasionally, though, a past-life regression does confirm
someone's spontaneous memories of a past life, and when this
happens the impact on that person is dramatic.

Jenny Cockell is a forty-five-year-old chiropodist living in
Northamptonshire. Born in 1953, she is one of the relatively
rare people whose past-life memories did not fade as she grew
older but intensified. For as long as she can remember, she has
had memories of a past life that she was convinced she lived
as "Mary," in Ireland, from about 1898 until the 1930s. "I
can't explain why or how," she says; "the knowledge was just
there in my consciousness." Jenny also studied a map of Ireland and felt drawn, again without being able to explain exactly why, to a place called Malahide, near Dublin. She "saw"
the cottage where she lived quite clearly, "the first on the left
in a quiet westward lane," and she even drew a map of the village where she lived, with the position of the cottage marked.

Much of Jenny's information about her life as Mary came
to her in childhood dreams. Jenny's childhood was not happy,
and as a child she would frequently dream that she was
"Mary," lying in bed, alone, and with the realisation that she
was dying and would be leaving her children behind. She remembered being desperately poor, with scarcely enough
money to buy food. Memories of her husband were vague and
peripheral.

Eventually, Jenny's parents separated, and after this she
seems to have become happier and to have thought much less
about her other life. She grew up, married and had two children. Then in 1987 she met a hypnotist who practised past-life
regression, and she decided to try to find out more about her

past life in a series of hypnotic-regression sessions. Under hypnosis Jenny was taken back to her past life as Mary, living in Malahide. She described a cobbled street, with market stalls down one side, and her dying moments (a scene she was already familiar with through her childhood dreams). She also recovered what she believed to be her husband's name (Bryan O'Neil) and the names of four of her children (James, Mary, Harry and Kathy). Jenny's most powerful memories had always been of her seven or eight children, and her desire to be reunited with them eventually grew so strong that she set out on a quest to find them.

It wasn't until some years later, in 1989, that Jenny could afford actually to make a trip to Malahide and try to find "her" family. From a detailed map of Malahide, she had managed to identify what she believed was the location of Mary's cottage, in Swords Road. Malahide in 1989, however, had changed considerably from her memories of it earlier in the century. The cottage had long since been demolished, though a butcher's shop still stood where she remembered it. But a former resident of Swords Road was able to tell her who had lived in the cottage that used to stand where Jenny remembered it during the 1920s and 1930s. This was indeed a woman called Mary—Mary Sutton—who had had seven children and died in 1932, soon after the birth of her youngest child. The children had been sent to orphanages.

Women called Mary who had borne seven children cannot have been too thin on the ground in Ireland in the 1930s, but this does not seem to have been a problem. Neither did the fact that Mary's married name was Sutton and not O'Neil, nor that her children were called Jeffrey, Philomena, Christopher, Francis, Bridget, Elizabeth and Sonny prove a barrier. Jenny was and remains convinced that she had found her family. Since then she has managed to trace most of these elderly children, old enough to be her own parents, and one at least (Sonny, the eldest) seems quite readily to have accepted Jenny as his reincarnated mother. What seems to have convinced Sonny was Jenny's memory of incidents from his childhood that he felt no one but his mother could have known about. One of these memories was of "Mary's" children surrounding a live hare trapped in a snare. Sonny, too, remembered this incident and confirmed that the hare had indeed been alive when they had found it. Jenny also told him that she could remember standing on a jetty waiting for a boat, though she could no longer remember why. Sonny told her that he often used to act as golf caddie on an island to which he had to take the ferry Whenever he did this, he would always find his mother waiting for him on the jetty when the boat returned.

Was Jenny's quest really successful? In terms of Jenny's personal needs (which, after all, is why she undertook the quest), one has to accept that it was. She feels at last that she has fulfilled her obligations towards her lost children. In her own words: "By his acceptance, Sonny has given me what I have searched for. The sense of responsibility and guilt has fallen away, and I feel a sense of peace that I have never really known before."

Is this anything more than a good story, a series of coincidences reinforced by hypnotic regression? It's easy to dismiss most of the details Jenny remembered, apart perhaps from the incident of the snared hare and her memory of waiting for Sonny's boat to come back, as coincidence. But should we dismiss as readily her strong conviction, the feeling, which has been such a constant and driving force in her life since early childhood, that she has lived before? True, her memories are not razor-sharp, and many of her facts are clearly wrong, including the names of her children, which she should surely have remembered. Does this matter? What it does suggest, yet again, is that even the "best" past-life memories are available only as snapshots, moments of a life frozen in memory. Whether we believe in the reality of Jenny's past-life memory probably depends on whether we attach more weight to the objective evidence—facts that check out—or to the subjective evidence—Jenny's inner conviction that this was a life she actually lived.

SEARCHING FOR PROOF

Someone who is searching for a past life under hypnosis is looking for proof. To help him or her the hypnotist will try to elicit as many details as possible—names, dates, places, anything that can be checked to see how well the past-life story hangs together. Perhaps one should not expect complete correspondence: after all, memory is never perfect, and these are past-life memories interpreted by a twentieth-century brain.

Disappointingly, very few of the past lives that have been disinterred under hypnotic regression stand up to close analysis—which is why the few that make a comparatively good showing are so well known. Most are full of historical inaccuracies, inconsistencies and anomalies.

Very occasionally, such apparent inconsistencies actually strengthen the case for a past life: Mrs. Smith (see page 154), for example, remembered the Cathar robes as dark blue when the accepted view at the time was that they were black. But much more often such inconsistencies simply destroy the credibility of the past-life memory and suggest very strongly that the memories produced have their origins firmly set in the twentieth century, that people see what they would expect to see from a twentieth-century perspective.

One subject of the hypnotist Harry Hurst, for example, remembered a life during the reign of Pharaoh Ramses III, regardless, or ignorant, of the fact that a system of numbering the pharaohs was not adopted until the nineteenth century. He also referred to a "sestertius," a coin not in use until 1,000 years later.

A subject of Arnall Bloxham, remembering a life as an American Indian, talked of coastal tribes who had brought tales of men with horns, carrying round shields and sailing in tall ships driven by huge blankets. To most casual listeners, this would conjure up a picture of invading Vikings in horned helmets, and the Vikings very probably did land on the American mainland some time in the eleventh century. However, they would not have been wearing horned helmets. Although many people associate these with the Vikings, the fact is that the helmet worn by the ordinary soldier was a simple close-fitting, often conical cap. Horned helmets were worn only occasionally, by high-ranking individuals, and usually for religious ceremonial occasions rather than battle or invasion.

Hypnotherapist Joe Keeton, who has conducted hundreds of past-life regressions, believes that only about two in every hundred regressions are not the product of imagination and fantasy. Sometimes errors and inconsistencies in a past-life

story are glaringly obvious. Very occasionally, a past-life regression throws up a personality who is a matter of historical
fact, and whose memories are largely verifiable. But even
then a sharp eye may spot inaccuracies in a story that seems
to stand up to analysis in every detail. And once this happens,
like a house of cards, the whole magnificent edifice collapses.
Such is the case with the story of Joan Waterhouse, the
Chelmsford witch.

THE TRIAL OF THE CHELMSFORD WITCH

In the library of Lambeth Palace, in London, is the only sur-
viving copy of the sixteenth-century chapbook recording the
trial for witchcraft, at Chelmsford Assizes in July 1566, of
Agnes and Joan Waterhouse, mother and daughter, from the
Essex village of Hatfield Peverel. The trial, presided over by
Judge John Southcote and with the Attorney-General, Gilbert
Gerard, taking the role of prosecutor, was one of the earliest
witch trials on record. Agnes Waterhouse was found guilty
and hanged; Joan was acquitted.

Joan's chief accuser had been another Agnes, a twelve-
year-old girl called Agnes Brown, and the charge against Joan
was that she had summoned a creature called Sathan, who assumed the form of a black dog to frighten and then haunt the
girl. Agnes had apparently fallen foul of the witch by refusing
her request to be given some bread and cheese.

In 1977 Jan, a twenty-three-year-old woman from Merseyside, answered an appeal by the hypnotherapist Joe Keeton
for volunteers for past-life hypnotic regressions. At her first
(and, as it turned out, her last) session, Joe asked her, while in
deep hypnosis, to go back to before her birth to search out a
memory. An extraordinary scene then unfolded as, before the
watchers' gaze, Jan seemed actually to *become* Joan Waterhouse, to live again the mental and physical agony that Joan
must have suffered during her trial, and eventually to show
such distress that Joe Keeton quickly brought her back to a
waking state. So horrifying had the experience been for Jan
that she refused any subsequent sessions and has never allowed herself to be hypnotised since.

What so impressed the watchers was not simply the wealth

of factual detail Jan produced—including the names of the presiding judge, the prosecutor, her accuser and those accused with her at the trial, all of which were corroborated by historical accounts of the trial—but the intense emotion she showed as she described the humiliation of the search to find the extra nipple every witch had with which to suckle her familiar, of being stripped and shaved and pricked all over with pins to find her witchmark (the one spot every witch was supposed to have on her body which was completely insensitive to pain). She held her hands curled up as if in intense pain, and when asked why she did this replied that they were burned by a "rod of iron," a reference to the hot iron bar victims were made to grasp while being interrogated.

After her regression, Jan was able to remember in detail all the events of the trial. In an interview with the writer Ian Wilson the following year, in November 1978, Jan told him that she had been shocked by her mother's appearance in the dock—"she looked too old to be my mother." Her face was "disgustingly spotted." Both these statements were true. Agnes *was* old to be eighteen-year-old Joan's mother—the record gives her age as sixty-four—and the record also mentions that "there were diverse spottes on her face and one on her nose." Now, *Jan* might well have been shocked by Agnes's appearance but why should *Joan* have been? After all, Joan had lived with it for eighteen years and must have been well accustomed to it. It does sound as though the woman describing the dreadful experience in the dock at Chelmsford was not Joan but Jan.

Other people have made similar observations about her speech. Language has changed so vastly in the last 400 years that it would be virtually impossible to communicate with someone who had been regressed beyond the end of the sixteenth century if they were really speaking as they would have spoken then. The words, the expressions used by "Joan" sounded archaic, but behind them Jan's native Merseyside accent could still be detected. Ian Wilson asked Stanley Ellis, of the School of English at Leeds University, an expert on English regional accents and the development of spoken English throughout the centuries, to listen to and comment on the tape recordings of Jan's hypnotic regression. Ellis regretfully concluded that there was nothing in the recording that persuaded him he was listening to genuine sixteenth-century speech. The phrases and sentence structures used were the kind of archaisms regularly used in the twentieth century to convey a period flavour in historical plays or novels: "I know not, sire," "'Tis a rod of iron," etc.

However, it was Joe Keeton's wife, Monica, who noticed what seemed at first like a small discrepancy but was eventually to show pretty conclusively that Jan's memories as Joan Waterhouse had their origins fair and square in more modern times. Early in her regression Jan had given the year in which she found herself as "the year of Our Lord 1556." Fifteen fifty-six was near the end of Mary's reign; Elizabeth did not come to the throne until two years later, in 1558. And yet later in the session, when Jan was asked the name of the reigning monarch, she insisted repeatedly that it was Elizabeth, not Mary.

There is no doubt about the actual date of the trial—the Lambeth Palace chapbook gives it as 1566, a full decade after the date mentioned by Jan, and well within the reign of Elizabeth. So how could Jan, so accurate about so many aspects of the trial, have been so wrong about its date?

It was Ian Wilson who discovered the probable answer, in a reproduction copy of the chapbook, produced in a limited edition by the British Philobiblon Society in the nineteenth century. The front page of the original chapbook reads: "The examination and confession of certain Wytches at Chensforde in the Countie of Essex before the Quenes maiesties Judges the xxvi daye of July Anno 1566." The front page of the Philobiblon Society copy, which became the most important resource for anyone researching or writing about the trial, is an exact copy—except that the date is given as "Anno 1556." The typographer responsible for setting the copy mistranscribed the date. No one has discovered the exact origin of Jan's Joan Waterhouse memories, but it seems certain that they must have sprung from some book, article or drama which used this nineteenth-century copy as its source, and perpetuated this simple error.

To round off the story, Jan should have been hypnotised again and asked under hypnosis whether she remembered such a source, as was done in the case of Blanche Poynings. Unfortunately but understandably, Jan had been so terrified by her experience that she refused ever to be hypnotised again, and so this opportunity was lost. Cryptomnesia remains a possibility, though we have no evidence of the source. The only other explanation is that she was somehow stepping out of time, a possibility that is discussed further in chapter 16.

Many of the past lives that come to light under hypnotic regression are notable for their richness of detail and data, which makes them seem far more convincing than most spontaneously remembered past-life memories. Most are probably the results of fantasy. But fantasy can't explain every case of supposed reincarnation. At best it is only a partial answer. It may explain the creation of a particular personality or the circumstances of a particular life, but it can't explain how it is that, in a very few cases, this fantasised past life is fleshed out with facts. Even if the character is a product of fantasy, the historical data which help to make it credible clearly are not. And nowhere has a wealth of historical detail proved more persuasive than in one of the most intriguing of all cases of apparent past-life recall on record—the story of Antonia Michaela Maria Ruiz de Prado and the Spanish Inquisition.

8

The Case of the
Spanish Adventuress

This is one of those cases in which the imagination is baffled by the facts.

Winston Churchill, remark in the House of Commons
following the parachute descent of Rudolf Hess
(13 May 1941)

THIS is one of the most interesting and arguably one of the most convincing cases of hypnotic regression on record—not because the story itself is convincing; on the contrary, it beggars belief. It is an extravaganza, a story so colourful, full of such torrid passion and high adventure—in fact, so thoroughly over the top—that common sense would suggest it had its origins in either fantasy or fiction. Its interest lies in the fact that hundreds of hours of diligent and painstaking research over a number of years not only verified the numerous historical facts of the story but found that some were so obscure that there seems no way in which the subject could have acquired them. Dr. Linda Tarazi, the hypnotherapist who has described the case, had many sessions with her subject and meticulously checked out every detail of her story. Eventually, she was forced to the conclusion that reincarnation had to be considered a possible explanation of the case, if only because no other explanation seemed plausible.

The central character in this story is Laurel Dilmen (pseudonym), a woman now in her late sixties who was born and raised in Chicago during the Depression years. Both Laurel Dilmen and her mother say that, in common with many children who remember past lives, she was a precocious child, claiming to have experienced life as an adult. Although there is no record that she actually talked in detail about a past life when she was a child, when she was about six she did show an unusual interest in clothing, weapons, buildings and artefacts of the sixteenth century. Her all-time favourite gift, which she had wanted for two years and received for her seventh Christmas, was a pair of fencing foils. She disliked history in school because, she said, "they made it dull, not at all like what really happened." She never studied Spanish history or learned Spanish. At college she majored in education and took courses in German, English and various sciences. After graduating from Northwestern University she went into show business for a few years before becoming a teacher. She married and had two children.

In the mid-1970s LD joined a club of amateur hypnotists, of which Linda Tarazi was a member, in the hope that hypnosis might help her lose weight and also cure her headaches. Some members of the club were studying past-life regression, and LD volunteered as a subject. Between June 1977 and January 1978 LD had eight sessions in which she regressed to several past lives. But only one seemed to hold any real interest for her—that of a woman called Antonia in Spain. She "remembered" other lives, happier or more successful than Antonia's, and yet it was to this that she returned again and again. This is Antonia's story.

ANTONIA'S STORY

Antonia Michaela Maria Ruiz de Prado was the daughter of a Spanish officer, Antonio, and his German wife, Erika. She was born on 15 November 1555 on a small plantation on the island of Hispaniola. For much of Antonia's childhood her father was away on military campaigns, and during his prolonged absences her mother, who was in poor health, suffered from depression. Antonia, a lively, intelligent child, nominally in the care of uneducated servants and slaves, was left to run wild, riding bareback in peasant clothes, climbing trees and swimming nude in the river or sea.

Antonia's mother spoke German to her, but when her father came home he expected her to speak Spanish and to behave properly. However, he also treated her like the son he knew he would never have, teaching her to ride and shoot, in case in his absence their home should be attacked by bandits, pirates, natives or rebellious slaves.

In 1569 Erika took Antonia to Germany to visit her brother Karl, a university professor who had left the priesthood to marry but was now a widower. Unfortunately, shortly after they arrived Erika died and Antonia was left in the care of her uncle. Karl not only educated Antonia but taught her to think for herself and make her own decisions. He took her with him to the Universities of Prague, Leipzig and Heidelberg and encouraged her to read widely. Here she started to show a propensity for cross-dressing, first of all sneaking into the libraries disguised as a boy, then into the lecture halls, and finally enrolling as a student and taking part in student activities such as brawling and fencing.

In 1580 they left Germany and went to Oxford. Karl himself had by now abandoned the Catholic Church and embraced the ideas of the Catholic humanists, Protestant reformers and the newly emerging scientific disciplines, but although he introduced these to Antonia he never tried to impose them on her and she remained a devout Catholic.

She also remained a loyal Spaniard, aligning herself with a group of rebellious Catholic students and on a few occasions acting as a courier for the Spanish ambassador, Don Bernardino de Mendoza, who was plotting with Mary Queen of Scots. Antonia seems to have been a most useful agent, able to assume a different nationality, social status and even sex at will.

After several of her friends had been arrested, tortured and executed, Antonia asked Karl to let her go to Spain. He warned her that if she did she would be in grave danger from the Spanish Inquisition, who would never accept her freedom of thought however devout she professed herself to be. Fate, however, stepped in. First, Antonia received a letter from her father, asking her to join him in Spain at Cuenca, where he now owned an inn. Secondly, in January 1584 Karl died. Finally, diplomatic relations between England and Spain were broken off. Antonia was arrested, but escaped to France and then made her way to Spain.

When she finally arrived in Cuenca in May 1584 it was to

discover from her father's attorney that her father had died ten days before. The inn was heavily in debt, and all the waitresses were moonlighting as prostitutes. The one piece of good news she was told was that her father had had a powerful friend who would help her if she proved worthy, although in the meantime he wanted to remain anonymous.

Antonia rose to the challenge. Her Spanish improved, the business slowly recovered, and she made various new friends, including a Jesuit priest, Fernando Mendoza, and a couple called Andres and Maria de Burgos. Meanwhile, she was under close surveillance by the Inquisition. In fact, the Inquisition already had a good deal of information about Antonia, largely gathered from her own father, who had been a close friend of Arganda, one of the two Inquisitors at Cuenca. It was this same Arganda who was Antonia's anonymous protector. Knowing that he was dying, that Antonia would then be left alone in a strange country, and that she had been exposed to many heretical ideas that might make her a very suspect figure in the eyes of the Inquisition, her father had asked his old friend to watch over her. He had also, somewhat rashly, passed over to Arganda Antonia's letters, in which she discussed these prohibited ideas and which also made it clear that her uncle Karl had indeed been a heretic. Her father's justification for this was that the letters also showed Antonia to be a devout Catholic and devoted to Spain. He had also assumed that the Inquisition would be made aware of their contents anyway, as Antonia would, as the law demanded, make inquisitorial confession when she arrived in Spain. But, ignorant of the law, she did not.

The Inquisitors of Cuenca soon felt it necessary to quash her freethinking ideas and rebellious spirit. She was summoned for questioning three times, and arrested and tried once. Eventually, she made a full confession and submitted to the instructions of the Inquisitors, paying a heavy fine and performing other penances.

In the ordinary course of events, trial by the Inquisition would have meant disgrace not only for Antonia but for all her descendants. However, both the Inquisitors seem to have grown fond of Antonia, appreciating both her piety and her beauty. With Arganda she already had a special relationship through her father; the other had tried several times to make Antonia his mistress. She offered numerous objections, none of which dissuaded him. "Finally, I decided to appeal to his honour as a conscientious Inquisitor: 'Can you honestly believe that such a wilful and deliberate sin will not alter your decisions as Inquisitor?' I asked coolly. He sighed. 'I suppose in a way it already has. In reviewing my cases recently, I noticed that they indicate a far more lenient view of fornication since I decided to indulge myself. To me the liberality was so striking that I feared it might arouse suspicion in the Suprema. I suppose I shall have to revert to my sterner judgements.'"

Antonia was reassured that her name would disappear from the records of the Inquisition. A bottle of ink "accidentally" spilled on her folio and rendered it illegible.

Despite her adventurous and unconventional life, Antonia, now 29, had so far remained a virgin. But now, in a steamy episode that seems to have been the climax of her life, she finally lost her virginity to a man she had secretly adored. The episode (which bears all the hallmarks of fantasy) involved a highly erotic and masochistic rape scene set in a torture chamber. Antonia's passionate and selfless love for her seducer did not go unrequited; her perfect love changed his own lustful feelings to an equally deep and powerful passion. Linda Terazi tells us that "They shared every faculty of mind, soul and body in a love that was both deeply spiritual and passionately erotic." Antonia's lover was a strong, dominant, powerful man. She became his mistress and bore him a son, and together they embarked on many more adventures around the world. Eventually, Antonia was drowned near a small unknown island in the Caribbean, her lover nearly dying in a vain attempt to save her. She was so wholly focused on his wellbeing that she was unaware of her own death until she realised that she did not feel his arms around her or his tears splashing on her face."

This passionate love affair lies at the heart of Antonia's story, and certainly seemed to be the reason why this life, above all the other past lives Laurel Dilmen remembered under hypnosis, became so important to her. In fact, it was more than important: it became an obsession. She started to have dreams and daytime flashbacks of Antonia's "life."

Eventually, it began to obsess her to the point that it came to seem more vivid and far more worthwhile than her normal life. So involved was she with "Antonia's" life, with the search for this one lost perfect love beside which all other relationships paled, that she realised she was in danger of jeopardising her present life as LD, neglecting her friends and activities. It was at that point, three years after the initial regression sessions in which "Antonia's" memories had emerged, that she decided to seek help and turned to Linda Tarazi.

Dr. Tarazi was intrigued by the case and felt that the best way to persuade LD to give up her obsession and return to reality would be to convince her that Antonia's life was pure fantasy. Between June 1981 and March 1983 she regressed LD 36 times to her life as Antonia. The tapes of these sessions contained a huge amount of information about Antonia's supposed life. Dr. Tarazi then embarked on a search for inconsistencies and errors, which involved hours of library research, consultations with historians who had specialised knowledge of Spain in that period, and a visit to Cuenca, during which she was able to examine the town's archives and Inquisition records. She also checked the ease with which LD would have been able to acquire the information that she "knew" as Antonia, had she set out to do so.

Any educated person would be expected to know many of the people who had walk-on parts in Antonia's story: Queen Elizabeth I, King Philip II of Spain, Mary Queen of Scots, for example. Fifty or sixty more facts were easily verifiable from most history books or encyclopedias, but another twenty-five to thirty Dr. Tarazi discovered only with difficulty in rare books found in specialised research libraries. Over a dozen facts were published only in Spanish, and a few were not published at all but could be found only by checking local archives. The names of the two Inquisitors of Cuenca, for example, whom Antonia correctly identified, and their biographical details, were verified only by checking the diocesan archives of Cuenca.

Much to her own surprise, instead of discovering a catalogue of errors and discrepancies, Dr. Tarazi's research simply confirmed Antonia's story. Of the hundreds of detailed facts that formed the background to her life, all were correct.

Antonia was able to recall and recount factual events of her life with apparent ease but found more difficulty in talking about emotional material related to those events. If her story were fantasy, one might have expected the emotional memory to be the "easy" bit, the facts to bolster the story to be elicited with more difficulty. For example, in Antonia's second regression session she recalled her death in the Caribbean on her way back from Peru, where she had visited her uncle, Juan Ruiz de Prado, an important official in Lima. She refused, however, to say what his position was and became defensive when questioned about this, asking why the hypnotist wanted to know. This meeting was apparently traumatic, but she did not reveal any details of it until a later session.

Dr. Tarazi found several aspects of Antonia's story particularly convincing. Most hypnotic regressions, she says, have a nebulous quality, but Antonia's was quite different. From the first she came through as a proud, independent woman who knew exactly who, what and where she was. Her account also presented an intriguing contrast between the extreme accuracy of the details that affected her personal life and her relative ignorance of contemporary events that did not affect her directly. At her very first session, for example, the hypnotist who questioned her was a Dutchman, knowledgeable in Dutch history. The Netherlands were at that time under Spanish domination. Antonia was able to give a detailed account of the assassination of William of Orange in July 1584 and the succession of his son Maurice because, she said, this was what the local intellectuals were discussing at her inn. She referred correctly to the Spanish governor of the Netherlands at that time as Don Alejandro Famesio, sometimes incorrectly referred to as the Duke of Parma, although he did not succeed to his title until 1586. More impressively she referred to the Duke of Alva, Spanish governor from 1568 to 1573, by his name—Don Fernando de Toledo—rather than by his much better-known title.

Particularly interesting was Antonia's mention of the Inquisitor who had attempted to make her his mistress. He had, she said, become more lenient towards people who had committed the sin of fornication. When Dr. Tarazi examined the Inquisition records of Cuenca she found that a much smaller percentage of those arrested for fornication were penanced, as opposed to being released for insufficient evidence or receiving a suspended sentence, during the time that one of the Inquisitors was supposedly enamoured of Antonia. The figures were:

Before Antonia's arrival:	1582	73% penanced for fornication
	1583	75%
	1584 (to May)	60%
After Antonia's arrival:	1584 (May–Oct)	10%
	1584 (end of year when Antonia was under suspicion)	100%
	1585	11%
	1586	35%
	1587	50%

She revealed in a later session that in a dispute between Inquisitor Ulloa of Peru and Viceroy Villar, her uncle, Juan Ruiz de Prado, had supported Ulloa. All these names Dr. Tarazi eventually found, though with some difficulty: it took her many years to trace the names of de Prado and Ulloa, eventually finding them in a very obscure old Spanish book.

Another convincing aspect of Antonia's story is that two of the facts she reported were at first uncorroborated by the authorities in Spain, and yet further research proved Antonia to be correct. One of these was her description of the building that housed the tribunal of the Inquisition in Cuenca: she described it as a castle standing above Cuenca and dominating the entire region. The Government Tourist Office in Cuenca sent a photograph of the building that had housed the tribunal, but LD was stunned when shown it because it did not even slightly resemble the one she'd recalled. Dr. Tarazi describes the moment: "All present observed her dramatic change in mood from eager anticipation to a deep depression. She made no attempt to reconcile Antonia's description with this building. It never occurred to her to question the authorities. In quiet resignation she said her whole story must have been imagination because this was nothing like the building that had played such an important part in the life of Antonia!"

However, because this was the only apparent error she had found in Antonia's account, and because Antonia had seemed so sure of her ground, Dr. Tarazi decided not to let the matter rest. Finally, she found, in an obscure Spanish book on Cuenca, that the tribunal had been moved in December 1583, five months before Antonia's arrival in Cuenca, to an old castle overlooking the town, a castle that fitted her description perfectly.

The second discrepancy concerned the existence of a college in Cuenca. Antonia had said that students at the college met regularly at her inn. But Dr. Tarazi found that there was no college in Cuenca, and could find no reference to there having been one. The archivist at the municipal archives said that he had never heard of one. Eventually, in a century-old seven-volume work in Spanish, Dr. Tarazi found a reference to a college having been founded in Cuenca in the mid-sixteenth century. The work quoted mainly from obscure sixteenth-century Spanish sources and was, Dr. Tarazi pointed out, difficult even for Spanish teachers.

A third oddity in the story was that although there were normally three Inquisitors at a tribunal, Antonia had mentioned only two. However, when Dr. Tarazi checked the episcopal archives in Cuenca she found that from 1584 to 1588—the entire period during which Antonia lived in Cuenca—there had been only the two Inquisitors she had named.

Dr. Tarazi describes one more piece of evidence which seems to support the view that if this were fantasy it was a fantasy with a very special and compelling quality. In the hope that it would help to cure LD of her obsession with Antonia's life and love, Dr. Tarazi decided to try to persuade her that her ecstatic love affair would, in reality, never have lasted. Had she not died such a tragic early death, her romantic love would have gone the way of most romantic loves, passion spent, tempered by time and familiarity to a calmer affection. If LD could be persuaded to live out the unfinished part of Antonia's life in her imagination, Dr. Tarazi reasoned, she might at last be able to let it go.

When she had undergone her regression analysis, LD had been asked to try to recapture impressions of a possible past life. This time, again under hypnosis, she was told to try to fantasise what the rest of Antonia's life would have been like had she lived. In trance she was told that neither Antonia nor her son had drowned but that her lover had revived her and they had gone on to have another child, a daughter. They returned to Spain, where she lived out her life happily until the death of her lover nearly twenty years later. She was then told to visualise the rest of her life and the upbringing of her two children.

Antonia could not accept the idea that they had all survived, but was told that this did not matter; all she had to do was to imagine what her life would have been like had they survived.

The life that LD imagined was of a quite different quality from her original life as Antonia. Her descriptions were far less vivid, she added no new facts and recounted no new adventures. She and her lover remained faithful to each other but never married, and they spent less and less time together as both became more involved in their own careers. She showed little emotional involvement with her story, except when she was talking about her lover's death.

In fact, this exercise served its purpose. After it, LD seemed reconciled to her own present-day life and even admitted that in some ways it was better than Antonia's. She was no longer interested in being regressed. Her last regression to her life as Antonia took place in March 1983.

There are a few barriers to a total acceptance of Antonia's story. The first and perhaps the most fundamental is that although Antonia's lover is a real historical character, there is no evidence at all that Antonia Ruiz de Prado herself ever existed. Dr. Tarazi did not even attempt to find records of her birth, believing that it would be impossible to find proof of her birth on an isolated plantation, or her baptism in a small local church she could not name. But the Inquisition is known to have kept meticulously accurate records, and she did expect that if such a woman had existed, some traces of her would be found in the record of her tribunal. It is true that Antonia had produced a plausible, though perhaps suspiciously convenient, explanation of this omission. But on checking the Inquisition records, Dr. Tarazi found no missing number where Antonia's folio should have been. When asked about this, Antonia replied that the Inquisitors had probably foreseen the desirability of eliminating her file and probably gave it a number identical to another, but with an "a" after it so that there would be no gap in the record. Dr. Tarazi comments that this practice was indeed sometimes followed, though probably not for this reason.

Another fact that is hard to explain is that Antonia spoke no Spanish. How could it be that so many memories of her past life are apparently accurate and intact, and yet apparently no trace remained of her memory of the language that must have been one of the most fundamental elements, one would have thought, of her whole life? She pronounced Spanish names very well, was able to recite the prayers required by the Inquisition in Latin, and composed words and music to a song in Latin. But when she told her story, when she recalled so vividly her life as a Spaniard, she told it entirely in English.

Was It Fantasy?

What do we know about Laurel Dilmen? Linda Tarazi describes her as someone who had a very active imagination and a great ability to fantasise. As a child she rarely played regular children's games, but used to entertain her playmates with stories about heroes and gods, witches and wizards, princes and princesses, knights and dragons. She would make up games of the "dungeons and dragons" type and often felt that she had actually experienced the pretended situations before. So in being Antonia was she simply acting out yet another role? If she had known the facts of Antonia's life, there is no doubt that she could have woven them into a story and created around them the life and the personality of Antonia.

So was Antonia's story all a fantasy, the product of a vivid imagination? Almost certainly fantasy played a part. But we still have to explain how she learned the facts to flesh out Antonia's life. The personality may have been a fabrication; the facts certainly were not.

Was It Fraud?

Clearly, Antonia's story could not have been entirely fantasy. But could it have been fantasy combined with a carefully planned fraud? If so, it would have required an incredible amount of effort and forward planning. To get her story right, to create a convincing and consistent life as Antonia, LD would have had to have worked her way through numerous obscure sources, many of them in Spanish, a few in sixteenth-century Spanish difficult even for those fluent in the language to decipher. Why on earth should she bother to do this? And where would she have found the time? Linda Tarazi collected evidence from Laurel's family and friends and found that in the three years before she consulted her Laurel had been heavily involved with work and further studies. Moreover, much of the factual detail that makes the story so convincing was revealed in the earlier hypnotic sessions, before Dr. Tarazi was consulted, although it was only later that it was checked out and found to be accurate.

What makes it even more improbable that she did this is the way in which she told her tale. To begin with, she herself seemed to regard facts as unimportant. She would reveal them when they were relevant to her story, but certainly didn't make a point of displaying what she knew, or seem as though she was trying to impress or prove that her story was true by the depth and breadth of her knowledge. In fact, she gave the impression that she probably knew much more than she bothered to volunteer and would get irritated when her narrative was interrupted by questions about mundane things such as money, household commodities or artefacts. All she really seemed to want was to make other people understand the depth and reality of her love—almost as though, Dr. Tarazi says, she felt that if enough souls sympathised with her plight it might influence the "powers that be" to mitigate her sentence of being kept eternally apart from the, man she loved so desperately.

It is also worth noting that some of the more obscure facts were reported very early. She mentioned the name of her uncle Juan Ruiz de Prado, for example, at a very early stage in her exploration of her past life—at only her second session. This was a name verified only with the greatest difficulty by Dr. Tarazi in an old and very obscure Spanish book. It is difficult to believe that LD would have had the opportunity to research her supposed background in this kind of detail at that early stage. Moreover, facts about the same incident confirmed from the same source were not reported at around the same time, as might be expected if LD were collecting information from an obscure library source. Details from the same source might be given months, even years apart, mixed with details that had to be verified from other sources.

Finally, where would she have found the time? Simply verifying the facts of LD's story took years: it would have taken even longer for her to collect the hundreds of facts involved in her story in the first place. In any event, if it were fraud, it is difficult to see what LD could have gained from it. She didn't want publicity for her story and has always refused to allow her real name to be published. She has never capitalised on her story by attempting to publish it as sensationalised fact or as fiction.

Here one also has to consider the possibility of fraud not on the part of the subject but of the past-life therapist. Linda Tarazi, who published her account of the case in the *Journal of the American Society for Psychical Research* in October 1990, has since written a novel based on the transcripts of her regression sessions with Laurel Dilmen. Might she have invented the whole thing? It seems unlikely. There were witnesses to the early sessions in which Antonia appeared, and so clearly neither Laurel Dilmen nor Antonia are figments of the therapist's imagination. One has to assume that the historical research that Linda Tarazi carried out is accurate—someone who has the same amount of time and energy will sooner or later check her research findings, and if there are inaccuracies they will be found. If Linda Tarazi had simply wanted to write a historical novel, she has gone about it in a singularly labour-intensive way.

WAS THIS A CASE OF HYSTERICAL DISSOCIATION?

Most modern psychiatrists believe that one defence mechanism of the mind, a way it sometimes deals with various painful mental processes, is to suppress them—a phenomenon known as hysterical dissociation. Very rarely, the person dissociates so completely that he or she escapes into what appears to be a quite different personality. A tendency to dissociate is known to be related to a variety of childhood traumas, in particular to childhood sexual abuse. Is there any evidence that the "Antonia" personality was an alternative personality in this sense, a psychological creation of Laurel Dilmen, created in response to some unhappiness or stress?

Certainly, Laurel's childhood does not seem to have been particularly happy. During her early high-school years she was a lonely and somewhat isolated young girl who studied hard and socialised little. She had different interests from her peers and felt that she had nothing in common with them, and to make things worse her family moved twice during this time, which must have added to her difficulty in making close friends and to her feelings of isolation. But she seems to have found her own positive ways of dealing with this by making a conscious effort to "rewrite" herself as a rebel rather than a recluse. She joined a street gang and proved not only that she could stand up for herself but also that she had potential usefulness to the gang as its "brains." She learned jujitsu and had a romance with a German prisoner of war. At fifteen she left home to live alone 2,000 miles (3,220 kilometres) from home and family. There seems to be no evidence that she dealt with any problems she had by dissociating.

Different personalities do quite often emerge during a hypnotic trance, but they are typically very different from the person's normal personality. Laurel Dilmen and Antonia do not fit this pattern. In fact, "Antonia" seems to have been very much a reflection of Laurel Dilmen herself, and Laurel speaks of Antonia not as if she is a totally different personality but much more as if the two of them are essentially the same person, as if "Antonia" is simply another, earlier stage of her own life. They have the same personality traits, likes and dislikes, interests and skills. There are numerous echoes of Antonia's independent, freethinking, erotic and adventurous life in Laurel's own life. But even if we did decide that dissociation was a possible explanation, we would still be left with an unanswered question—how did Antonia find her facts?

WAS IT CRYPTOMNESIA?

Cryptomnesia (see page 16) is the most usual explanation for past-life memories. So perhaps at this point in the story we should look a bit more closely at Laurel Dilmen's background to see if there is any obvious way she could have acquired such detailed and convincing knowledge of sixteenth-century Catholic Spain. Linda Tarazi went to enormous lengths to examine Laurel's life and discover how she could have acquired her knowledge of, and feeling for, the Catholic practices of sixteenth-century Spain. She had no Spanish or Roman Catholic relatives or ancestors, and didn't attend a Catholic school or church.

The usual sources for cryptomnesic past-life memories are historical novels and films. Laurel claimed that from adolescence onwards her reading had been limited to non-fiction; she had read no novels, historical or otherwise. She did, however, admit that she enjoyed historical plays and films and watched all that she could of these. Linda Tarazi used hypnosis to try to discover whether Antonia's story had its roots in any such sources. She first asked Laurel (under hypnosis but not regressed to Antonia) to search her memory and list all the books she had read relating to history. She also checked several indexes of historical fiction dealing with the period and read those that were available in any Chicago area library. She found nothing that could have provided the meat of Antonia's story, let alone the significant, obscure historical facts.

Dr. Tarazi also asked Laurel under hypnosis if she could recall any possible source for the material reported for Antonia's life. She replied: "No, not really." When pressed to recall when she had become interested in the sixteenth-century conflict between Spain and England she responded immediately that it was when she was eight or nine and had seen a movie, *The Sea Hawk*. But although the period—1584—of the film was right, nothing in it corresponded to Antonia's life. She was also asked under hypnosis when she had first heard of the Spanish Inquisition and replied that it was when she was about twenty and saw the film *Captain from Castile*. But although the Inquisition played an important part in that, the tribunal was set in Jaén; Cuenca was never mentioned. Moreover, the film was set in the early part of the sixteenth century, before Antonia was born. Antonia did, however, say that when she saw the film, she had a vague feeling that it didn't give an accurate picture of the Inquisition, though she didn't know why. When, many years later, after the emergence of "Antonia," she saw the film again, she was able to spot various inaccuracies.

If cryptomnesia deriving from some fiction was truly the explanation for "Antonia," her attitude towards the Inquisition is particularly interesting. In fiction and in the public's mind generally, the name of the Spanish Inquisition is synonymous with atrocity and terror. Antonia's view seemed to be entirely at odds with this. She describes it respectfully and depicts the Cuencan Inquisitors as moderate men who rarely imposed the Inquisition's severest penalties. During her lifetime, for example, they never sent a living person to the stake.

Modern research on the Inquisition records bears this out. Henry Kamen, in his book *The Spanish Inquisition: A Historical Revision*, has pointed out that the Inquisition was not the killing machine that it has often been assumed to be: the numbers of those executed has been greatly exaggerated. Neither is the image of the Inquisitors as ruthless and sadistic thought police a fair one. For the most part they were career lawyers. As for their reputation as torturers, we must not forget that torture was common practice in every state at that time; in fact, the Inquisition used it more sparingly than most.

So the picture Antonia paints is not only an unusual one but is unexpected in view of what we know of both Laurel Dilmen and Antonia. If this story is purely fantasy, one might have expected Laurel's vivid imagination to have taken the opportunity to create at least a scene or two of mild torture.

However one tries to explain the Antonia story, whether as

a case of cryptomnesia, or fraud, or simple fantasy, one comes up against the same problem every time. Even if any one of these explanations is true, or partly true, how did Laurel Dilmen come by her information? And yet even to suggest that Laurel Dilmen is a reincarnation of Antonia raises at least one other unanswerable question: why was such apparent total recall of another life not accompanied by recall of another language?

There is another reason for feeling uneasy about accepting reincarnation as an explanation for the Laurel Dilmen story. It is, if not too good to be true, too good to fit comfortably into the normal pattern of past-life memories. Even the most persuasive accounts of past lives—the memories of Shanti Devi, for example, or Bridey Murphy or Jenny Cockell—give us the mere skeleton of a life, with occasional scraps of flesh clinging to the bare bones. Antonia's story, with such total recall of a life, such an accurate memory for detail—names, dates, places—is in a quite different category and, so far, it is in a category of one, unparalleled in the annals of past-life stories.

For Linda Tarazi reincarnation is still the explanation that most easily fits most of the facts. The only alternative explanation she feels might be plausible is that some discarnate entity—Antonia herself or possibly her lover—communicated the information telepathically to Laurel Dilmen, whose ability to fantasise created the Antonia personality as a fictionalised vehicle for the information she received. You may want to reserve judgement on this, but for the time being at any rate the story of Antonia and the Spanish Inquisition is a case—perhaps the only case—of past-life regression under hypnosis that so far defies rational, scientific explanation.

9

A Question of Fraud and a Case of *Folie à Trois*

A little credulity helps one on through life very smoothly.
Elizabeth Gaskell

FRAUD suggests a deliberate intention to mislead others. Almost certainly, such cases are very rare. To set up a reincarnation scenario which is accurate and consistent enough to be convincing would require an enormous amount of time and effort. The financial rewards, at any rate, would hardly make it worthwhile. However, self-deception, an overzealous interpretation of the facts, could be considered equally fraudulent and is almost certainly much more common. Whether one regards Alfred Howard Hulme, for example, as the perpetrator of a fraud or a deluded victim of his own wishful thinking makes little difference. He was persuasive enough to make many people believe his account of what appeared to be one of the most remarkable cases of xenoglossy ever recorded.

ALFRED HULME AND THE BABYLONIAN PRINCESS

Alfred J. Howard had two main interests in life: art and spiritualism. It was his love of art which in 1911, when he was forty-one, led to a job as curator of the embryo art collection of the wealthy industrialist Lord Leverhulme which at that time included a few Egyptian antiquities. Howard's connection with the collection lasted only a few years; by 1922 another curator had been appointed, and Howard had moved to

Ovingdean, near Brighton. But those years had left their legacy—a fascination with ancient Egypt which changed the course of his life.

On his move to Brighton Howard seems to have reinvented himself as a professional Egyptologist. He bought a cottage whose name he changed from "Eagle's Way" to "Egypt's Way." He acquired a smattering of ancient Egyptian, probably from Gardiner's *Egyptian Grammar*, published in 1927. He even awarded himself (for there is no record of the university in question ever having done so) an "Hons. Cert. in Egyptology, Univ. of Oxford." And he changed his name, thereafter styling himself Alfred J. Howard Hulme.

In 1931 there occurred an event that was to be pivotal in Alfred Howard Hulme's life, giving him the opportunity to combine his passion for Egyptology with his interest in spiritualism. He read, in a spiritualist magazine, an article by a Dr. Frederick Wood, a doctor of music who was deeply involved with spiritualism. The article described the reincarnation of "Vola," a young temple dancer in the reign of the eighteenth-dynasty pharaoh, Amenhotep III, in the twentieth-century person of Rosemary, a spiritualist medium living in Blackpool. During Dr. Wood's sessions with Rosemary, Vola had started passing him messages from Nona, a Babylonian princess who was living in Egypt as a member of the pharaoh's harem.

The article clearly fired Alfred Hulme's imagination. Immediately, he wrote to Dr. Wood expressing his own interest both in spiritualism and as a "professional Egyptologist" (a somewhat exaggerated claim) and asking if actual ancient Egyptian words ever came through during the consultation. Not one to undersell himself, he also led Dr. Wood to believe that he was the author of a unique Esperanto-Egyptian grammar and dictionary.

So far all Nona's messages, transmitted by Vola/Rosemary, had been in English. But to Dr. Wood's delight, some weeks after he had received Alfred Hulme's letter (whose contents one assumes he had shared with Rosemary) Vola reported that messages from Nona were coming through in ancient Egyptian! Dr. Wood does not seem to have found anything suspicious either in this serendipitous event or in the fact that Nona, having abandoned her surprisingly good English, should have chosen to communicate in ancient Egyptian rather than her native Babylonian tongue. What Rosemary had actually said sounded, to Dr. Wood's attentive ear, like "ah-yita-zhula." That, at any rate, was as near to its phonetic transcription as Dr. Wood could get. Immediately, he wrote this down and sent it off to Hulme. One can imagine his excitement when the verdict came back—Nona had undoubtedly been speaking ancient Egyptian!

The two then set up a strange collaboration. Over the course of the next five years Wood wrote out phonetic transcriptions of around nine hundred phrases uttered by Rosemary and sent these off to Hulme, who analysed them and assured Wood that not only were they in ancient Egyptian but showed an "infallible use of Egyptian grammar." He also transcribed each phrase back into its original hieroglyphics. In 1937 the pair published the result of their labours, *Ancient Egypt Speaks*, a book that claimed to have "completely restored the spoken language of ancient Egypt."

One might have expected the world of Egyptology to be set alight by this achievement. Scholars had been able to decipher Egyptian hieroglyphics for more than a century, but these conveyed only the consonants of the words. The vowel sounds, and therefore the actual sound of the spoken language, could only be guessed at. Alas, when academic Egyptologists examined *Ancient Egypt Speaks* their judgement was scathing. In a review in the *Journal of Egyptian Archaeology* in June 1937, Battiscombe Gunn, Professor of Egyptology at Oxford, pointed out that not only was Nona's grammar far from infallible but that Hulme had manipulated Wood's transcriptions to fit what he imagined the original Egyptian to have been, by arguing either that Nona's pronunciation was at fault (despite her excellent grammar) or by amending Wood's transcription on the grounds that it was inaccurate. If Nona was reported, for example, to have said *a va stee vong tu*, which was meaningless, Hulme would amend this to *eph e; stirf o(ng) tu*: "to enumerate, now, the items."

One can see that the possibilities for translation are infinite.

Ian Wilson re-examined this case for his excellent book *Mind Out of Time*, an investigation of reincarnation. Aware

that academics are no more immune than the rest of us from
spite and professional jealousy, he decided to ask a modern
Egyptologist to look at Hulme's work to see if the original
criticisms of it were fair. He approached John Ray, Reader in
Egyptology at the University of Cambridge, to give his view
of *Ancient Egypt Speaks*. Ian Wilson describes the result.

> As John Ray was able to confirm, there could be no
> mistaking Hulme's incompetence. In a number of sen-
> tences Ray found inexcusably bad grammar, and he
> pointed out that Hulme had frequently confused Middle
> Egyptian and Late Egyptian in his translations of
> Nona's phrases, despite the fact that these languages
> were as distinct as classical Latin and present-day Ital-
> ian. In any phrase sent to him by Wood, Hulme had in
> fact a wide choice of Egyptian words that could be
> made to fit the consonants to give his preferred mean-
> ing. To give an English example: if the word "bend"
> were received, for instance, the possible words to be
> matched against this would be any with the letters "b,"
> "n" and "d." Thus, Hulme's possible choices would in-
> clude band, bend, bind, bond, banned and boned, to
> name but a few . . . On this basis Hulme could conjure
> up an ancient Egyptian meaning for any set of sounds
> produced by Rosemary . . .

John Ray also confirmed, another of Professor Gunn's observations—that although Rosemary/Vola had described visions
that included camels being used as domestic transport, the
camel was not used in this way in eighteenth-dynasty Egypt.

So was this fraud? Or was it simply a *folie à deux* between
Wood and Hulme? And what about Rosemary? Rosemary's
identity was closely guarded by Wood during her lifetime, but
after her death in 1961, at the age of sixty-nine, he revealed
that her real name was Ivy Carter Beaumont and that she had
been a schoolmistress until she retired in 1953. Did she deliberately set out to dupe Dr. Wood? Or was she merely, and
probably unconsciously, trying to please him? Rosemary and
Wood had known each other for many years; it was through
her mediumship that Wood had contacted the brother whose

sudden death in a car accident had sparked off his own interest in spiritualism. It is well known that when people are in analysis they tend to dream the kind of dream their analyst expects of them—Freudian analysands, for example, will have Freudian dreams, clients of a Jungian analyst will have Jungian dreams. One can well imagine that the same kind of situation might arise between medium and client.

Ian Wilson notes that Wood, although eventually disillusioned by Hulme's claims to be an Egyptology expert, went on to learn ancient Egyptian himself and remained convinced that many of Nona's messages were authentic. But a gramophone recording made of some of Rosemary's/Vola's utterances suggests that they are similar to the "speaking in tongues" of various Pentecostal and charismatic sects—that is, they are meaningless babble.

Speaking in tongues (glossolalia) is a curious phenomenon. It can vary from meaningless and incoherent sounds and emotional exclamations, which are usually uttered in a state of religious ecstasy, to the fabrication of words—neologisms—which occurs sometimes in children attempting to invent a new and a private language, sometimes as a symptom of mental illness, and sometimes in dreams (see Chapter Six). These dream neologisms are probably the explanation for the strange phenomenon described to us by Chris Tidy—something that puzzled first her mother and then her husband.

When I was in my late teens/early twenties my late first husband John asked my mother if I spoke German, as he had heard me speak it in my sleep. My mother was not surprised by this question (to my surprise) and informed John that I was speaking backwards! At the time I never thought to question this reply, nor did John. Now I wonder if maybe I can speak German and not know it. I have never mentioned this to anyone before for obvious reasons, but I have often wondered if in a past life I was imprisoned, as a Jew, in one of Germany's concentration camps. I was born in 1955. 1 have no idea why I think this. I have always had an intense interest in this subject and did attempt to read about the Holocaust but had to stop as it played on my mind too much.

Speaking in tongues can also occur in the trance state. In February 1896 a French medium, Hélène Smith, started to speak, and later to write, in a language that seemed to her hearers utterly foreign and incomprehensible—not surprisingly, as it soon transpired that she was speaking Martian. Happily, each Martian hieroglyphic had its exact equivalent in the French alphabet, which made translation relatively easy. Over many months an impressive body of Martian texts was built up which, together with the many visions which Mlle. Smith also experienced, gave a never-to-be-equalled portrait of life on the red planet.

Mlle. Smith and many of the *habitués* of her seances were as convinced of the reality of the Martian language as Wood and Hulme were that they had unlocked the secrets of ancient Egyptian. However, Théodore Flournoy, a professor of philosophy and psychology who attended Mlle. Smith's seances and transcribed and translated her words, believed that although she had indeed created a language, in that the sounds she made formed words that expressed definite ideas and were consistent in meaning, it was, in his opinion, just an infantile travesty of French. But Flournoy, who described the case in his book *From India to the Planet Mars*, did not believe it was an intellectual creation in cold blood but rather an automatic product of the unconscious activity of the mind. It looks as though the only real difference between Rosemary/Vola and the medium with the message from Mars was that the messages from Mars fell on slightly less gullible ears.

A Case of Folie à Trois

Reincarnation experiences convincing enough to be regarded as "proved," in Ian Stevenson's words, are rare. Professor Erlendur Haraldsson of the University of Iceland has made a serious study of such experiences over the last decade, mostly in Sri Lanka, where reincarnation is part of people's cultural expectation and so might be expected to be relatively common. And yet even his intensive and widespread searches in this potentially fruitful territory managed to find only four or five new cases each year.

It does, therefore, require a certain suspension of belief to accept the unfolding saga of Arthur Guirdham and the Cathars, in which first one, then two, then three reincarnated Cathars finally became a veritable torrent of heretics who had lived together under Roman Catholic persecution in thirteenth-century France and discovered each other anew in their present-day incarnations, in Bath, in twentieth-century Britain.

Was this any more than an intriguing and unusual case of cumulative lunacy in which each member fed on and reinforced the beliefs of the rest of the group? Two things make this story interesting enough to look at in some detail. The first is the historical accuracy of some of the information provided by the first of the reincarnated Cathars. The second is the central character, a respectable retired NHS psychiatrist called Arthur Guirdham.

The Cathars were a heretical Christian sect which flourished in Western Europe in the twelfth and thirteenth centuries. One of their heresies was a belief that good and evil had two separate creators. In this dual creation the spiritual world of goodness was created by a good God; the material world was evil and was created by Satan, the evil god. Their other heretical belief was in the transmigration of souls, either from man to man, or from man to animal, as animals too, they believed, had souls. Persecution by both the Roman Catholic Church and the state, perhaps combined with their lack of popular appeal (they believed passionately in celibacy and the renunciation of all worldly and sensual delights), led to their gradual demise. Although traces of the heresies lingered on until the early fifteenth century, as a sect they had virtually disappeared by the end of the thirteenth century, most of them being massacred in 1244 at the Siege of Montségur.

Two facts must be noted about Arthur Guirdham. before his story is told. The first is that although he was a qualified doctor and had had a conventional scientific training, he had another, psychic side to his nature, a side that was very important to him and which became ever more dominant over the years. He had a long-standing interest in the subject of reincarnation and for many years had been a close friend of

Joan Grant, a woman who had written several books about her memories of her own past lives.

The second fact to be taken into account is that he had been fascinated by the history of the Cathars for several years. In his own words, "Anything to do with Catharism had a magnetic effect on me." He had had powerful feelings of *déjà vu* in Toulouse and other places in the Languedoc area of southern France which had been centres of Cathar heresy.

Throughout most of Guirdham's adult life he had suffered a recurrent nightmare in which he was lying down when he was approached by a tall man. So when, in 1962, one of his patients, a housewife in her early thirties, confided to him that since adolescence she had often had a similar nightmare, he was intrigued, especially as both of them found their nightmares ceased after she became his patient. He was more than intrigued when, about a year later, Mrs. Smith (the pseudonym Dr. Guirdham gave her for the sake of medical confidentiality) confided to him that she had also for many years had dreams and daydreams about her life as a girl in thirteenth-century France. In these dreams she had been the lover of a young man called Roger de Grisolles. She showed Guirdham notes she had made in her diary at the time. "I could write a book about Roger and it would not take any effort at all . . . It is a comfort to know that other girls dream of lovers. I wish I didn't have the uneasy feeling that this is different. I don't want to live in a world of fantasy and that world is so real to me, but if I write it maybe I shall get it out of my system."

By the time she left school, Roger was such a constant presence in her thoughts and dreams that he seemed almost real. Persecuted by the Roman Catholic Church, Roger died in prison, and she was burned at the stake. At around this time she recorded a dream that gave a graphic description of her own death:

> The pain was maddening . . . [but] not half so bad as the pain I felt when I knew he was dead. I felt suddenly glad to be dying. I didn't know when you were burned to death you'd bleed. I thought the blood would all dry up in the terrible heat. But I was bleeding heavily. The blood was dripping and hissing in the flames. I wished

I'd had enough blood to put the flames out. The worst
part was my eyes. I hate the thought of going blind . . .
I tried to close my eyelids but I couldn't. They must
have been burned off . . . The flames . . . began to feel
cold. Icy cold. It occurred to me that I wasn't burning
to death but freezing to death . . . I started to laugh . . .
I am a witch. I had magicked the fire and turned it into
ice.

When Mrs. Smith first consulted Dr. Guirdham she had (he
says himself) "no realisation whatever that she had been a
Cathar." It was, in fact, Arthur Guirdham himself who "realised" this and, having suggested it, set in motion the whole
intriguing saga.

Once prompted, memories of Cathar life and rituals
poured from Mrs. Smith. From Dr. Guirdham's own knowledge of the Cathar period, several things Mrs. Smith said impressed him. She said, for example, that the robes worn by the
Cathars were dark blue. Dr. Guirdham believed, as most historical sources maintained, that they were black. However, he
decided to check this information with the French scholar
Jean Duvernoy, an expert on the Cathars, and discovered that
more recent evidence confirmed that the Cathar robes had indeed been dark blue at that particular time.

Mrs. Smith also described how Roger had a chest complaint that was treated with loaf sugar, a commodity so rare at
the time that it was kept under lock and key. To Guirdham this
seemed an unlikely remedy. But in 1969 it was discovered
that sugar was imported from Arab countries in loaves at that
time, and was recommended for diseases of the chest by the
Arab doctors whose influence was particularly strong in that
part of France.

But perhaps the most astonishing thing that Mrs. Smith
told Arthur Guirdham was that as soon as she met him she had
recognised him as the "Roger" of her dreams.

So strong was Guirdham's conviction that the story he had
been told was a matter of historical fact, and so deeply did he
become involved, that the next step seems almost inevitable.
He, too, became convinced that he was indeed the reincarnation of the Roger of Mrs. Smith's Cathar life. What is more,

he wrote a book about this, *The Cathars and Reincarnation*, which was published in 1970.

So far, so good. It is subsequent developments in this tale that start to stretch credulity. To begin with is the arrival on the scene of Miss Mills, a woman with whom Guirdham apparently struck up an acquaintanceship one day when she happened to be passing his house in her car. They had not known each other long before she asked him whether the words "Raymond" and "Albigensian" meant anything to him. Indeed they did, as they would to anyone who knew anything about Cathar history. Raymond VI, Count of Toulouse, was a friend to the Cathars—a French nobleman who resisted the attempts of Pope Innocent III to coerce him into helping him put down the heretics. And Albigensian is simply another word for Cathar, meaning "men of Albi," Albi being one of the Cathars' main centres of influence in southern France.

It transpired that Miss Mills, too, had two vivid recurring dreams that seemed to indicate a previous life among the Cathars. In one she was walking along a rough, stony path down a hill, on the summit of which was a medieval castle in which something horrible was happening. In the other dream she, too, was about to be burned at the stake. As she was walking towards it, she was struck on the back with a burning brand. With all of this she regaled the fascinated Dr. Guirdham. She also allowed him to discover, quite by chance (she had developed a pain in her hip and had asked him to examine her), an extraordinary—and highly significant—birthmark. This is how Guirdham describes the occasion:

> When I looked at her left hip I saw slightly above it a belt of strange protuberances arising from her skin. I have never in my life seen anything comparable . . . In shape and appearance they looked like large blisters produced by burns. The difference was that there was no fluid in their interior and they were semi-solid. The distribution of these semi-solidified vesicles was significant. They extended from above her hip across her back to the midline.
>
> "I suppose this is part of your dream? This is where

the burning torch hit you?" I spoke lightly and not at all insistently.

"Yes," she said simply.

To Dr. Guirdham the conclusion was inescapable: Miss Mills, too, had been his companion in a previous Cathar life.

Miss Mills's nightmares ceased soon after her friendship with Guirdham began in 1968. But events then took an even stranger turn. To this odd trio other reincarnated Cathars soon gravitated, most either born or living in the same area of the West Country, some still alive, but many of them dead, and, according to Guirdham, establishing communication from the next world, enabling him to acquire Cathar memories by telepathy and clairvoyance.

Many of these people apparently had some connection with Miss Mills, who began to produce a host of much more detailed memories of the Cathars' life under siege at Montségur, the Cathar fortress in the Pyrenees which was besieged by the Roman Catholics between May 1243 and March 1244. Gradually, Miss Mills came to realise that her thirteenth-century persona was Esclarmonde de Perella, a plucky woman who, although an invalid, stayed in Montségur throughout the siege, and afterwards chose to die at the stake rather than recant. Two women friends of Miss Mills, it transpired, had also formerly been Cathars, and so, too, had the mother of one of these friends. It appeared that Miss Mills's 80-year-old father had been a Cathar bishop, and an old boyfriend of hers had been a Cathar sergeant-at-arms. This strange group reunion is described in Guirdham's second book, We Are One Another, published in 1974.

Two years later, in 1976, Guirdham published the final and most bizarre volume of his reincarnation trilogy, The Lake and the Castle. This revealed his conviction that not only had this doughty group fought shoulder to shoulder against the persecutors of the Cathars but that they had been reincarnated together in other stirring times as well: in Roman Britain in the fourth century AD and in France during the Napoleonic era, for example.

There are innumerable difficulties in accepting the saga of the Cathars at face value. The first and most profound is that,

save Arthur Guirdham himself, none of the characters involved has ever been identified. All appear in the trilogy of
books which Dr. Guirdham wrote about this group and their
reincarnation experiences, but all have their anonymity carefully preserved by him. Ian Wilson made persistent attempts
to identify and make contact with some—any—of these people, but each approach was blocked "politely but firmly" by
Dr. Guirdham. We have, Ian Wilson says, only Dr. Guirdham's assurances that these people ever existed. The author
Colin Wilson, who became friendly with the Guirdhams while
researching his book *Afterlife*, did manage to meet Miss Mills
and says that she confirmed everything Arthur Guirdham had
said. And like most people who met him, Colin Wilson insists
that Arthur Guirdharn was "a perfectly normal, honest, well-
balanced individual, not a crank."

However, it is worth noting that as well as being a psychiatrist, Guirdham was also an occasional writer of fiction.
While the scientist's role is to report facts as he finds them
and interpret them with cautious diligence, the fiction writer's
job is to entertain and intrigue. One cannot ignore the possibility that in Arthur Guirdham's case the two roles may have
overlapped and, in the last book particularly, one may have
largely supplanted the other.

Lynda Harris, author of *The Secret Heresy of Hieronymus
Bosch* and a writer who has a particular interest both in reincarnation and the Cathars, has talked to several people who
were Guirdham's neighbours near Bath. What she was told
suggests very strongly that what began as an interest finally
became an obsession.

Apparently, during the early 1970s Guirdham spent
many hours trying to convince the ageing mother of
one of his neighbours that she had been an eleven-year-
old girl who had lived through the siege at Montségur.
He never managed to get her to agree with him on this
point, and no one today remembers the reasons he gave
for believing it himself. Most likely he based his idea
on information that had been communicated through
Miss Mills. As the saga of reincarnation continued to
unfold, Guirdham clearly accepted the "facts" that were

passed on by his Cathar communicants with less and less questioning.

An explanation which is sometimes advanced is that Guirdham, who had acquired some considerable knowledge about the Cathars, was transmitting it telepathically to the rest of the group, who then relayed it back to him. Certainly, members of the group were consistent in their memories of events, people and places; their stories always tallied, and they always seemed to mirror Guirdham's own beliefs—even when these were historically inaccurate, as they sometimes were. (Miss Mills, for example, remembered her Cathar initiation as taking place in a cave, a romantic idea that was current at the time but is now known to be fantasy and not fact.) But telepathy seems an unlikely explanation. There is now considerable evidence that telepathy does exist, but not that it exists on that kind of scale. The best experimental evidence suggests that some people, some of the time and under some conditions, are telepathic. To suggest that a whole group of people could transmit such a wealth of accurate and detailed information to each other at more or less the same time goes way beyond evidence and even beyond anecdote. Two far more likely explanations are either that members of the group were colluding with each other or that there was no group—that the origin of the whole story lay with Guirdham himself.

Let us suppose that Mrs. Smith and Miss Mills *did* exist outside the world of Arthur Guirdham's imagination: how far can their past-life memories be trusted? Of the bevy of Cathars, Mrs. Smith sounds by far the most convincing. Her memories were much more individual than those of the rest of the group, more rooted in the personal details of an everyday life and less in Catharism, about which it is said she knew little.

From Arthur Guirdham's first book, *The Cathars and Reincarnation*, we learn several interesting things about Mrs. Smith. The first is that she had an excellent memory—so good, in fact, that it resulted in her being accused of cheating in an examination at school. "I had a photographic memory and scrawled off yards of a commentary on Wordsworth word for word as in the textbook." It is at least possible that much of her intimate knowledge of the Cathars derived not from a past life but from some twentieth-century source, once read and then apparently forgotten. There is even some evidence for such a source, In 1954 Mrs. Smith had begun to write a novel, not about the Cathars but about the troubadours in France. Guirdham had many times asked to see the novel but had been refused. Finally, she confessed that she had burned it, her explanation being that she had recently come across an article in a back issue of a journal which contained a passage identical to one she had written in her novel. What she called her "unconscious plagiarism" of something she believed she had never read so terrified her that she felt compelled to destroy her novel.

So far as Guirdham was concerned, the only significant thing about the article was that he, too, had happened to come across it and read it for the first time at about the same time as Mrs. Smith did so. This, for him, was yet another example of the "synchronisation of action and thought between Mrs. Smith and myself." Much more significant, though, is the fact that although Mrs. Smith did not mention this, and Guirdham apparently considered the fact unimportant, the article was about Catharism, a topic in which the author, a theosophist, had been particularly interested. Unfortunately, Guirdham doesn't mention its date of publication, which would have helped to work out the sequence of events. But at least we know that Mrs. Smith had at some time read an article about Catharism and that, although she had apparently forgotten having done so, she had reproduced at least one passage from it accurately in a novel she had started to write long before she met Arthur Guirdham.

She also started to read about Catharism at the time of Guirdham's revelation to her that she had been a Cathar—he mentions that she was reading a library book on the subject the very day he broached the topic. Again, his only comment is to marvel at the synchronicity of this; he doesn't seem to consider the book as a source of apparent Cathar memories.

The second fact worth noting is that Mrs. Smith may have had epilepsy (the diagnosis seems to have been in some doubt, but she certainly had three unexplained attacks of unconsciousness during adolescence). She also suffered from migraine. Both of these conditions are sometimes accompanied by the feelings of *déjà vu* which often characterise past-life memories. In a letter to Guirdham dated 10 January 1965 she wrote of "this terrible affliction of 'going out of time.' I am sometimes so confused that I cannot honestly be sure if a person has just said something or whether they will say it one day, or did so in the past."

This statement tells us a great deal. The kind of feelings she describes are typical of a partial complex seizure (minor epileptic attack). Such episodes of confusion in adulthood, together with the probable history of generalised seizures with loss of consciousness as a child, suggest that she may have had temporal-lobe epilepsy. The commonest cause of temporal-lobe epilepsy is damage to the hippocampus—a structure deep in the temporal lobe of the brain which is involved, among other things, with memory. Damage to this structure may lead not only to seizures but, more important, to odd mental states in which the person finds difficulty in distinguishing whether experiences are real or due to imagination. In epilepsy clinics one often comes across patients with epilepsy who have very strong *déjà vu* feelings which make them feel they have been in that particular place or situation before. Occasionally, this may lead to a strong belief in reincarnation.

The most plausible explanation is that Mrs. Smith was perfectly genuine and recounted perfectly genuine experiences of apparent past-life memories to Guirdham, and that he interpreted these to accord with his own beliefs (not an uncommon practice among dream analysts). The well-known phenomenon of transference, whereby a patient may transfer his or her affections to the therapist, is enough to explain Mrs. Smith's identification of Guirdham with "Roger," and his own obsession with Catharism would have made him only too happy to accept the identity.

The mandatory celibacy of Cathar priests does not seem to have been considered a problem by either of them, but this is probably fair enough, as it has never been a problem for a good many other supposedly celibate priests either. Guirdham at one time seems to have decided that Roger was only a trainee priest, though his books are very inconsistent on this point. The blue Cathar robe is always cited as the most convincing evidence that Mrs. Smith's was a true past-life memory. And yet a dream priest has to be dressed in something. A blue robe seems as appropriate as anything else. In this case coincidence seems a more plausible explanation than genuine past-life memory.

Miss Mills is a different matter. Here it is hard not to believe that the good doctor was being duped, though certainly he would have been a willing victim. So many strands lead back to Miss Mills. So many of her friends and relations were part of the Cathar reincarnation circle. Neither is there any doubt about a probable source for her "memories" of the Montségur siege. All the information given by Miss Mills was readily available to her. A vivid, popular and historically accurate account of the siege of the Cathars at Montségur was given in *Massacre at Montségur* by Zoe Oldenbourg, published in French in 1959 and translated into English in 1961, seven years before Miss Mills started to recount her Cathar memories to Arthur Guirdham. Arthur Guirdham himself owned a copy of the book, and Miss Mills might very easily have had access to it. The book mentions many of the details of the siege remembered by Miss Mills and includes the names of many of the individuals she mentioned, among them Esclarmonde and her family.

So was this whole affair fraud or was it self-delusion? Whenever it is suggested that the Cathar reincarnation is fraudulent, it is assumed that Guirdham himself perpetrated the fraud. Although most people who knew Guirdham personally testified to his honesty and good character, we have talked to one person who knew him who is convinced that the man was an out-and-out fraud. What is generally acknowledged is the strength of his own beliefs in reincarnation and psychic experiences. Certainly, by the early 1970s he had clearly lost all sense of perspective on the matter.

Anyone who holds such strong personal beliefs may fall victim to self-delusion and would be an easy target for fraud. If fraud were perpetrated, then if Miss Mills did indeed exist she seems an equally likely perpetrator. But even here fraud seems too harsh a judgement. A more charitable explanation is that Guirdham's own personality (which was acknowledged to be attractive and charismatic) might have inspired the tacit agreement by a group of people who were under his spell to give him something they knew he would value— proof of his own belief in reincarnation.

10

Soul Mates

So, friend, when first I looked upon your face,
Our thoughts gave answer each to each, so true.
Opposed mirrors each reflecting each,
Although I knew not in what time or place,
Methought that I had often met with you,
And each had lived in others' mind and speech.

Alfred, Lord Tennyson

ARTHUR Guirdham and his fellow Cathars are by no means the only examples of people drawn together by the conviction that they have shared a past life. The feeling that we live out our destinies over and over again with the same companions and the same behaviour patterns but in different ages and in different relationships is a common one. And from this follows naturally the idea that we each have a soul mate, a partner who is made for us, without whom we are incomplete, who is our destiny. The feeling of inevitability is often a normal part of falling in love—how could one *not* love this particular, this unique human being? And how could a feeling this strong arise out of nowhere, sometimes almost instantaneously? For many people, especially if they have apparent memories of a previous life, it seems more logical to believe that their empathy, their knowledge of each other, must derive from several lifetimes together.

Wendy McClymont had experiences as a child which convinced her that she had lived before (see chapter 14, page 244). When she met her husband she felt almost immediately that she had known him in a previous life. They both felt they had found the person they had been looking for. Frances Marie Preston met her husband on a train, and they married three months later. "We both feel that we have known each other in many lives, as women and men, maybe even as brothers or sisters. We cannot explain this, but I know in my heart that this is true. We have known each other for only two and a half years in this life, but thousands of years in others."

Chris Warner says her belief in reincarnation has been strengthened since meeting her husband two years ago. "We both feel that we have been together before as we are so close and so attuned. We discovered very early on in our relationship how alike we are, and we frequently start talking about a subject at the same time . . . The relationship is truly idyllic, and we both feel that we have never been apart."

American psychiatrist Brian Weiss had the odd experience of hypnotically regressing two of his patients, who were unknown to each other, and discovering that they seemed to have had a relationship in their previous lives. One described a life in which Roman soldiers tied him to their horses and dragged him along the ground, finally leaving him to die in the arms of his daughter. The other described a past life in which her father died in her arms after being dragged behind Roman soldiers' horses. Dr. Weiss believes strongly in the power of twin souls to find each other in different lifetimes, and he decided to help destiny along by rearranging their appointments so that they were given an opportunity to meet in his waiting-room. They did indeed meet but at that time did not apparently recognise that this was a meeting of twin souls. Soon afterwards, however, they recognised each other in the departure lounge of the airport, about to board the same plane to Mexico. This time they started to talk, sat next to each other on the plane, and are now apparently happily married and living in Mexico.

One can only rejoice at the reunion of twin souls who rediscover perfect happiness. Perfect happiness, however, is a rare human condition. There is always the chance that we may find ourselves in an action replay of a more troubled relationship. Within any group of close friends alliances tend to shift, and tensions arise, and a new incarnation does not, apparently, always resolve these. This is a cautionary tale of four friends, Rick, Dave, Nick and Olwen, who each felt that they remembered parts of a life they had lived together, probably some time in the seventeenth century. We were given two accounts, one from Rick and one from Olwen, describing the way in which this quartet discovered their mutual past. Their story begins in the 1970s when Rick met a stranger, Dave, with whom he had an immediate rapport.

> Some time back around 1970 I was at a friend's house one afternoon, talking with his wife, when he came in with a stranger in tow; only he wasn't a stranger. As soon as we saw one another we both said "I know you" almost in unison. We didn't need any introduction, we sat down and swapped histories. His name was Dave and he had met my friend in a coffee bar. Back in those days us hippie types were more open and friendly than people are today, and my friend had invited him home to meet other people he thought he'd get on with. We established that we could never have met before, but we knew that we were, or had been, brothers. Over the next couple of years we were pretty close, and from time to time, when I looked at him, I had flashes of something like memory of him dressed in bright colours, blues, greens, and reds, and always laughing. One very complete memory was of us as we stood with some other men on a hill overlooking a forest and some open stretch of greyish sandy soil. He was laughing, as usual, brightly dressed and hung with weapons. I was dressed more soberly in black and white. (Several years after this flash I drove for the first of many times through les Landes de Gascogne in southern France and recognised the area and the soil.) The worst memory I have is of running and then riding for my life, with the impression that I had just murdered a woman who had somehow been responsible for my brother's imprisonment and execution.

Olwen Bowen's first past-life memory is a dramatic one. "I have an abiding memory of an execution. My execution. It was a hot, dusty day and I was up quite high and lots of people are looking up at me. They are dressed in seventeenth-century clothes, quite ordinary, peasant types. I know I'm about to die, but I'm not really afraid even though I didn't do whatever I've been condemned for."

It was only when Olwen one day decided to tell her friends about her execution that the friends realised that Olwen's "vision" was just one part of a life they had all had a role in. They all remembered different bits of the same picture. Dave revealed that for years he had had a vision of being thrown into a cell and laughing at his captors even though he knew he was going to die. Rick not only remembered that incident but knew who had caused it. He and Dave had arrived in a town where they were strangers, and where a war, possibly the English Civil War, was raging. Olwen was married to a "Puritan type" who in this life was Nick, with whom she was living.

Back (or rather forward) to the 1970s and to the Southampton University bar. Here another serendipitous meeting enabled Rick to fill in another piece of the jigsaw. A mutual friend introduced him to a girl called Carrie. Olwen Bowen describes what happened next. "When Carrie turned to look at Rick, she turned white and with a look of absolute horror on her face ran off into the Ladies and refused to come out while Rick was still there. All very odd until Rick remembered why. She had caused the events in the previous life through jealousy and rumour-mongering. She had a liking for Dave which was not reciprocated. He had formed a friendship with me even though I was married. She mistook this for an adulterous affair, and we were both condemned, my husband apparently believing every word she said. After our deaths Rick wanted retribution. He followed her out of town one day and killed her with his sword." No wonder poor Carrie had locked herself in the Ladies.

Olwen, however, had an intuitive feeling that this was not the end of the matter. The drama, she felt, was shortly to be played out again in this life—in two weeks' time. She told her friends of her foreboding, but they reassured each other that, no matter what, nobody would die this time. "I was living with Nick then. Dave and I had formed a friendship but nothing more. Carrie wanted Dave, but he had no interest in her. She went to Nick and said that Dave and I were sleeping together. He believed it all, again. Silly man, never learned! I came home one day and he attacked me. Not badly, but just lashed out accusing me of all sorts. I was screaming that none of it was true and also, 'You can't kill me this time, you b—' He was totally confused, but it stopped him dead and he calmed down. Needless to say, that was the end of the relationship in this life! All this happened two weeks after my announcement, just as I said it would. It was as if everything had come full circle. The sense of relief was overwhelming."

And the aftermath? Olwen and Rick are still the best of friends and about to go into business together. Nick and Dave are long gone. So, too, is Carrie, who was, Olwen rather unfairly maintains, the cause of it all.

There is no question of verifying this story and even the participants are not particularly interested in establishing their previous personal identities. What is intriguing is to conjecture how far the past-life scenario which the group had created became a self-fulfilling prophecy, in exactly the same way as happened with the reincarnated Cathars. One has the impression that by the time poor Carrie appeared on the scene the whole thing had developed into a game in which they were all deeply involved, and in which she was unwittingly allotted a role. But however much one feels that they were locked within the story, there is still the question as to how the story first began, and here they are very clear that it started as a past-life memory.

The recognition of a past-life relationship is not always so happily reciprocated. Helen Bedford described to us an incident that happened when she was in her early teens. "My father was taking me to buy my Christmas present when we bumped into someone he had been in the army with. We stopped to pass the time of day, and my father introduced me. This man put out his hand to shake mine and as our hands touched I was transported. The whole thing could have only lasted a split second or two but was very powerful and intense. This man was about 40 or so, plain and wearing a cap and raincoat."

Helen says that at that moment she felt older, but still young, and as though she knew him very well and had not seen him for some time. The feeling of complete happiness and joy she felt at seeing him was totally overwhelming, something she had never experienced before. She felt she had someone with her, a woman older than she was, to whom she was emotionally close, though she was not her mother. She could not see her properly because her vision was obscured by something dark which framed her face. She was aware that she was wearing a long dress, which felt "puffed out."

The man coming towards them was in uniform, a high black hat, red coat with gold trim and buttons, black trousers, and carrying a sword at his side. And Helen had the feeling that although he was happy to see her his feelings were nowhere near as intense as hers. She has always believed that if this was indeed a glimpse of a past life, she was a spurned love.

Helen never told her father about the incident (he would have thought it all rubbish). She is now fifty-seven and says that although she has had plenty of happiness in her life, that was the first occasion and one of the very few times in her life when she has felt complete and total joy. It was very powerful and very memorable.

However, that story should sound a warning note for anyone who is searching for a reincarnated soul mate in their present-day existence. The soul mate may not recognise you. And sometimes the feeling that you have found your soul mate can be so overwhelming, so compelling that occasionally it can become an obsession. Suppose you believe you have met your past-life love again and he or she does not share your memories and has no wish to restart the relationship? And suppose you remember your soul mate in a past life but never meet up with him or her in this? There is a danger that the memory of a past-life love can become more real and more important than any present-day relationship. This is what happened to Laurel Dilmen (see page 134), whose remembered passion for her sixteenth-century Spanish lover so obsessed her that no mere twentieth-century man could match her memories.

There seems to be no guarantee, either, that if you *do* meet your soul mate from a previous life, your relationship in this lifetime will necessarily follow the same pattern. One of the most interesting accounts of a reunion with a soul mate was told to us by Rachel J. (pseudonym), herself a psychotherapist. The story starts in the autumn of 1970.

I was twenty-three and going off to sleep one night in my bedroom in Wales. I was thinking about my new French boyfriend Claude, whom I had met at the beginning of August in Tunisia. I went out with him then for four years. Claude was Jewish, lived in Paris and had black hair, good looks, like a typical Gitanes advert. I went on to think of the one before him and then the one before him and the one before him, and so on, going backwards until I fell asleep. A few hours later, the next thing I knew was that I felt a man's hand brushing my forehead, so vividly that I woke up. It seemed that when I opened my eyes I could see this dark-haired man looking down at me with a very deep expression of love on his face. I wondered who he was, for although he looked very much like him, it was not Claude. I tried to ask him telepathically who he was but to no avail. (I was in the body in the bed which was either asleep or unwell; for some reason I was not able physically to speak to him.) To myself I was saying, You are not Claude, you are not Richard, etc., etc. I could see his face clearly, even the wrinkles on his forehead. Then I looked around. I was in a strange room, in a four-poster bed. The floor was of stone slabs, there were swords and shields on the walls, armour, a big wooden door, and window slits. I think there was grass outside, but I couldn't be sure. The period seemed to be the sixteenth or seventeenth century.

The man was dressed in a white round-necked shirt with big billowy sleeves, and black high-waisted trousers. It was not the way any casual male acquaintance of that period would be dressed, particularly in a lady's bedroom, so I presumed that he was either a husband or, more probably, a lover. Whichever it was, there was a great feeling of love between us. At this point I thought, I must be dreaming. So I tried to wake myself up, but however much I rubbed my eyes, the vision would not go away. It seemed I was wide awake.

This seemed to last for ages, and I began to panic. I thought, I know I am not really here, I think I have gone back in time. But I can't remember where I really should be. I had never experienced any mental or astral travelling or recall of previous lives before. It was also clear to me that this did not have the quality of a dream. Often when I am dreaming I can wake myself up if I want to, or change the dream if I want to. This was not the same. I kept trying to ask the man who he was, mentally, but he could only see the body in the bed, which was either ill or asleep, she certainly could not talk physically at that time. Neither did I "see" the body, for I was in it. Also I was too busy looking around at everything else. Now I became frightened and I think I started knocking my head to try to wake up to come back. Then all of a sudden, my eyes still wide open, the vision in front of them suddenly changed or clicked back, and there in front of me was my "real room," the light shining through the window from outside. I put the light on, got up and walked around, shaken and amazed by the whole event. I could still remember absolutely every detail, and I could "see" it in my mind's eye. But I could not actually see it as I had seen it then. I was remembering it, imagining it. When it was actually happening there was a quite different quality about it: I say I did actually "see" this vision, because my consciousness was there, in that dimension. When I remember the scene now, the vision is qualitatively different from the actual experience, although it is the most vivid memory I have. The more I thought about the scene, the more I thought it seemed to be mid-Europe.

The next morning I mentioned the experience to my mother, and possibly my sister, but I never talked to anyone else about it except a Sufi friend who said I must have gone back to a previous incarnation.

The appearance of Rachel's dream lover is easy to explain. As she was drifting off to sleep she developed a mental "set" by thinking about her boyfriends, particularly Claude. This is a recognised technique for inducing a dream about someone or something you want to dream about—you make sure you are thinking about them as you go to sleep. The man in her dream was not Claude, but he was very much the same physical type as Claude—clearly a type Rachel finds attractive. But this doesn't explain the strange medieval setting of the dream.

What happened next was that she had an episode of sleep paralysis (see page 105). She was able to look around the room but was not able to move or talk. Although she felt she was awake, what she was seeing was the very real-seeming hallucinatory world that accompanies sleep paralysis (often the imagery in these experiences is terrifying, but on this occasion it was positive and full of love). Even though nothing had the normal dream-like quality, she was aware that she must be dreaming but couldn't wake herself. The paralysis, the inability to speak or to wake up, together with a very "real" hallucinatory world, all indicate that this was an episode of sleep paralysis.

So we can understand what happens in terms of brain function: we can explain most of the sensations she felt, the imagery of the strange room, the mental "set" that produced the dream lover. If the story ended there, there'd be no need to look for any other explanation. But that wasn't quite the end of the story, which now moves forward five years to the summer of 1975.

I had been having some heart muscular problems, and my homoeopathic doctor admitted me to a hospital for a month, during which time I fasted, rested, analysed myself and my life, trying to establish where I was at that point in my life and where I was going. I believe I underwent a tremendous psychological and spiritual change.

For some time I had been thinking of making some extra money through having a market stall. An old school friend was enthusiastic about the idea, and we started the weekend of 16 August. The next day, Sunday August 17, I felt some kind of anticipation. When the market closed, three or four of the other stallholders asked Sue and me to go for a drink nearby. A group was playing jazz and someone was selling wine and chilli con carne from a barge. We all went round and sat on the floor listening to the music and chatting.

After about ten minutes my attention became forcibly drawn over to the far side of the yard, where there was a man standing looking over at me. He looked just like Claude: dark hair, dark glasses, jeans, French-looking. Every time I looked at him he was looking at me, and I inwardly wished that he would come closer. As I thought this, so he started walking towards me. I then wished that he would take his sunglasses off so that I could get a better impression of his face. The next time I looked, he had taken his glasses off. Then he walked over to our side of the yard and came to stand right in front of our circle. He was carrying a packet of Gitanes. I asked myself, Why has he come over? I knew that there was some kind of interaction between us and that a meeting was inevitable. But before I had time for conjecture, I heard the man sitting next to me saying: "I like that guy's shirt. I'm going to ask him where he got it from." I was amazed. Not only is it extremely unusual for men to remark on other men's clothes, but unheard of for a normal chap to go up to a stranger and ask him where he bought his shirt.

The next thing I knew the two of them were walking towards our circle and he sat down with our group. He had a slight foreign accent, and as soon as there was a pause in the conversation, I asked him if he was from France. He said yes, he had been living there. I asked if he was Jewish. "Yes," he said, "but how do you know? No one has ever asked me that." His name was Bene, a name I had never heard of before. I was quite astounded. He, too, looked just like a Gitanes ad. It was obvious that Bene didn't really want to talk to the others, and he soon asked if he could come and try on a pair of the boots I was selling on my stall. These were, of course, either too big, too small or whatever—that is, he obviously didn't want a pair of boots at all. But he did invite me out to dinner that evening. I actually accepted, and surprised myself. Normally, I wouldn't accept an invitation that quickly, but there was nothing normal about this—the speed with which things were happening, for example. On a rational level I thought he was good-looking, but there was something rather odd about him, a sort of nasal voice, a strutting walk. I suppose I had a question mark about him. He was an artist and had a studio in the area, and so we agreed to meet at 8.30 p.m. after I had gone home to wash and change. I returned there later, quite excited at the prospect of the evening. Eventually, I found the right studio. He and I left and went to look for a restaurant. We picked a French one nearby which neither of us had ever been to before. As I sat down at the table and faced him properly for the first time alone, I was suddenly dumbstruck. His face was the same face as my "experience" five years before. I couldn't believe it. I thought I was going mad. Was it my imagination? I did not, of course, say anything to him, because I thought he would have thought I was bananas.

I tried to concentrate on the conversation, but my being was reeling, my heart beating overtime at the excitement and vulnerability that I felt at this totally new experience. As the evening progressed, it became apparent that we were very much "in tune." We appeared to like the same things, think in a similar way about things and so on. Then he said: "Do you know, it's funny, but I have this feeling that I've met you before? I feel I know you, you are very familiar to me." I still didn't say anything. He went on: "It's strange, because usually I never go to listen to the band on Sunday, but today something drove me out there, and as soon as I got outside I only saw one thing: you. Or rather, I didn't notice your physical form but I 'felt' you and knew that we had to meet. It was as if I was magnetised." The conversation continued more normally. Then I asked him how he had got the scar on his cheek, a dark red thin line about three inches [7.6 centimetres] long. "What scar?" he said. I pointed to it. "But I haven't got a scar," he said. But I can see it, I thought. Then I dropped the subject. Some time later he said: "Have you noticed the décor here?" I hadn't, because I had been totally spellbound by his face. I looked around and was taken aback. Swords and shields on the walls, bits of armour, stone flooring, etc.—the same sort of period as I had seen in my "vision."

Bene said: "I would have liked to have lived at that time. I can just imagine myself as a swashbuckling cavalier . . .' By this time I was bursting to tell him. So I started, "Well, actually, I think you did live then," and went on to tell him of my experience. I was a little apprehensive about what his reaction would be; it is not every day that one meets a girl who tells you that you have been her lover in the sixteenth century! But he seemed to take it quite coolly, neither outraged nor overwhelmed by it. He just said that he did not know if it were true because he had not had his own recall, but he did know that he was irresistibly drawn to me, felt that he knew me, and that he had had a recurrent dream in which a girl would come up to him and say: "I've met you before, a long, long time ago." I must add that by the end of the evening the scar that I had "seen" had disappeared. There was nothing on his cheek. Was I hallucinating, I thought?

Eventually, it was time to go home. I wanted to be alone. I could not take any more. When I did get to bed I couldn't sleep anyway. It was as though I had been struck by a thunderbolt. The whole experience had shaken me. I'd never had such a strong, vivid and important experience before. I tossed and turned, trying to make sense of the whole thing, wondering what had happened, and what was going to happen. I felt that things were coming to me from the outside rather than things that I was instigating. Suddenly, in bed, my eyes being wide open and I was fully awake, a "face" appeared before my eyes—not a flesh face; it was what I can only call a spirit face, greyish white and non-material. I began to wonder if I really had gone crazy. Immediately, I intuitively knew it to be my paternal grandmother, who had died before I was born. Her name had been Catherine, which was my middle name. I say I "intuitively" knew it to be her because I could not recognise her in the usual way. I had only previously

seen photographs of her but they were of material flesh.
This vision did not look like her photograph at all.
Again I thought I must be imagining it and I tried to
alter features, which I could have done if I had been
simply imagining it, but nothing could be changed. It
was there, outside me, or outside my creative faculties,
existing independently of me, and there was nothing I
could do to make it go away. I inwardly asked why she
was there, appearing to me, and I was left with the impression that it was she who had been responsible for
the meeting with Bene that day. Eventually, that vision
went, and I was left in even more of a confused state.

The next day, Monday, he rang and asked if I would
like to go to Paris with him that evening. How exciting,
but I, cautious as ever, refused, saying I couldn't because of my other work commitments. He came round
to my flat later that day with a bunch of flowers. We
talked and talked, each being excited by the other, feeling very much in harmony. Neither of us had to explain
what we meant by a word or phrase. There was mutual
understanding. It seemed that I felt every sensation he
had, or thought every thought, even before he voiced it.
I knew what every facial expression of his meant.

How did the relationship progress? The initial intensity lasted
only for a few weeks. Gradually, Rachel began to realise that
this was not a story with a fairy-tale ending. The two still felt
very drawn towards each other, but the relationship proved to
be a difficult one. Bene was not an easy person; he was subject to violent emotional outbursts, and Rachel would bear the
brunt of these. She still had a strong feeling, though, that they
had been brought together for a purpose, but she realised that
although it was a relationship that had something to teach her,
or even something to teach them both, it wasn't destined to be
a lifetime partnership. They parted, then eventually came together again as friends before finally drifting apart altogether.

If Rachel had not had the dream, this part of the story
would need no explanation. We'd see it simply as an immediate attraction of such intensity that the people concerned had
to believe that they were destined to be together, an empathy

so strong that it seems to have been built up over previous lifetimes. Even with the knowledge of the dream, an obvious explanation would simply be that Bene's face wasn't the face of the man in the dream, that she thought it was only because he was the same type of man—the type that Rachel often found attractive and would have noticed anyway. After five years she might not have remembered the dream face clearly, but a similar face might have triggered the memory of the dream.

But this doesn't explain all the facts. It doesn't explain Bene's recurrent dream, or his feeling that he had met Rachel before, or the similarity of the restaurant to the room in her "vision." For that we have to fall back on coincidence. Is it too much of a coincidence that she should have met that particular person in those particular circumstances?

Even if we don't like the coincidence theory, or if we believe that Rachel was not mistaken—that Bene's was indeed the face she saw in her vision—we don't have to accept reincarnation as the only explanation. An equally plausible and equally non-scientific explanation would be that her first vision had been a precognitive experience of their future meeting. This would fit nearly all the facts except his feeling that he had known her.

Perhaps the real lesson to be learned from this experience is that you can't rely on history to repeat itself. Common sense would dictate that even if you think you have met your soul mate, and whatever you believe went on between you in a past life, you'd be wise not to assume that it will be recapitulated in this. Even soul mates who have managed to find each other for a second time around have to be prepared for their relationship to undergo tough times as well as tender.

11
Using the Past to Heal the Present

The best of prophets of the future is the past.

Byron

JOE Keeton is a hypnotist who has conducted several hundred past-life regressions. One of his most intriguing cases is that of Ann Dowling, a housewife from Huyton, near Liverpool, who during sixty hours of regression recounted her life as Sarah Williams, an orphan living in the slums of Everton in the first half of the nineteenth century.

Ann originally approached Joe Keeton in the hope that he might help rid her of two recurrent nightmares that had plagued her for many years. In one she was sitting alone in a small bare room, bewildered but filled with a terrible and growing sense of apprehension. In the other dream she was standing in a sordid basement with a roughly dressed stranger who was brandishing a knife. Both dreams left her feeling very disturbed for many hours afterwards.

Joe Keeton's experience of past-life regressions is that it is memories of the most traumatic events in a previous existence which tend to emerge first. During Ann's first regression the events that formed the stuff of her nightmares seemed to be spelled out in horrifying detail.

Q: You have a complete set of memories . . . you are free in all time. . . . You can remember everything . . . Where are you?

A: *Instantly a terrified panting.* In . . . a . . . basement.

Q: What is your name?

A: *Frightened whisper.* Aha . . . Aha . . . Sarah . . . aha . . .
       I . . . ca . . . ca . . . *Hysterically.*
       I . . . don't . . . like . . . this . . . room.

Q: Who is with you?

A: Lindy . . . and Tony . . . and Jimmy an' Jacky.

Q: If all of these people are with you, why are you so afraid?

A: I . . . don't . . . like . . . this . . . room.

Keeton then told Sarah to go into a deep sleep and brought her
forward five years in time. Her head dropped and her breathing became deep and regular, but she would no longer respond to any of his questions. This, says Keeton, is usually an
indication that the personality is dead. Keeton told her to return to the previous period; her chest began to heave with terror, and her face became contorted with fear.

Q: Where are you now?

A: *Breathless with fear.* In . . . that . . . room . . . I don't
       like . . . this room.

Q: I know you don't, Sarah, but why are you so frightened?
       Why don't you like this room?

A: It's that man . . . it's . . . that man.

Q: What man? Remember.

A: Aaah. . . . *Breaks down in bitter crying.* Get the kids out.

Q: All right, Sarah. We'll get the kids out.

A: Oh . . . he's . . . got . . . got a big . . . it's like . . . a knife.
       Screaming. He's hitting me . . . He's coming . . . coming.

She gave a cry of anguish and became silent. But first, at Keeton's insistent demands, she gave a vague description of a
rough man, someone she thought was an Irish navvy from the
railway building, whom she had seen once before lurking in
an alley as she took the four children she was minding back to
their parents.

Does this suggest that Ann's nightmare consisted of fragments of a dimly remembered past-life? Or that she had constructed a past-life memory that was an elaboration of the
nightmare that had troubled her for so long? An even simpler

explanation is that under hypnosis she had recovered not the memory of a past life but a more complete memory of the dream itself.

Virtually all children suffer from at least the occasional nightmare. In Western culture nightmares are attributed to unresolved conflicts or anxiety or stress. Often a nightmare doesn't seem to relate to any concern of the dreamer which can be identified, but we explain this by saying that we tend to dream in symbols, and our dream are much more a reflection of our emotions than a straight rerun of events. Many people have a specific dream that recurs whenever they are anxious. In cultures where a belief in reincarnation is widespread, it is natural for such dreams to be accepted as past-life memories.

Ian Stevenson (*Children Who Remember Previous Lives*) has noted the similarity of some children's vivid and recurrent dreams to their spontaneous, apparent past-life waking memories. And occasionally even Western families with no belief in reincarnation conclude that past-life experiences might indeed be influencing their child's nightmares. Antonia Mills describes a case in which a child whose nightmares seemed to bear no relationship to any events in her present life was helped by the explanation that they might relate to some experience in a past life.

Heidi Hornig (pseudonym) was born in British Columbia in July 1982. She was a healthy, normal baby, but her mother noticed that she cried whenever anyone touched the top of her head. As she grew older she still hated having her head touched or her hair washed. When she was four she was thought to have "perceptual problems"—she had, for example, a very odd reaction when playing with blocks. She would refuse to build block towers, and when asked to copy a tower she would instead make a horizontal structure along the floor. When her younger sister made a brick tower and knocked it down, Heidi would get very upset.

In the autumn of 1987, when Heidi was five, her kindergarten class was involved in a project to make a house out of cardboard blocks painted to look like bricks. Heidi avoided going anywhere near this, and whenever it was knocked over (which happened frequently) would become very upset. Fi-

nally, and very fearfully, she was persuaded to add a single
block to the structure. That night she woke up and went running into her parents' bedroom trembling and saying that
bricks had fallen on her head. She insisted that her head hurt,
that there was blood on it, and that she could not see. She told
her parents that the house had fallen on her head, that the animals were very hungry, did not have enough to eat, and were
dying. This nightmare, always followed by the pain in her
head after she awoke, recurred about three times a week for
four months. She then began to experience the same distressing feelings while she was awake.

There seemed to be no medical reason for Heidi's odd
symptoms, and doctors concluded that she was suffering from
night terrors. The family doctor eventually suggested that the
child might be remembering some incident from a previous
life in which bricks had fallen on her head. He suggested that
Heidi's mother should try reassuring her by telling her that
she had no need to be frightened any more because what she
remembered had happened in a previous life and could not affect her now.

The idea of previous lives wasn't something Heidi's parents had ever thought about; indeed, her engineer father found
it quite unacceptable. But her mother was prepared to give it
a try, even though she was not convinced it would work. She
started a bedtime routine of massage and soothing music, and
reassured the little girl that she need not worry about bricks
falling on her head now because it had happened in another
life that was over. She told her that only she, Heidi, could
make the unpleasant feelings stop. She also asked Heidi to tell
her a little more about her dreams, and Heidi told her she had
been big, like her mother, when it happened.

Four months after the onset of the nightmares. Heidi woke
up early in the morning, went to her parents, and announced:
"It is over. I'm not having that any more." Her behaviour
changed; she no longer minded having her hair washed or her
head touched, she no longer became tearful and anxious when
her sister built towers and knocked them down.

Two days later she asked her mother how you knew when
someone was dead, a question her mother interpreted as Heidi
trying to integrate the concept of death with her experience in

the nightmare. Two years later, when a neighbour died unexpectedly, Heidi took the news calmly and later said that the neighbour had left her body for a while but that some people return after being away for a time. Heidi's mother felt that her daughter understood and accepted the concept of past and future lives more readily than she herself was able to.

Do we need the concept of a previous life to explain Heidi's fears? Many small children hate having their hair washed; on its own, this is not particularly significant. Many small children have fears that seem to be quite irrational. And many small children have nightmares or night terrors. Is it possible that Heidi's phobia about bricks arose from a nightmare or night terror, and not that her nightmare was a memory of being injured by falling bricks in a previous life?

Night terrors are not like ordinary dreams. The imagery in night terrors is not clear visual imagery as in a dream but consists much more of feelings—and a terrifying feeling of being trapped, or of the walls of a house collapsing in on one, is quite commonly part of night-terror content. But night terrors are not usually remembered, and in Heidi's case the memory of the nightmare/terror persisted into waking life in a way that does not occur with a night terror and is rare even with a nightmare. Finally, phobias do *not* usually arise from nightmares, though nightmares certainly do arise from phobias.

It is impossible to say whether Heidi's fears really did have anything to do with a past life. But from a practical point of view, using the past-life explanation worked and got rid of both the nightmares and the phobia.

Past-life therapy is becoming increasingly popular. People are often anxious to explore their past lives under hypnosis out of curiosity, or just for fun, but most reputable hypnotherapists now will refuse to regress someone for this reason alone. They offer past-life regression only if they think it might help to solve someone's present problems. But it is still a controversial area. Is it really good therapy to look for the origins of present-day problems in a past life? As a general rule, the origins of most of our problems, both physical and emotional, lie fair and square in this life, which is where they should be tackled.

A common belief among healers is that some present-day

illnesses originate or are carried over from a previous life. There is no known way in which any physical problem could be caused by something that occurred in a past life. But there are areas in which looking for the cause of a problem is difficult or unproductive. It is often difficult to find the source of a nightmare or a phobia, for example, or to eliminate the stresses that trigger psychosomatic illnesses. Here, any kind of psychotherapy which can change the patient's mental "set" and attitudes may work. Regression therapy is one way of doing this.

Gillian Goddard described to us the way in which recognition of past lives had helped her. From the age of about seven Gillian suffered a recurring nightmare followed by sleepwalking, panic attacks, hyperventilation, etc. When she was 45 she decided to go to a spiritual healer, feeling that she had nothing to lose. She says: "The depression and panic attacks went away. The cause—three past lives—started to come to the surface in several ways: dreams, meditation, etc." In one of these lives she was accused of witchcraft, ducked, tortured and burned. In another she was burned as a heretic; in a third she seemed to see a human sacrifice. Discovering traumatic past-life episodes would probably have been enough to make anyone feel grateful for whatever the fates may have dealt them this time around.

Elizabeth Royce (pseudonym), herself a healer, described an experience she had during a meditation which involved not only herself but another healer. In the experience:

> I was a very small child in America, and I was on a very long walk or trek. My father was with me, and I recognised him as my friend and mentor in this life. The scene then changed, and I was a few years older, about nine or ten, and I was playing in a very large field. Suddenly, five Red Indians appeared in war paint, whooping and circling. I turned and ran and at the same time I saw my father on horseback galloping frantically towards me to save me. Just as he got to me I was brought out of the vision or memory by a sudden intense pain in my right lung (I felt this as a real physical here-and-now pain, not a remembered one), and I knew I'd been

hit by an arrow. I felt, although I didn't actually see it, that my father had also been hit.

Elizabeth's "friend and mentor" in this life is another healer, Barry, a man who is a strong Roman Catholic and did not believe in reincarnation. A few months after her experience, Elizabeth and her husband called to see Barry and found him feeling unwell. He explained that he had severe recurrent chest pains for which no explanation could be found, and he asked Elizabeth for some healing. This she did, but didn't say a word about her experience because, she says, "I was afraid he'd think I was off my head or worse."

A few months later they again met Barry and this time Elizabeth suddenly decided she would tell him about the Indians. To her astonishment, as soon as she mentioned feeling the pain in her lung, Barry abruptly broke in and said: "I always knew I was shot in the chest." He then told her that every time he had this pain he felt it was because he'd been shot or hurt in some way but didn't understand how or where or when. "He completely accepted the fact that we had probably shared a life together as father and child: hence the connection in this life, albeit in very different circumstances." Can one prove that these two really did share a past life together? Of course not, but certainly Barry hasn't suffered any chest pain since.

David Bryant has also described how he found past-life healing effective. For over sixty years David had suffered from "an extremely nervous bowel." Finally, after trying many different medicines he plucked up the courage to see a hypnotherapist. In a trance state he was taken back to what he saw in his mind's eye was 1700. He saw a young man standing before a big house in the country and "just knew" it was himself. Then he watched a man whose face he could not see coming towards him, attacking him. They fought with swords, and his assailant was killed. He himself was taken away and locked up somewhere very dark. He feels pain in his lower abdomen and knows that he is dying. At this point the hypnotherapist brought him round and said: "Now, we do not know if that is fact or fiction, but all will be well now."

And indeed it was. That was three years ago, and Mr. Bryant has not had any problems with his bowels since.

Phobias, too, seem to respond well to past-life therapy. Phobias are irrational; most people who have a phobia have no idea how it arose and accept that their fear is illogical. Invoking a past life may at least make them feel there is a reason for their fear.

Denise Chamberlain's mother remembers that as soon as Denise could draw, she would spend many hours unaccountably drawing image after image of people dying from stab wounds. Understandably, this troubled her mother. Denise remembers drawing the pictures but had no idea why she drew them, only that she felt she needed to. She had, she says, "a feeling of an awful shadow hanging over my life, but nothing more tangible than that. As I grew older, the compulsion gradually ceased." She wonders now whether the experience could be indicative of a past life. As an adult she continues to have a great and unexplained fear of knives. Although she is not usually squeamish, once when she cut her hand chopping vegetables she became nearly hysterical, although she knew the wound was only superficial.

Sometimes recognising the apparent origin of an anxiety is enough in itself to help resolve it. Marion Pearn had had a number of hypnotherapy sessions in the past in which nothing had emerged to indicate a past life. Then she spent a week at Findhorn at a workshop that was concerned with spiritual growth and quite unconnected with reincarnation. In a relaxation session at the outset of the workshop, "I found myself on the Somme, in the First World War, as an ambulance stretcher-bearer. All around was utter desolation, bodies everywhere, and I felt so bad at knowing I could not save everyone. But I tried my hardest and saved all I could. As this was happening, I actually felt a cracking feeling in the groin area and almost heard it too. It was the release of tension that was manifested when my mind was accepting I could not help all the casualties of the war on the Somme." For Marion, the effects of this release of tension on her anxiety problems continued for months afterwards.

Although the regression therapist may explain present-life fears in terms of past-life traumas, it is, of course, equally logical to say that a fantasy past life is very likely to embody present-life fears. The following account by Dr. Wambach, an American hypnotherapist who believed that she herself had had a past life and who, before her death in 1985, had conducted at least 1,000 past-life regressions, demonstrates this very clearly. Here she is describing the regression of one of her patients, Betty, to a fifteen-year-old girl in England in the seventeenth century.

> She was despondent because she had just escaped from a fire that destroyed her home and that of many others . . . Because all other members of her family died in the fire, she was apprenticed to a tavern-keeper, and thereafter led a very difficult life as a barmaid. Although her personality as a feisty wench who fought for herself came through, she was repeatedly abused and mistreated, and eventually died, very painfully, after being raped and beaten by several drunken men.
>
> Betty experienced considerable emotion . . . after she came out of the hypnotic session. "You know, I smelled the alcohol on those men," she said, "and I felt the same feeling that I've had in this life . . . I've always been unusually afraid of people who are drinking. Now I feel I understand why. It's because I died at the hands of drunken men."

That Betty's terror of drunkenness had its roots in her rape by drunken men in a previous incarnation is one way of looking at it. But just as valid and perhaps more credible is to conclude that her past-life memory was a fantasy that took that particular form because of her fear of drunkenness. "I felt the same feeling that I've had in this life," she says.

A literal belief in reincarnation is not necessary for regression therapy to work. How credible someone finds the past life they are regressed to will depend more on the beliefs, attitudes and expectations they hold before the therapy starts, or which are transmitted to them by the therapist, than on anything they experience during the regression. Some hypnotherapists present reincarnation from a point of view that assumes some notion of ongoing self. Others find it more helpful to suggest that the past-life experience is fantasy or metaphor.

Robert Jarmon and Roger Woolger are two of the most experienced practitioners of regression therapy. They use it because they have discovered it works. Whether or not their patients are literally regressed to a past life is of secondary importance to them.

HEALING THE SOUL

Robert Jarmon is an American psychiatrist who had never been particularly interested in reincarnation until he was consulted by a woman, Anna, who wanted him to help her lose weight. Dr. Jarmon had previously used hypnosis to help patients lose weight, and Anna proved to be a good hypnotic subject. However, after two months of successful treatment, she suddenly developed abdominal pain, swelling and tenderness on the right side of her lower abdomen. She also stopped menstruating. Despite extensive tests, no medical reason could be found. Then, during a session with Dr. Jarmon five months after her last menstrual period, Anna started to talk about her mounting, though vague, feelings of anxiety and depression. She seemed to have some personal problem that she could not or would not put into words. Dr. Jarmon decided to put her under hypnosis and instructed her to go back to where her problem started. In deep trance, Anna held her right side and began to moan as Dr. Jarmon questioned her, asking what was troubling her, and where and when it was happening.

Anna then started to talk about a different lifetime in which she was a nineteen- year-old girl, Elizabeth, in her fifth month of pregnancy. She said little about the time and place, apart from the fact that she was in Europe and that the time was "centuries ago," but was much more concerned about the specific scene she was remembering—her difficult, painful pregnancy and the priest and physician she could hear talking at her bedside. The doctor wanted to remove the unborn child from the womb to save Elizabeth's life; the priest was insisting that it was wrong to take life even to save a life. "If God wills that the woman die," he said, "then she dies."

At this point Dr. Jarmon noticed that Anna became visibly

weaker, and a look of serenity came over her face. Suddenly, she became absolutely still. Asked what was happening, she replied: "I've died. I'm floating now. I'm floating up—into a tunnel of light." Dr. Jarmon then talked to her soothingly, reassuring her that the pain of her previous life had died when that body had died and would no longer afflict her. When Anna was brought out of her trance the pain had gone, and so had the swelling and tenderness. And that evening she started menstruating for the first time for five months.

What is interesting in Dr. Jarmon's account of this experience, described in his book *Discovering the Soul*, is that, although the patient is evidently "cured," he does not let matters rest there. The following week, in another session with Anna, he again regressed her to "Elizabeth's" deathbed scene. He explains his reasons thus: "Without her consciously realising it, something in her mind or soul had been awakened or activated, had prepared her to go more deeply and in a more direct way into that life and death she had experienced centuries ago."

What happened this time was a surprise to them both. Anna was Jewish, Dr. Jarmon a practising Roman Catholic. As Anna/Elizabeth lay on her deathbed once more, she began to recite what Dr. Jarmon recognised immediately as the Act of Contrition, the prayer a Catholic says at the end of confession or during last rites, a prayer that Anna, born and brought up in the Jewish faith, did not know and claimed after the session that she had never heard before.

For Dr. Jarmon this was a revelation. For him, regression therapy is a form of spiritual medicine, a way of "discovering the soul" and healing it. He accepts that the underlying concepts of the soul and the afterlife which are central to his work may not even be valid, but believes that this is irrelevant to healing effectiveness. His attitude is: if it works, it works. And he also accepts that it is not a cure-all; not all problems are purely or even mostly spiritual by nature. But he believes that the goal of healing should always be *total* healing, and that by working through past lives he has found a way of working on the whole human being, body, mind and soul.

Roger Woolger, in an interview with *Reincarnation* magazine, also maintains that he practises regression therapy simply because he has found that it works. He is not trying to "prove" reincarnation, though he gives the impression that he himself believes in it. But this is incidental to his work as a therapist, which involves using stories that may or may not be true. He says: "When the unconscious mind is given the opportunity to play stories *as if they were past lives*, it comes up with staggering solutions, releases, and spontaneous healings which you don't get in other therapies!"

In the workshops he holds, Roger Woolger finds that one of the quickest ways to get people into past lives is to start from the idea that everyone has within them inner characters, secondary or sub-personalities which appear in our dream life. If you dig into these characters with a slightly different perspective, he says, you find that they have past-life biographies. Participants are asked to do very simple exercises to call one or two of these characters up. Then they try to find one or two places in the world which either attract or repel them, and to imagine they are living there in another lifetime. These countries are, he says, "charged" because the soul remembers them at some very deep level.

Although he believes that between 10 and 30 percent of what comes up is fantasy, he also believes that he can distinguish between a fantasy reconstruction and a genuine past-life memory. This goes for his own past-life memories too. Some of them he can't accept but treats as fantasies; others seem to him to be parts of himself, but not his whole self, just as his dreams are part of him, but not him. It is as if a sub-personality within him has a memory of being, say, a thirteenth-century soldier, so that he will say, "I have the remnants of such and such in me today," rather than, "I *was* such and such. . . ."

Regression therapy very seldom provides any evidence of reincarnation. It is used as a tool to help the patient achieve insight into a problem, in the same way as dream therapy is often used by psychotherapists. The questions the therapist asks have only one aim—to discover whether traumatic events in a past life lie at the root of difficulties in this. A past-life regression that is attempting to prove reincarnation will take a quite different form. The hypnotist will try to elicit as many details as possible—names, dates, places, anything that can be checked to see how well the past-life story hangs together. It seldom does. Neil Robinson, however, has told us of one occasion when both therapist and client were taken aback when he decided to check out the memories of a past life.

Neil is a professional hypnotherapist and member of the National Society of Professional Hypnotherapists, practising in Edinburgh, who uses both past-life and present-life regression to resolve problems. Sometimes he finds that a client in a present-life regression will regress spontaneously to a past life. One day when he was regressing a client:

> Under hypnosis she regressed to a past life in the 1920s and recounted details of her life—her name, where she lived, what she did and names of her relatives. She particularly mentioned her favourite aunt, Aunt Aggie. The client's previous life ended in 1934. She was born in this life in 1946 and so therefore it seemed likely that some of her previous relatives were still around.
>
> This lady had never been to England, and yet she had given specific details about names and addresses in Burnley. After the session, with the client present, I telephoned Directory Enquiries and gave them the surname and address that she had relived. I was given two telephone numbers for that name in that street in Burnley. One was identical to the house number that she had said she lived at. With the client's permission, I telephoned that number and asked for Aunt Aggie. I was told by the person who answered the phone that Aunt Aggie had died about five years ago.
>
> My client was freaked out by this and, understandably, did not want to continue any further.

Neil Robinson adds that his client had no relatives in Burnley—in fact, hadn't even heard of the place. After the session was finished, one of the first things she asked was: "Is there such a place as Burnley? I have never heard of it before. Where is it?" Coincidence is really the only rational explanation for this, and yet the account would involve *four* coincidences: name, house number, street name and town all checked out. Is this really that much easier to believe than the idea that Neil's client had somehow tuned in to memories of a past life, whether her own or someone else's?

There are dangers in past-life therapy. The psychological effects of a past-life regression can be dramatic and can create emotional reactions that an inexperienced or inadequately qualified therapist may be quite unable to deal with. The following two accounts hold a warning.

Christine Pye told us that she had been fascinated by aircraft ever since a boyfriend first took her gliding at the age of seventeen. She became a regular attender at airshows and "spent many hours crying underneath the belly of aircraft unable to move, racked with emotion and totally unable to explain just what I am crying about." She became involved with spiritualism and in a trance state one day experienced the horrific death of an airman. "The burning explained why I have always felt something different about one side of my face, why my face changes when I stare into the mirror, why I fear flames."

After several past-life regression sessions with a hypnotherapist, Christine eventually relived in the spiritualist circle the exact death sequence she had experienced. For her it was a healing experience. "Since that experience of going back I have become my 'own' person. I am able to cope with situations I once feared, stand up for myself . . . I believe my insight into my past lives has given me much strength and inspiration to better this one." She also adds that her belief that we live many lives has eliminated any fear she may have had of death. But she also adds a warning note for anyone who contemplates exploring their own past lives. "The state I was in after that session was fairly distressing—taking a few weeks to settle. I was sweating, crying and terribly emotional and had vivid dreams for several weeks."

Katherine Callaghan (pseudonym) also questions the wisdom of anyone who decides to have hypnotic regression out of curiosity. She herself went to a hypnotherapist looking for stress relief. After four or five sessions in which she recounted her dreams, one day in a session she found herself in a quite different state, "in a dream, but it wasn't one":

My name seemed to be Irmgut, and I was driving a buck wagon home. My dress and the stuff it was made of was so important to me. I could feel the fine cotton petticoat against my lap, and my hands with the bridle in them were on my lap. I just loved the dress. It was blue and white fine gingham with small red rosebuds sewn around the hem. My young child, about six months, was in a carrying crib and was dressed in a linen bonnet and dress that was creamy white with fine embroidered trims my mother had done. I was on a country road with a slow gradient down. On the right was tall grain, corn or maize, which was golden. It was a beautiful Sunday evening in summer, and I could smell and feel all of it more pronounced than in any waking dream. To the left the grass was green and sloped down to the small group of trees on the horizon. I saw one young brave come over the horizon on horseback, followed by another three. I was in terror because I could see they were either drunk or drugged. I looked at the baby and lifted the gun under the seat. I checked it was loaded and went on. I fired at the Indians first and brought one of them down. They came screaming and yelping. I woke up in terrible pain; my baby lay dead by the upturned wagon. My dress was all torn, which upset me so much, and I had obviously been beaten and raped. When I next awoke I was lying on bracken and wood. They'd cut my beautiful long golden-brown hair and I knew they had brought me to a village. I could see a totem pole, which terrified me because it was so tall. I realised that the crackling sound I could hear was the fire below me. I was more terrified than ever, although very dopey as if half-conscious. Thankfully, the smoke started choking me as I felt my feet and legs burning, but I could smell the burning skin. I never wanted to experience it again.

At this point Katherine came out of the trance state, very agitated. At the next session the same thing happened. At that point she told her therapist: "I'm pulling the curtain shut on this—this is enough." The effects of the experience persisted for several weeks—at one point, she says, she came across a totem pole at a garden festival and had "an intense and frightening reaction to it." The whole experience made Katherine question the wisdom of anyone who wants to explore their past lives out of curiosity.

Was this imagination, cryptomnesia or a past-life memory? Had the whole scenario been lifted from some episode of *Wagon Train*? Katherine doesn't know. She says herself that she has a vivid and lively imagination and always has had. But cowboy stories have never been of much interest to her.

Katherine does also remember that when she was four years old and looking at an old *National Geographic* magazine with her granny, she told her granny that she could read Chinese. She insisted that she had another granny who watched her in a parade with lots of other little girls, and she could take only tiny steps. She remembers that her Chinese granny sat on a seat to the left of the parade, which took place under a closed terrace. In this memory, too, she was immensely conscious of what she was wearing—a green silk outfit. This is one clue that the experiences may owe at least something to Katherine's present life rather than a past one— when she was a small child her mother was a seamstress and tailoress and Katherine grew up very aware of materials.

Predictably, Katherine's Scottish granny told her not to be so silly and to forget the whole thing—and, she says, she more or less did.

How effective is past-life regression as a form of psychotherapy? In the hands of an experienced and qualified hypnotherapist, past-life regression can be a useful tool to help patients deal with fears and emotions that may be too difficult or painful for them to face in full consciousness. By distancing them from reality, the therapist can make it safe for them to face and deal with these emotions. The whole process of hypnosis, which involves physical relaxation and rapport with the therapist, together with the fact that the patient is being offered an explanation for his or her experiences are all likely to have a therapeutic effect.

In the hands of a good, charismatic therapist, almost any therapy—or even none at all—will probably work. The placebo response is good evidence of this. But in the hands of non-professional therapists who themselves have a strong belief in past lives, and who may try to persuade vulnerable clients of the truth of the memories induced, regression therapy has huge risks.

Perhaps the greatest danger is that regression therapy is too easy. It is not difficult to induce a hypnotic-trance state—virtually anyone can learn to do it. In the UK this area is not controlled by legislation: anyone can set himself up as a past-life therapist. An unqualified or poorly trained therapist may unintentionally reinforce or encourage or even implant a belief in false memories. When these memories suggest an innocent belief that you have been a thirteenth-century Italian peasant, this doesn't much matter. But belief in a false memory of sexual abuse in this life, for example, may devastate families and ruin lives. There is also no doubt that some patients are severely traumatised by the lives or memories that are evoked. Handling traumatised people requires professional training: an inexperienced or unqualified therapist may not have the skills to help the client deal adequately with any traumatic memories or strong negative feelings that arise.

12

Hidden Talents

Work is futile if we cannot utilise the experience we collect in one life in the next.

Henry Ford

ALL kinds of explanations have been suggested to account for the information about a past life which people apparently acquire. False memory, fantasy, fraud, even telepathy have all been suggested. But none of these can explain adequately another strange phenomenon of the reincarnation experience—that sometimes people exhibit a skill that seems to be a talent reborn, something they feel they knew in a past life but claim they have had no opportunity to learn in their present life. Is there any evidence that what we call a natural talent, an inborn talent, may sometimes be a talent reborn?

Stephanie Wilson describes how several years ago she started to learn calligraphy at her local college:

> We were taught several different "hands"—foundation hand, italic and uncial. However, towards the end of the course the tutor asked if anyone would be interested in learning copperplate writing. We were told it was entirely different from the other scripts, required a different nib, etc.
>
> The tutor would come round and write a few letters of a particular script, and we would copy them (I should add it took several terms to learn one script properly). However, on this particular occasion, after the tutor had

demonstrated how some of the strokes of copperplate were formed, he walked round the class checking on our progress. By the time he came back to me, about ten minutes later, I had written a full page of copperplate script! The strange thing was, with the other scripts I *learned* them, but with copperplate I was *remembering* it. I was explaining to the girl who sat next to me in class that the strokes of the "f" and "p" were shorter than the loop strokes, and there was no way I should have known that.

The tutor smiled and said: "You've done this before, haven't you?" I replied, Yes, I'd learned it at school. However, when I was telling my mother about it several days later she said: "What do you mean? You never did any copperplate writing at school!"

It was only then that Stephanie began to think of reincarnation as a possible explanation. As she said to her mother, if she didn't learn it at school, where did she learn it? Stephanie says she can distinctly remember someone instructing her in the script and saying, "Always start the letter 'c' with a dot." She remembered how to join the letters in certain ways—it all came back to her when she started the class.

Quite recently Stephanie bought a book, *The Universal Penman*, a book of examples of engraving and copperplate writing, which shows how bills were made out. Stephanie says: "I can remember writing out bills in just the same way, yet these are dated between 1730 and 1800."

Jo Gordon (pseudonym) describes how when she was nine years old she visited a fairground in London and decided to have a pony-ride. "I had nil experience of horses but knew I loved them. As soon as I sat on the pony and confirmed that I wished to trot, I knew how to rise in the saddle like an *aficionado*, and the man leading me commented that I knew how to ride well. At the spot we turned, I laid the reins across the neck of the pony, and my fairground friend said the pony was not trained to 'neck ride,' saying they only ride like that as far as he knew in America. My brain seemed to click into another 'radio programme,' and from that moment I had no doubts that we have many skills and talents gained from experiences in our other lives."

In the early 1960s Donald Galloway was told by some friends about a mystic who produced, for a fee of 30 shillings, "incarnoscopes" giving details of people's past lives. So impressed had his friends been that Mr. Galloway sent off his 30 bob and some weeks later received his reading.

I am not artistically gifted but can fully appreciate beautiful art in many forms. Mrs. Helen wrote that in one previous incarnation I had been trained in the artistry of making stained-glass windows; in another my training was in the area of architecture, but only in regard to designed churches, temples, places designed to the glory of God, and in another lifetime I had been schooled by apprenticeship in the design of rich carpets and textiles generally.

This rather took me back to my childhood and something I had completely forgotten about in the many years since. When very young, after I had done my school homework and if there was nothing to interest me on the radio, I would take paper and crayons and most meticulously set about drawing great buildings, or patterns for carpets and rich draperies, and sometimes intricate designs for stained-glass windows! Growing older, I let all this go quite naturally and, as I said, completely forgot about ever doing it at all—until Mrs. Helen prompted my memory!

Don Adams is fifty years old, and for most of his life he has been convinced that he has "lived" before. "When I started making medieval longbows forty years ago there was very little information available on how to make one. It seemed, though, that I knew intuitively a lot about it as I went along over the years, even though I was much criticised and ridiculed by others. I was using techniques which I could not possibly have read about. When the *Mary Rose* was raised and the bows examined, all became clear."

About sixteen years ago Don decided to have a past-life regression. People who have a strong conviction about a past

life often hope that a past-life regression will confirm their belief. More often than not, the experiment from that point of
view is a failure—the life they are regressed to is not the one
they expect or have memories of. Don, however, was not disappointed. His past-life regression revealed that he had lived
in around 1415, and that he was an archer who died at the age
of sixteen in the Battle of Agincourt, killed by a lance.

Where did these odd, unexpected talents come from? Was
Donald Galloway, for example, right in thinking his artistic
skill came from a past life or can we find an alternative explanation? The most straightforward explanation would be
that he was brought up in an artistic family, that his parents
encouraged him to draw these intricate patterns and stimulated his interest in art. But Donald is very clear that he drew
these great churches, stained-glass windows and intricately
patterned carpets entirely for his own satisfaction. This certainly suggests a talent and probably a well-developed spatial
sense too. But still one would expect there to have been a trigger of some sort to fire his imagination—a teacher or maybe
a book he had read. He has no recollection of this. So what are
we left with? A talent and an interest. What is missing is the
initial stimulus that fired his interest. He knows of none. So
do we have to look more widely than that? And is his explanation more economical than the others?

Don Adams is quite certain that he had never learned about
the construction of a longbow. But here the devil is in the detail. If there are principles involved in the construction of a
longbow which cannot be intuitively grasped by someone
wanting to make one, then we have to look for an external
source for this information.

Like Donald Galloway, one can argue that Don Adams has
good spatial skills and understanding of spatial relationships.
But many people have such talents and yet don't feel, in the
way that Don did, that they have privileged information in a
particular field. When you have a talent and can do something
easily, there is always a tendency to feel that it must arise in-
nately. You can grasp the concepts easily and learn them almost unconsciously—you don't have to struggle. This would
be a better explanation for Don's ability to make a longbow.
It does have testable features. If Don were in general a cack-

handed chap who could barely wield a screwdriver, then one would certainly have to look for some other explanation for his ability to make a longbow. But let's assume that he is someone with good spatial skills and a good eye for the way things work who happened to be interested in longbows. In that case, unless the principles behind the making of a long-bow are extremely complex and not at all obvious, by work-ing out from first principles how a longbow *ought* to be made, it is not surprising that he arrived at the same solution that those early longbow manufacturers reached.

However, Stephanie Wilson's knowledge of calligraphy seems to be in a different category, because she seemed to have not only the knowledge but the memory of actually being taught the skill. She attributes her knowledge to a pre-vious life because there seems to be no other easily available explanation, unless she did indeed have early lessons in cal-ligraphy at school which her mother had not known about.

Here is an account given by a man who has no intellectual belief in reincarnation and yet who had an experience of it so powerful that it shaped the whole future course of his life.

For Robert, the violin has always been a powerful source of memory. The first time he ever saw a violin he felt an in-stant recognition; he knew that he had to play it. For a pro-fessional world-class violinist, Robert was a late starter; it wasn't until he was eight that he began lessons. He joined the class half-way through its first term, and so at his first lesson the teacher told him he had missed so much it would be hard for him to keep up; he had better just sit and listen for the rest of this class. Towards the end he finally turned to Robert. "I picked up the fiddle, and it was just as if I knew what to do." When he went home that evening he told his mother: "I'm a violinist!"

A few years later, when he was about eleven or twelve, Robert was at boarding-school. One day he was practising his violin, and as he was playing he drifted into a semi-dream-like state. He was aware suddenly that he was playing a piece he did not know, in a hall he did not recognise, and that he was playing with a full orchestra, all its members dressed in what seemed to him to be old-fashioned clothes. He was also aware that his playing had changed; he was making a sound on the fiddle that as a child he simply could not make. His vibrato had changed: it was much stronger. In fact, he was playing like an adult. His whole body felt different, too: his chest felt deeper, he was breathing quite differently.

When he came out of this altered state he was on cloud nine, almost hysterical with joy. It was, he says, the most wonderful experience of his life. He then made the mistake of trying to explain what had happened to him to his music teacher and was promptly sent off to matron and the sickbay.

At that stage of his life Robert was a very unhappy, very introverted little boy, and he accepts that all manner of rational psychological explanations might account for what happened to him. And yet it had so much meaning, and has had such an influence on his life, that he believes it had to be more than simply that. Intellectually, the idea of reincarnation is still one he can't accept. And yet, as he says, whatever questions we have about the nature of existence, in the end all we have to go by is our own experience.

Other people have told us of similar experiences. In 1945, as a child of three or four, Mary Balaam moved with her family to a small farm in Wales. Next to the house was a field with many clumps of rushes growing in it. "I pestered my mother to attend to them. 'Shouldn't we be making something with them?' I continually enquired. I vividly remember worrying and never having my anxieties assuaged."

Many years later, in 1982, Mrs. Balaam happened to turn on a schools television programme, *How We Used to Live*. "The hairs on my neck and my whole spine seemed to shiver when the candle-making was explained. The inside pith from rushes was used as the wick, being rolled in tallow and dried repeatedly until sufficiently thick to form a candle. I do not claim to have lived before but do wonder whether we have 'ancient knowledge' imprinted in our hindbrains. I still remember a terrible sadness as the rushes died and turned brown in the autumn."

THE CHANNELLERS

When people with a special talent feel that it originated in a past life, usually they mean their *own* past life. Equally interesting are the people who have a different but closely related experience—they believe not that they are reincarnations of dead artists but that they are being used as "channels" by those artists to communicate their posthumous works through automatic writing or drawing or musical composition. The experience is essentially the same, but the interpretation is different.

The physicist Dr. Vernon Harrison, a forensic and photographic expert, has studied several of these cases of "channelling," of which the most interesting is that of the psychic and healer Matthew Manning. During his adolescence Matthew was plagued by poltergeist activity and found that he could reduce this by allowing himself to be used as a channel for automatic writing and drawing. Matthew, a teenager with no particular artistic gift, "received" dozens of very creditable drawings very much in the style of several artists, including Albrecht Dürer, Picasso and Aubrey Beardsley.

Dr. Harrison considered the possibility that Matthew's drawings might have been the result of either eidetic imagery (the ability to take a quick glance at a picture and retain it in memory) or cryptomnesia. So far as eidetic memory is concerned, he pointed out that even when the source of a drawing could be identified, Matthew's version was not simply a copy of it but a "transcript, paraphrase, reworking of a theme or composite."

Was Matthew unwittingly reproducing pictures that he had seen but forgotten? Cryptomnesia is notoriously difficult to prove or to disprove. Matthew *could* have seen some of the pictures that were obvious sources for his work, though Dr. Harrison thought this was unlikely. But again, his own pictures were not direct copies, and cryptomnesia would not explain the ability of this untutored boy to reproduce so accurately the styles and techniques of the various artists, or to draw as rapidly and competently as he did.

It is interesting to read Matthew's own description of what happened the first time he found himself producing automatic writing. He was writing an essay that he didn't find easy and had to keep stopping to think about what he was going to write next. "As I sat with my pen poised above the paper ready to start writing whatever I thought of next, my hand went down on to the paper in a completely involuntary way and began to write. While thinking about what I was going to write, my mind had wandered from the subject on to nothing in particular. I watched, startled, as I wrote words in a handwriting different from my own. Then, becoming momentarily frightened, I pulled my hand away and looked at what I had written. The words were incomprehensible and sprawled across half of the page."

Matthew later tried to repeat what had happened, sitting down with the express intention of allowing his hand to be used for automatic writing. This time he produced a legible and coherent sentence. This process of practice making perfect seems to be common to most channellers. But does it mean that Matthew was learning how to produce "automatic" writing? Or was some outside influence "learning" how to use Matthew as a channel? Clearly, there was a willed action on Matthew's part.

Channellers seem to operate in an altered state of consciousness probably very similar to the light trance state of a hypnotic regression. It's possible that in this state natural talents are enhanced, and certainly inhibitions would be lessened. Musicologist Melvyn Willin has a special interest in what he calls "paramusicology," which includes the phenomenon of channelling, and once conducted a regression experiment with a Dutch didgeridoo-player who believed he was an Aborigine in a previous life. He could certainly, reports Mr. Willin, play considerably better when in a light trance than in his normal state.

The case of Patience Worth is the one that Dr. Harrison himself considers one of the most important examples of channelling produced this century. Between 1913 and 1938, when she died, Pearl Curran, a medium, was the channel through which one Patience Worth communicated a voluminous oeuvre of poems, plays, novels, and a book, *The Sorry Tale*, set in the time of Christ. This last was a volume of 325,000 words, dictated at great speed. Patience gave little information about her life, except that she had been born in Dorset in the seventeenth century and brought up a Quaker. Her family emigrated to America, and shortly afterwards she was killed by Indians. Dr. Harrison points out a difficulty here. "Patience" spoke not in a Dorset but in a Northumbrian or Borders Scots dialect—and, moreover, a dialect that Dr. Harrison maintains can be dated with some precision to 1623. The Quaker movement did not start until 1646, which would make it impossible for Patience to have had a Quaker up-bringing. She might, however, have sailed on the *Mayflower* (1620) and been killed in the massacre of 327 settlers in Virginia in 1622. But this is all conjecture. There is, in fact, no evidence that "Patience" ever actually existed.

Mrs. Curran was an unlikely choice as an alter ego for Patience Worth. She lived in St. Louis, Missouri, and had never travelled. She had had only a limited education, had little interest in books and owned only a few, some whose pages had never been cut; she disliked reading and had no literary ability. Dr. Harrison, who has published a study of the case, maintains that her work is distinguished by quality as well as quantity. In his words: "To be appreciated, Patience Worth has to be *read*—and read with a small library of reference books close at hand ... Whoever she is, I know that [she has] ... witched me by her wit and verve; by her keen observation of human foibles; by the swiftness and deadly aim of her repartee; and above all by the beauty of so much of her writing and her philosophy ... To me she seems as 'real' as my well-loved Walter de la Mare ..."

For his own working hypothesis to explain these phenomena, Dr. Harrison draws on the teachings of Swedenborg and the Theosophists, which suggest that at death only the physical body disintegrates. "Kama," the motivating force of man—desire, emotions, memories, passions—can survive for hours or even years after death before it, too, is sloughed off, leaving man's true individuality, the permanent, growing, reincarnating self. When Kama is shed, however, it can be re-activated in the presence of people like Matthew Manning, who act as a power source. Kama may re-create the personality, prejudices and emotions of the former life, but, lacking man's higher principles, shows no sign of creativity, imagination or moral judgements. The alter ego remains a second-rate shadow of its former self.

Professor Stephen Braude, Professor of Philosophy at the University of Maryland, has suggested that an alternative, and perhaps more fruitful, way of looking at these cases is by assessing the lives of the people involved (lecture to the American Society for Psychical Research, March 1998). He suggests in particular that investigators ask a very simple question: Who benefits? In the case of Pearl Curran, for example, he points out that her own creativity seemed to be enhanced or liberated while she was in the altered state of consciousness. Pearl herself was a housewife who did not express her own opinions; Patience Worth held very strong views and was a feisty woman. By assuming this alter ego, Pearl was able to express views she might have hesitated to admit to as her everyday self and avoid taking responsibility for her own work.

Professor Braude's approach certainly helps to explain the case of "L"—a man who feels he could be the best tenor that ever lived. "L" claims that the spirit of Enrico Caruso inspires his voice, that when he is practising he has clairaudiently heard Caruso giving him instructions, and that when he sings his own voice is augmented by the spirits of Caruso and Mario Lanza. Mediums, he says, have seen the spirits of these illustrious gentlemen standing beside him.

Melvyn Willin has interviewed "L" on several occasions. He says that musicians who have heard "L" sing agree that he does indeed have a powerful tenor voice, though he lacks musicianship and polish. Willin's view is that, with further training, "L" has the talent to become a professional tenor in his own right. So why should this talented man be so keen to share the credit for his own admirable voice with the spirits of two long-gone tenors? Willin points out that "L" has a compulsive need for public recognition, which may be due both to self-aggrandisement and to a genuine desire to spread his message of personal conviction that there is life after death.

Rosemary Brown is the best-known example of musical channelling. She is generally acknowledged to have limited musical ability and knowledge. And yet for over thirty years composers of the past have apparently been channelling their music through her. It has to be said that most of these composers' afterthoughts have not greatly enhanced any musical reputations—Vernon Harrison has described them as "of inferior quality . . . more . . . sketches or memoranda jotted down for future reference by the composers concerned."

He does, however, make one exception. There is, he says, "at least one of Rosemary's pieces, attributed to Liszt, which is not a pastiche, paraphrase, reworking or copy of anything that Liszt actually wrote. However, it could well be something that he would have written had he lived another two or three years. In other words, it shows knowledge of the direction Liszt's work was taking at the time of his death. The piece in question is *Grubelei*. It is interesting, complete in itself and far from easy to play, with its persistent five-in-a-bar in the right hand against three in the left. My attention to this work was first drawn by Humphrey Searle, composer, musicologist and authority on Liszt . . . *Grubelei* is very Lisztian in feeling—and late Liszt at that."

Vernon Harrison does not take this any further, but we can ask if this is a sufficient explanation. Could such a piece be produced by someone who has a naturally good ear for music but no musical education?

We know that a natural talent can sometimes reach prodigious heights. Charlton Greene passed his GCSE maths at nine years old—the youngest pupil ever to do so. Ruth Lawrence gained first-class honours in maths at Oxford at the age of 13. Wesley Chu, of Calgary, Alberta, has been a charismatic concert pianist since the age of three and before his fifth birthday had completed nine grades in one year with the Canadian Royal Conservatory of Music. These children have such a stupendous natural talent, so far beyond the experience of most of us, that it seems to demand some explanation beyond the normal. Even though none of them has claimed past-life memory of discovering the principle of gravity or the laws of relativity, or of composing a clarinet concerto, it is perhaps surprising that no one else has suggested that they, or others like them, are reincarnations of Newton or Galileo or Einstein or Mozart.

And yet there is no need to invoke the paranormal as an explanation for such gifted children. Dr. Valsa Koshy, of Brunel University Able Children's Unit, believes that: "The difference between an exceptional child and a child who is just bright is that the truly exceptional can process information so quickly that they basically teach themselves." Most experts on gifted children believe that prodigies are created when a natural, genetically inherited talent is matched by a powerful environment that nurtures and encourages it. Dr. David Feldman, a professor of child development at Tufts University and an expert on gifted children, believes that even a modest inherited talent can still be a key to developing prodigious skill. Of the many musical-prodigy families he has studied, many have had only one musical parent, but he has come across no families where neither parent was naturally musical.

When one looks at what the truly gifted can achieve, entirely under their own steam, the achievements of channellers such as Matthew Manning and Rosemary Brown seem less astonishing. Why should it surprise us that some natural talent, combined with a good ear for music, enables Rosemary Brown, for example, to produce her imitative but generally mediocre compositions, even though she does produce an occasional work of a higher standard? What is usually lacking in these communicators of the great and gifted is innovation and consistent quality. Channellers never exhibit genius. They are usually a second-rate approximation to their source, without any real creative talent. One imagines it must be a source of great irritation to the likes of Beethoven to see what channellers produce in their name.

THE SAVANT SYNDROME

A supreme talent looks even more inexplicable, even more demanding of some paranormal explanation, when it appears in someone who is grossly handicapped in almost every other way.

Nadia was the child of Polish parents living in Britain. She was thought to be autistic, and in 1974, when she was six years old, she came to the attention of Nottingham University psychologists Elizabeth Newson and Loma Selfe. She was a clumsy child, large for her age, and almost totally lacking in normal speech development. However, she had one extraordinary talent. From the age of three she had been producing astonishingly mature drawings. These were inspired by pictures she had usually seen only once. They had great vitality, and she was able to handle perspective, foreshortening and movement and use shading and shadow to create three-dimensional representations. Nadia particularly liked drawing horses, and when doing so would begin not with the outline of the head, as virtually all children and most untrained adults would, but with the neck, in the manner of a trained artist. And while everything else about her was clumsy, her whole hand–eye coordination was far in advance of that of the normal five-to six-year-old. Loma Selfe describes the way Nadia drew: "her lines were firm and without unintentional wavering. She could stop a line exactly where it met another despite the speed with which the line was drawn. She could change the direction of a line and draw lines at any angle towards and away from the body. She could draw a small but perfect circle in one movement and place a small dot in the centre."

Nadia was described as seeming like a different person while she was producing her drawings; after finishing a drawing she would sometimes lapse into a "staring reverie" lasting for several minutes. On other occasions she talked jargon to herself that no one could understand. From the age of about six, Nadia's drawing skills started to fade, though the drawings she made at 8½ still seemed far in advance of what a normal 8½-year-old could produce.

Nadia never talked about a past life—indeed, she did not have the language with which to do so. But there are interesting parallels between her story and children who *do* have apparent past-life memories, which have led some people to suggest that Nadia's very special talents originated in some other lifetime. It has been suggested that one drawing in particular, of an eighteenth-century horse and rider, may have had its origin in some memory of a past life because, unlike all her other drawings, its source has never been found. Then there is the trance-like state Nadia seemed to enter while she was engrossed in her drawing. Other children (see page 268) have been observed to enter a similar "staring reverie" when something seems to remind them of a past life, before suddenly snapping back to normality. The final parallel is the fact that, just as past-life memories fade and eventually disappear, Nadia's ability seemed to wane after about the age of six.

However, we don't need to postulate a past life to account for Nadia's special skill. We can explain it instead by saying that Nadia is one of a very unusual group of people, the "savants" (in less pc times they were known as "idiot savants"). The savant syndrome is an extremely rare condition in which people with profound mental handicaps show spectacular islands of genius in some narrow but very consistent range of skills. Many of these children, like Nadia, suffer from early infantile autism, a disorder present from birth. Autistic children are profoundly withdrawn, show an obsessive desire for sameness, and an inability to empathise with other people and to show or feel emotions for them.

Savants have difficulty with abstract thinking, and seem able to think only in terms of concrete visual images. But they have phenomenal memory and are able to recall something they have seen or heard in minute detail, though only within a very narrow and limited range. Identical twins George and Charles, for example, are "calendar calculators." They can tell you, within a span of 40,000 years backwards or forwards, the day of the week on which any date you choose to mention fell or will fall. And yet they cannot perform simple additions. Leslie Lemke is blind and severely mentally handicapped. But he has only to hear a piece of music once, however long or complex it is, to be able to play it back perfectly.

Darold Treffert, in his book *Extraordinary People*, suggests that the fundamental cause of the savant syndrome is either impaired brain development before birth or brain injury during or after birth. The damage is to the left hemisphere—the hemisphere which in normal right-handed people is dominant, and in which speech develops. Another factor then comes into play to produce the savant: there are changes in the structure and wiring of the brain in an attempt to compensate for the damage, and the right hemisphere, due to increased interconnectedness, becomes larger and takes over as the dominant hemisphere. In addition, and probably due to the same brain damage, there is abnormal brain function and circuitry, which is responsible for the prodigious memory of the savant.

Savant memory is very different from ordinary memory. We all of us have tremendous storage capacity in our brains,

but under normal circumstances we can recall only a fraction
of the vast amount of data we have tucked away somewhere
in the memory filing system. Savants seem to use some alternative memory filing system which allows them automatic
and unlimited access to some narrow set of concrete and non-
symbolic data. The savant does not have the capacity to work
things out in the normal way. Instead, the savant uses an unusual and highly developed "habit" memory to compensate
for the damaged or absent "cognitive" memory pathway. Certainly, music, a skill that tends to be very marked in the savant, is associated with right-cerebral dominance. Verbal and
language skills, which are associated with left-brain dominance, are usually poor in the savant. Maths does not fit into
this pattern, but Treffert suggests that mathematical processing may move to the right hemisphere in the savant. It is well
known that speech migrates from the left to the right hemisphere if the left hemisphere is seriously damaged before the
age of five to seven. Possibly maths processing in the savant
does the same.

The final factors probably needed to produce the savant,
just as is the case with the non-savant musical prodigy, are
some genetically inherited ability and at least some degree of
encouragement from those around them.

Even among savants, Nadia is unusual, because savants
rarely display artistic talent. Lorna Selfe suggests that Nadia's
drawing ability was linked to her almost-complete lack of language. Selfe's hypothesis is that visual imagery is used as the
initial "language" by all children but that, as we mature, this
mental imagery is supplanted by language and decays through
lack of use. According to Lorna Selfe's theory, if Nadia developed language, her spectacular drawing ability would disappear. And, indeed, this is exactly what happened. When she
was seven Nadia went to a special school for autistic children.
Her language improved and as it did so her genius deterio-
rated and, sadly, finally vanished. She seldom drew spontaneously and, when she did draw, her drawings showed none
of the skill of her earlier drawings.

However, Darold Treffert points out that a sudden appearance and disappearance of a skill also happens in other savants and, indeed, in normal children, who quite often seem

to show, for a brief period, some precocious talent that fails to flower but simply fades away.

The dying back of a savant's talent is not inevitable. A look at other savants shows that even though their extraordinary abilities may have developed because of some gross neurological deficit, they can and often do learn other skills and develop in other areas without any diminution of their special genius. Stephen Wilshire, for example, is another gifted autistic savant artist, who, after once seeing a building or even a photograph of a building, is able to draw a detailed and accurate three-dimensional representation of it from memory. Stephen, who was described by Sir Hugh Casson as "possibly the best child artist in Britain," has managed to retain his extraordinary artistic ability even though he has learned some language and acquired other skills.

THE REBIRTH OF LANGUAGE

It seems to be quite common for people undergoing past-life regression to develop an appropriate and consistent accent while they are under hypnosis. Bridey Murphy (see page 4), for example, developed an Irish brogue that grew more pronounced as she became more involved with her previous life. Some of the words she used were contemporaneous with her past life—a "linen" for a handkerchief, for example, "ditched" for buried.

Very much rarer are the people who, when they recall a past life, seem to have the ability to speak in a language they have apparently never learned (the phenomenon known as xenoglossy) and to understand when they are spoken to in that language (which is called responsive xenoglossy).

One might suppose that everyone who recalls a past life as someone of a different nationality would have this ability. Language, after all, is one of the most fundamental skills we have, an ability programmed into us, learned as soon as we are out of infancy, retained even in old age. If we are to recall memories of *any* aspect of a past life, surely we could expect to recall the language we spoke throughout it. And yet this doesn't seem to happen, or at least it happens very seldom.

This is why the few convincing cases of xenoglossy which
have been recorded are of very special interest.

In a letter to us, Dorothy Smith described how, twenty-two
years ago, she was on holiday with her twelve-year-old son
Peter on a cruise around the Greek islands. Every day they
stopped at a different port and did as much sightseeing as possible.

> On one of these sightseeing trips we were approached
> by a friendly gentleman who had a little girl with him,
> and I became engaged in a conversation with him. We
> talked about trivial matters: the weather, how we were
> travelling, etc. I was totally unaware of his nationality.
> However, when he asked me which part of Germany I
> was from I was quite startled. I became ill at ease, and
> because of this the conversation came to a hasty con-
> clusion.
>
> As we walked away my son was agog. He was
> amazed that I had such a lengthy conversation with a
> German gentleman and that I could speak fluent Ger-
> man—I was born in England and I have never been
> able to speak any other language. My conversation with
> the German gentleman had lasted for approximately
> twenty minutes.
>
> I was shaken and horrified. Although my son was
> rather young to judge my capability in speaking Ger-
> man, he was at the time studying both Latin and French
> at school. Even if we allow for the fact that my son had
> been wrong, how could a stranger from Germany think
> that I was a native of Germany? I was at the time per-
> plexed, and I still am.

Mrs. Smith's account is all the more interesting and convincing because she herself was apparently quite unaware that
there was anything unusual about the conversation she was
having. She was also clearly able to understand the language
and respond to questions rather than simply to reproduce odd
words or phrases, which most of us could probably do in
many European languages. It is as if the language, triggered
by the meeting, sprang from some quite different level of

memory and consciousness. Mrs. Smith has no explanation, and certainly she has no conviction that it was due to a past-life memory; it is simply that it is difficult to think of any alternative explanation.

Another equally interesting case, which has been extensively investigated by Professor Ian Stevenson, also involves an unexpected talent for German.

THE CASE OF GRETCHEN GOTTLIEB

One day in May 1970 the Reverend Carroll Jay, a Methodist minister in Gretna, Virginia, who had been practising hypnosis for 16 years, was hypnotising his wife, Dolores, in an attempt to cure her backache. Suddenly, she replied to a question he had asked her with the German word "Nein." Carroll Jay had previously experimented with past-life regression under hypnosis, and he now decided to hypnotise his wife again to see if he could encourage this German-speaking personality to emerge further. The experiment was successful. Gretchen manifested, and during a series of experiments over the course of the next year spoke almost entirely in German. Carroll Jay, who knew no German, spoke to her in English, which she seemed to understand, but he, of course, could not at first understand her. With the help of friends who did know some German, and a German–English dictionary, he managed eventually to understand the general drift of what she was saying.

Under hypnosis, Dolores claimed that her name was Gretchen Gottlieb, that she had lived in Eberswalde, Germany, and that her father, Hermann Gottlieb, had been the mayor of the town. Her mother was dead, and she was cared for by a housekeeper. She did not go to school and could not read or write. During the experiments Carroll found that he could persuade Gretchen to assume different ages between eight and sixteen, but not beyond that age. She said she had died at sixteen but seemed unable to give a coherent account of exactly how.

Gretchen rarely spoke spontaneously, but would answer questions. She couldn't name any political leaders but did return repeatedly to the theme of religious strife. In fact, it was difficult to get her to talk about any other topics. She was evidently a Roman Catholic, as she identified the head of her church as Pope Leo. She usually seemed rather depressed and seemed to live in constant fear of persecution by the Bundesrat (federal council), which suggested that she was remembering a life at the time of Bismarck's persecution of German Catholics in the 1870s.

In the summer of 1971 Professor Ian Stevenson learned about the case and visited Carroll and Dolores Jay. As he himself knows the language, he was able to converse with Gretchen in German during several of the trance sessions. He found that Dolores understood the questions he asked her in German and was able to give sensible answers. He then enlisted the help of three native German-speakers who attended sessions with Gretchen. Two of the three signed statements to say that in their view Gretchen could speak German responsively—that is, give sensible answers to questions she was asked in German. The third felt that though Gretchen answered the questions put to her, she had doubts about whether Gretchen really understood what she was saying.

However, although Stevenson made extensive enquiries he failed to find any trace of the Gottlieb family. Eberswalde had had no mayor by the name of Hermann Gottlieb. "Gretchen" had apparently never existed. But what still needed explanation, and what was by far the most interesting aspect of the story, was Dolores's ability to speak German.

Although Dolores spoke German, she spoke pretty poor German. Her grammar scarcely seems to have been at the level of schoolgirl German. She seemed to have no knowledge of how to use the past and future tenses of German verbs, and her word order (very important in the structure of German sentences) was often incorrect. It was interesting that her grammar did not improve over the course of the next three years, although, during the experiments, people who spoke correct German often talked to her. Most of the time her pronunciation was satisfactory or good; sometimes it was excellent; occasionally it was dreadful. Her vocabulary was limited, and she spoke in short phrases of a few words, often omitting words altogether. In the transcribed tapes of nineteen sessions (altogether there were twenty-two sessions, but tapes of the remaining three were either not recorded or lost), Ian Stevenson counted 237 German words used by Gretchen before anyone else had spoken them to her. About half of these were words very similar to their English equivalent ("Mutter" for "mother," for example), although she also used a few rather obscure and somewhat archaic German words.

On one occasion Gretchen wrote a few short phrases in German. Some were spelled correctly; others were not, and looked as though they had been written by someone who had only heard the German word and was trying to reproduce it phonetically. The phrases were difficult to translate, because words were omitted, as they were when she was speaking, but they, too, referred to the theme of religious persecution, her main preoccupation.

Stevenson made extensive enquiries to discover whether Dolores had ever been exposed to German or German-speaking people, but he could find no evidence that she had. German hadn't been taught in the schools she attended, and there were no German-speaking people in the community she grew up in. She passed a lie-detector test in which she was asked about her previous knowledge of the language. The only clue he could discover was a dream she reported after the development of the case, in which she saw herself in her grandmother's house examining a German book called *Greta*. Stevenson questioned Dolores's family but couldn't confirm that this was based on any actual event, or that any book called *Greta* had ever existed. One possible source that Stevenson does not mention is cinema. Many Second World War films, for example, contained snatches of German dialogue.

The impression one gets from reading Stevenson's account of Gretchen's German-speaking ability is of someone who has heard the language spoken, picked up a few words and phrases, but has never formally learned it. If Dolores were truly reliving a past life as a native German woman, or somehow accessing memories of such a person or even if (Stevenson's alternative hypothesis) she were "possessed" by some discarnate German entity, one might expect her to speak rather better German than this. Even if she did not have total recall of the language, it is surprising that the phrases she did remember were not structured correctly. If cryptomnesia were the explanation, if she had seen a book in German about religious persecution, she might have been able to reproduce the text but would not have understood it. Understanding could have come only through being taught German, but there is no evidence for this. Against this are Stevenson's two explanations of discarnate possession or reincarnation. It is up to the reader to decide which is the more likely explanation.

UTTARA HADDUR

Far more impressive than Dolores Jay's German was the nineteenth-century Bengali spoken by Uttara Haddur in her "Sharada" incarnation (see page 85). Uttara's native language was Marathi, but during the times when she was taken over by Sharada's personality she spoke Bengali, a language she claimed never to have learned. She spoke it not only when she was awake, but muttered it in her sleep and when she was suddenly awakened by a splash of cold water on her face. When family or friends spoke to her in Marathi, Hindi or English, "Sharada" did not seem to understand.

It has always been difficult to judge just how much Bengali Uttara herself spoke, and of course this is crucial in looking at her "Sharada" personality. Marathi, Hindi and Bengali are all northern Indian languages which derive from Sanskrit, just as French, Italian and Spanish derive from Latin. Knowing one language may facilitate the learning of another, as it does with these European languages, but they are not mutually intelligible. Uttara had studied Sanskrit for three years in high school and had then had one year's private tuition in the language. She had learned Bengali script and had expressed a strong desire to learn Bengali.

Although there were rumours that she had once passed an examination in Bengali, Dr. Akolkar, one of the researchers who investigated her case, checked university and other records carefully and found no evidence that she did. However, we do know that in her matriculation year at school, Uttara did have some Bengali lessons with a classmate, F. Exactly how much they learned, though, is in some doubt. F. has said that "we had progressed enough to read a Bengali primer." He also told Akolkar that he had challenged Uttara, asking how she could deny that she had learned Bengali when, in fact, they had learned it together. She had, he said, replied dismissively: "Is that to be called learning Bengali?"

So how does Uttara's knowledge of Bengali compare with Sharada's? It is generally acknowledged that although Sharada's command of Bengali was impressive, she did not speak it like a native. However, she was said to be fluent in the language. Ian Stevenson obtained testimony about Sharada's ability to speak Bengali fluently from six native speakers of the language. Some pointed out imperfections in her Bengali, but all agreed that she had an excellent command of the language. Professor Pal, who had long talks with her on four separate occasions, noted that her intonation and pronunciation closely resembled his own, and this, he believed, was because they had both lived in the same district in West Bengal.

What is perhaps most interesting is that the Bengali Sharada used was not modern Bengali. Modern Bengali contains about 20 percent of English loan words, but Sharada did not use a single English loan word in the course of long conversations with Professor Pal. She did, though, use archaic expressions, and her Bengali had more Sanskrit words than modern Bengali has, as did Bengali in the eighteenth and early nineteenth centuries. We have to remember, however, that Uttara herself had learned Sanskrit.

When Sharada wrote Bengali she made spelling mistakes: sometimes a letter from the Marathi alphabet or a Hindi word would creep in. She wrote certain letters of the Bengali alphabet as they used to be written in old Bengali manuscripts contemporary with her existence as Sharada, not as they are written today. She also wrote the letters of the Bengali alphabet anticlockwise, as was customary at that time, but, again, this is not done today. All this suggests that she did not pick up the language through casual contact with modern Bengali-speakers.

Uttara was an intelligent woman, and no one denies that she was proficient at languages. Moreover, she lived in a city with a large number of Bengali-speaking people. Uttara certainly *could* have learned Bengali—but did she? Given Uttara's fascination with Bengali, her natural flair for languages, and the boundless opportunities she must have had both to improve her basic Bengali and to talk with Bengali-speaking people, it is almost inconceivable that she should not have done so. But to attain this level of proficiency would have required hours of secret study, and to have learned to speak nineteenth-century Bengali so effortlessly would have been even more difficult, and would suggest a deliberate attempt at fraud. It would also have taken considerable time and required long-term planning, and all the evidence is that the Sharada personality emerged quite suddenly in response to a particular emotional trigger.

In short, a jury might decide that there is a reasonable probability that Uttara knew more Bengali than she was prepared to admit. But there is no evidence that she had studied it seriously and, in particular, no evidence that she had an opportunity to learn nineteenth-century Bengali. Equally, there is no evidence that she did not.

Everything else in this strange story is explicable purely in terms of Uttara's life, her passionate interest in Bengal and all things Bengali, and her emotional state of mind. But yet the language still remains a problem, an uneasy glitch in what is otherwise a perfectly satisfactory explanation. We must also remember that past-life memories seldom come with the amount of detail displayed by Sharada.

Xenoglossy is a piece of the reincarnation puzzle that is hard to fit in whichever way you look at it. If memories of a past life really do occur, then language should be recalled along with memory. Hypnotherapist Joe Keeton has found that this certainly happens when he regresses someone to an earlier stage in their present life. One client of his was a woman who was brought up in Italy and spoke only Italian until she moved to England at the age of 12. When she was regressed back to the age of eight Joe found that he could not wake her from her hypnotic trance—she simply didn't understand the English he was speaking to her. It wasn't until he spoke in Italian that she responded. However, other hypnotherapists do not normally report this kind of literal age-regression.

Even in the most compelling cases of past-life regression,

people seldom manage to "remember" the language of their past. Usually they will utter a few words or phrases as if to give convincing colour to their character, or remind us of the period or the nationality of the life they are apparently living. Joan Waterhouse, the Chelmsford Witch (see page 125), used language that often sounded appropriately archaic to twentieth-century ears. When Joe Keeton asked her age, for example, she replied "nigh on my eighteenth year," and asked who she was she replied, "I am the daughter, sire, of Mother Waterhouse." And yet the truth is that language has changed so much in the past 400 years that if she were genuinely speaking as she would have spoken in the sixteenth century, in the time of Queen Elizabeth, she and the twentieth-century Joe Keeton would have had so little language in common that easy communication between them would have been impossible. Perhaps most surprising of all, Laurel Dilmen, in her persona as the Spanish adventuress Antonia (see page 139), had a detailed knowledge of sixteenth-century Spain but could neither speak nor understand Spanish, though she could pronounce Spanish names very well.

In those regressions that do exhibit xenoglossy, the language spoken is never entirely unfamiliar. There are no convincing cases of xenoglossy in which the subjects speak obscure languages quite unrelated to their own. There is a further puzzle. Why do all the reported reincarnation cases that show xenoglossy involve adults? If xenoglossy really does occur, children would surely be equally likely to show it—indeed more so, as this is the time when past lives seem to be experienced most vividly. In children, too, it would be much easier to believe that they had had no opportunity to learn the language, or even had much exposure to it. And yet this does not seem to happen. Ian Stevenson has studied a group of twenty Burmese children who remember past lives as Japanese soldiers in Burma, but, strangely, none of them spoke any Japanese at all; they could not say where they lived in Japan or even remember their Japanese name. One of these children would apparently sing songs in what her parents said sounded like a foreign language, but there is no evidence that this was Japanese, or indeed any particular language.

Sharada's story, in fact, is a one-off. No other reincarnation account provides anything like such good evidence of xenoglossy. Both Ian Stevenson and Dr. Akolkar made extensive enquiries among those who knew Uttara well and remain convinced that she could not have learned Bengali in the normal way. They are quite certain that somehow Uttara acquired memories of a previous life.

But we are left with too many if onlys: if only Uttara had not shown such an interest in the language . . . if only we did not know for certain that she had learned even a minimum amount at school . . . if only she had never learned Sanskrit . . . if only she had never lived in a community where Bengali was spoken frequently around her . . . if only . . .

13

"My Other Mummy"

"Don't talk about this—folk'll think you're daft."
Scottish grandmother to four-year-old granddaughter who
has insisted that she can read Chinese

ONE is sometimes spoiled for choice when looking for a rational explanation for the memories of adults who claim to remember a past life. The emergence of forgotten memories, suggestibility, fantasy or imagination, hysterical dissociation, wishful thinking, self-delusion—all these have to be considered and eliminated before one can even begin to accept that such people might be remembering another life another time and another place.

Children's past-life memories are another matter. Children who start to talk about a past life usually do so when they are very young indeed—in fact, as soon as they are able to talk. And almost always memories seem to fade between the ages of five and eight. The child stops talking about his or her "other life," either because he or she had forgotten about it, which seems most often the case, or because he she has been discouraged from talking about it.

So some of the explanations that are credible for many adult experiences—for example, cryptomnesia—simply don't hold up for children. Their memories appear spontaneously, usually long before the child has a substantial "memory bank" to draw on. It is difficult to see how they can have acquired such a wealth of information and then forgotten it. It is also much easier than it is with adults to see the possible sources they could have for the origin of these memories in their present life.

Of course, it is true that many children are imaginative, prone to fantasy, and find it hard to draw a clear-cut line between a real and a fantasy world. But despite all this, the past-life memories of children are more difficult to explain and seem more convincing than those of adults. Young children, much more than adults, live in the moment. The past doesn't concern them much, and they have very little concept of the future. Even their fantasies and imaginings are usually set in the here and now. This is why a story like Tammy's is so intriguing.

TAMMY'S STORY

Tammy was born on 26 December 1990. When we met her she was six years old, a very bright little girl who gave the impression of being mature for her age, transparently honest and not at all prone to fantasising or exaggerating. She learned to talk very early—her mother says she was able to say "hello" when she was only four months old. By the time she was eighteen months old she was talking very well.

When she was about this age she visited Longleat, with her mother and grandmother, and saw an exhibition of old doll's houses. Tammy stopped in front of a Victorian doll's house and, her mother remembers, said: "Look, that's like the house I used to live in." She was transfixed by a model of a woman in Victorian dress with short brown hair and pointed to it, saying: "That's my mummy." Going round the exhibition she seemed to know things that it is hard to see that any child of that age would have had the opportunity to find out about. She talked about the "feather pen" she used to write with, for example, and knew the uses of various pieces of old-fashioned kitchen equipment. She explained what a spit was for—"you put bits of meat on that and it turn around over the fire"—and identified as a writing-desk a piece of furniture that had both her mother and her grandmother baffled, saying "That's what I used to do my writing at." She described the kitchen in "her" house, saying that there were shelves where cups hung on hooks. The house had no bathroom; the bath was just a tub that you poured water into.

From that time on, Tammy upset her mother frequently by talking about her "other mother," her five sisters and the other life she had lived a long time ago. Her mother used to tell her not to be so silly, that *she* was her mother. Tammy would then also be upset, insist that it was true and describe what her other mother looked like. Her mother says: "Most of the time she would be playing like a normal two-year-old, but now and again she would just get this vacant look on her face and say to me, 'Mummy, can I tell you something?', and I'd know she was going to tell me about 'years ago'." It seems as though these episodes occurred only when Tammy initiated them; her mother says that on the occasions when they have tried to get her to talk about them, or to elaborate on what she has said, she doesn't respond.

Tammy is very consistent in her memories. She has a doll's house for which she is gradually collecting old-fashioned furniture, so that it will look like her "other" house. In the bathroom is a Victorian bath, the kind with little clawed feet. When we admired this, forgetting for the moment what she had said about the bath in her "other house," she was very insistent that it wasn't like the bath she had known; that had been a tub with no taps, so that you had to pour the water in. Whe Tammy was told (as she often was) not to talk about her life "years ago," her reply was that she wanted to talk about it, because otherwise she would forget all about it. She told us that she liked to remember it and didn't want to forget it.

Tammy's mother is a single parent and Tammy has never known a father. However, they live with Tammy's grandparents, and she has always called her grandfather "Dad." Her mother says that the word "father" was never mentioned. But when Tammy was describing her "other" family, she talked about "my father." Her mother and grandmother found this very puzzling. Tammy remembers her father making her a wooden toy which she described in some detail. It was a circle with a pole in the middle, and round the edges were the letters of the alphabet. Again, her mother and grandmother could think of no toy that Tammy had ever had which looked anything like that, and nobody who had ever made her any wooden toys. We asked her if she could describe the kind of clothes her father wore. Twice she started off telling us he wore leggings, then looked confused, shook her head and said she meant trousers. So we asked her if they were tight trousers that looked a bit like leggings, and she nodded and agreed with this. They might have been something like plus fours, perhaps, or lederhosen—Germany was a recurring motif in Tammy's memories, and her mother "went to Germany" when she was ill. Again, the family say they never talked about Germany, had no connections with Germany and had never even mentioned Germany so far as they could remember.

Tammy has no memory of dying, but her past-life memories stop at around the age of three. She does not remember being an adult in her other life. She says simply that she went to heaven but knew she had to come back, and so came back as a seed, choosing her present mother because she was the best one.

Because Tammy started talking about her other life very early, one might expect her mother and grandmother to have a good idea of any experiences she had had which might have corresponded to her past-life memories. Might she have been in the room when her mother was watching something like *Upstairs, Downstairs* on TV, for example? It's possible that parents may underestimate the extent to which a baby or child can pick up information, but Tammy's mother says that she can't remember any occasion when this could have happened—she very rarely watches TV now and when Tammy was a baby watched it even less. The TV was never on when Tammy was being nursed, cuddled or played with, only after she had gone to bed.

Her mother is quite sure that none of the books Tammy was reading or had read to her when she started talking about these experiences were about "the olden days" or had this kind of information in them. Since then, however, they have looked at picture books of Victorian costumes, visited museums, etc., all of which Tammy is fascinated by, so any new memories that she produced now would be suspect. But, in fact, her mother and grandmother say that Tammy hasn't produced any new memories as she has got older, and we got the impression that this wasn't a story that had been elaborated at all.

Even if a source could be found for some of Tammy's memories, this wouldn't explain some of the detailed knowledge she apparently showed. The concepts of the quill pen, the writing-desk or the rotary spit would be too advanced for a young child to understand even if she had somehow seen them before. And far from encouraging her to elaborate her memories, her mother seems to have been very threatened by the idea of Tammy's other life, and to have positively discouraged her from talking about it. In fact, her mother says when she has tried to get Tammy to talk about it, this hasn't worked and she hasn't responded. It has been Tammy herself who has been determined to try to keep her memories alive by talking about them.

One of the oddities about Tammy's memories is her observation that there were no bright colours in her other life. Everything was black or grey or brown or white. Her mother's clothes and her own clothes were all in these monochrome colours. She described a dress of her own as white, indicating that it had black frills around the shoulders (it sounded like an old-fashioned pinafore dress).

Tammy is a normal, intelligent little girl. But she is unusual in one respect—she has a rare condition in which her heart and some other body organs are reversed. Her heart lies on the right and not the left side of her chest; the positions of her spleen and appendix are also reversed. She was born a month prematurely, and it was a long labour and a difficult birth, during which she suffered some lack of oxygen. At one point her heart stopped beating. Might she have had a near-death experience, and could this be the source of her apparent past-life memories?

When adults have near-death experiences we know that they often see complex and vivid visual images—of people they have known, for example, or of beautiful pastoral scenes. These scenes seem absolutely real and are remembered with total clarity long afterwards. But such experiences are firmly rooted in the culture of the person having them. The images they see are clearly drawn from their own lifetime's experience. A newborn baby *has* no such experience, and probably does not have the memory capacity to retain any impressions. So even if we speculate that Tammy might have had some kind of near-death experience, it is very difficult to see how it could have taken that particular form—unless one accepts that these were indeed memories from a past life to which, in the near-death state, some part of her consciousness had access.

When children start to talk about a past life it is nearly always their "other family" that they focus on—often much to the chagrin of their parents in this life. Ian Stevenson has suggested that sometimes these children may feel conflicting loyalties towards their past and present families, but this is probably only a problem when the child is actually faced with the other family, when there has been a successful attempt to track down the previous incarnation and "solve" the case. Certainly, none of the children in our sample who have these memories seem to feel any such conflict, and they seem to be quite capable of distinguishing between their past life and their present.

Jean Cape's son Nicholas was three years old when he talked about another life. "Nicholas was sitting on our bed while my husband, Harry, was painting the window frame. After a while Nicholas began to speak to him as follows. *Nicholas*: 'I wonder where my mummy and daddy are now?' *Harry*: 'Mummy is at work and I am here painting.' *Nicholas*: 'Not you, I had a mummy and daddy before you, and my name was not Nicholas Cape; it was Peter Amies and I lived in Weston. I had a twin brother, and Mummy and Daddy died in St. Thomas' Hospital. I died, and God asked me if I wanted to stay and help him. I said I wanted a new mummy and daddy and that's why you got me.'"

His parents are convinced that there is no way Nicholas could have heard any of the names he had mentioned, and he never referred to the matter again. It was the utterly straightforward way he talked about this previous life that made his father, who had always been a sceptical man, believe him.

Sue Harris is not a sceptic. For her, the conversation she had with her three-year-old daughter one day was simply confirmation of her own belief in reincarnation. Even so, this little girl's apparent past-life memories evidently arose spontaneously and were not just a reflection of her mother's own beliefs. She is now seven and has little recollection of the conversation, so it seems unlikely that her mother continued to talk about it with her or encouraged her to elaborate it. "She was having her bath when she suddenly stated that I looked like her other mummy. We all know that three-year-olds have extremely fertile imaginations, and it is easy to find out if they are lying by asking questions such as 'Did you go to the supermarket? Where did you sleep? What food did you eat?', etc. She explained to me, very clearly, that her family lived in America, in the desert. There were no houses, only tents, and they slept on animal skins. The men hunted for food, and the women stayed home to me for the children and cook. She also told me her 'other mummy' used to clean the skins of the dead animals to make clothes. She described the food, mostly meat, but also nuts and berries mixed with fruits."

As a general rule, most children who have these memories seem to have been of the same sex in their previous life. Ian Stevenson, in a survey of American children who remembered past lives, found that only 15 percent remembered life as someone of the opposite sex. Nearly all of these were girls who remembered life as a boy; only one boy remembered life as a girl. Nearly all of our sample of British children had memories of a same-sex life, but one little girl had memories of life "when I was a boy." Nicola Gilpin recounts how, when her daughter Sophie was about two (she is now nine), she suddenly told her: "When I was here before, when I was a boy, I was really good at football." This was the first of many references to a life with her "other mummy." Over several months she told her parents that she had died when she was seven, along with some of her friends when the school fell down. "She said she lived in a house that was also a shop and had to do lots of jobs to help her other mummy, and that she had lots of brothers and sisters. She spoke of a man who used to come into school who wore a black hat, and she mentioned a place-name which I forget now but I did write down somewhere." At a friend's suggestion Nicol taped a programme about the Aberfan disaster and showed it to Sophie quite casually one evening. But, she says, Sophie showed no reaction out of the ordinary. Sophie, too, is a very bright child and was a very early reader.

Very few children remember life as an adult. One explanation is that they have experienced their present life only as a child, so if their memories are a fantasy they are most likely to see themselves only as children. Another explanation is simply that in a previous life they died young. It is often suggested that a past life is more easily remembered if it ends in a violent or unnatural death. In his study of American children who remembered past lives, Stevenson found that only 43 percent mentioned their mode of death, but, of these, 80 percent remembered dying violently.

Of our own British sample, just over a quarter of the children who remembered a past life mentioned their own death, but only three had a specific memory of a violent death. Mrs. Andrews's (pseudonym) youngest daughter April is five years old. "When she was about three we were driving along, just myself and her, when she suddenly said, out of the blue, that she used to live with a different mummy and daddy, then she died and she was born again. After correcting the swerve I'd gone into I said, 'Oh did you?' in as normal a voice as possible! Later I asked her what her name was before, but she couldn't recall it. She told me she used to wear long dresses, and she had a horse. The next statement convinced me. She said she remembered running away from people, but they caught her and shot her. She got the whole sequence of events in order, quite something for a three-year-old, and I can't accept that she picked up all this from TV or books."

It seems to be characteristic of these experiences that the language these children use and the concepts they express are often way beyond their chronological age, and certainly more advanced than their current level of language. Wilma Cunliffe describes an incident that happened twenty-two years ago, when her youngest son Nicholas was about two years old. Nicholas was a late talker and at this time, his mother says, "He could just about manage 'mamma' and 'dadda.' Even these words were hard to decipher for anyone other than close family. I was very worried about not only his inability to talk but this reluctance to even try. I consulted the doctor and a speech therapist to see if there was a medical condition, but was assured there was nothing wrong; he was not deaf, and he would speak in his own time. I was unconvinced, but there was nothing else I could do but wait and carry on encouraging him." She went on:

Shortly after the medical tests, my eldest son Gary, then almost five years old, started school, and every Monday his best friend John came for tea. When it came time to take John home one Monday, Nicholas threw a tantrum to come in the car with us. I usually left him at home with his father, but to keep the peace he came along.

That particular evening I took a different route for reasons I cannot remember. This route went past the back gate of the cemetery, and only a few yards from the grave for stillborn babies. It was in this grave that my first baby boy was buried after being stillborn. At this very spot Nicholas suddenly said in clear, concise speech: "Mummy, is that God's garden?"

Completely shocked, I stopped the car, and Gary and John were as speechless as myself. Nicholas's eyes seemed fixed and slightly glazed when I glanced in the driver's mirror, but when I turned to face the back seat his eyes were back to normal. I asked him to repeat what he said, but he went quiet again.

What is still very hard to understand is the term "God's garden." This was not something we had ever said in the house—indeed, neither my husband nor myself ever recalled hearing this expression. We could not recollect reading it in a story book or using it at any time. It was the same with other members of the family—no one recognised it as part of conversation.

For all these years it has preyed on my mind that such a young child should utter his first words at the very place his brother was buried. Is there any other way this can be explained other than reincarnation?

Another incident happened with Nicholas a few months later when we were having tea one evening. For some reason I looked across the table and his eyes were fixed and glazed (more than the previous incident) and staring over my left shoulder. Almost trance-like he said: "Mummy, there is no need to worry, someone in white is looking over your shoulder, they're looking after you." Almost as fast as he said it he carried on eating his meal as if nothing had happened.

The parents of these children were not believers in reincarnation. They were puzzled by what their children said, and sometimes quite upset by it—competition from an unseen "other mother" isn't always easy to deal with. But there seems very little evidence that they reinforced what the children were saying in any way.

One of the most fascinating cases suggestive of reincarnation, because it involves the dual reincarnation of two young children, reborn into the same family, is that of the Pollock twins. The difference, though, between this case and the others mentioned so far is that one of the parents not only believed in reincarnation but was expecting it to happen. This is something we have to bear in mind when reading about the case of the Pollock twins.

THE CASE OF THE REINCARNATED TWINS

On Sunday 5 May 1957 two little girls, Joanna (eleven) and Jacqueline (six) Pollock, set off to church with a nine-year-old friend to attend a special Mass for the pupils of the local Roman Catholic school. But as they walked along, a car, driven by a woman who was suffering from depression and had taken a drug overdose with the intention of committing suicide, lost control of her car and drove it on to the pavement, straight at the three children. All three were killed.

The girls' father, John Pollock, was a devout Catholic but an unconventional one in that he had always had a strong belief in reincarnation—a belief his wife Florence did not share. He had even prayed to be given a sign that would offer him proof of rebirth.

After the girls' death, their father became convinced that somehow they would be returned to him. And so when, several months later, his wife became pregnant again, John Pollock knew unquestioningly that this was to be his sign. He was convinced that she would give birth to twins, and that these baby girls would be the reincarnations of Joanna and Jacqueline. His wife found this hard to accept—not least because she had been assured by her doctor that she was carrying only one child.

John Pollock, however, stuck to his guns, and to everyone's surprise but his on 4 October 1958, seventeen months after the deaths of their daughters, his wife gave birth to twin girls, Gillian and Jennifer.

When Jennifer was born, her father noticed that she had a birthmark on her forehead, just above her right eye. He remembered that when his dead daughter Jacqueline was three years old she had fallen and hit her face on a bucket. She had to have three stitches in the wound, and it left a scar, just above her right eye, which was still there when she died. This was enough to confirm her father's belief that Jennifer was indeed a reincarnation of Jacqueline. For him, further proof was provided by the fact that both Jennifer and Jacqueline had another birthmark on the left side of the waist, a roundish area of increased pigmentation about 0.4 inches (1 centimetre) in diameter. No one else in the family had such a birthmark.

As the twins grew older, various other incidents happened which seemed to add further weight to the possibility that they might be Joanna and Jacqueline reborn, so that even Florence Pollock, albeit somewhat reluctantly, came to believe it. After the deaths of Joanna and Jacqueline, their toys had been packed in a box which was put in an attic. When the twins were about three, the box was opened and the toys taken out and left lying around. Among them were two very different dolls. When the twins saw the dolls, Gillian claimed the one that had belonged to Joanna and Jennifer the one that had belonged to Jacqueline. The children even named the dolls correctly—Mary was Gillian's doll, Suzanne Jennifer's. They also said that Santa Claus had given them the dolls—and, indeed, Joanna and Jacqueline had received them as Christmas gifts.

Also in the box was a toy wringer. Gillian immediately went for this, saying "Look! There's my toy wringer." Both parents commented that although the girls usually disputed ownership when one had something the other did not, in this case both of them accepted happily that the wringer belonged to Gillian.

When the twins were nine months old the family had moved from Hexham to Whitley Bay. Some three years later, when the twins were about four years old, the family went back to visit Hexham for the day. As they were walking along a road in Hexham near the park, both girls said they wanted to go across the road to the swings in the park. Florence said they mentioned the swings before the park itself was even in sight, and when there was no way they could have seen the swings or known they were there. The twins also apparently recognised the house where the family used to live, telling their parents, "The school's just around the corner," even though it was still out of sight.

The girls were very close, as twins often are, and to some extent they showed various personality traits that seemed to correspond to the characters of their dead sisters. Their mother believed that Gillian's behaviour resembled Joanna's more than Jennifer's resembled Jacqueline's. Jennifer was described by her parents as "fiery" and "wilful," whereas Jacqueline seems to have been a docile child. Gillian behaved much more as the older sister, seeming more mature and tending to "mother" her twin.

Before the death of his daughters, John Pollock had had a milk delivery business. Florence helped him and used to wear a smock when she worked. Soon after the deaths of Joanna and Jacqueline she stopped working with him and the smock was put away. One day, when the twins were about four and a half years old, John Pollock happened to take it out and put it on to protect his clothes while he was doing some painting. The twins had never seen it before, but Jennifer said immediately: "Why are you wearing Mummy's coat?" She also said that her mother had worn the smock while delivering milk. She became annoyed with her sister because she didn't seem to recognise the smock. However, although Jacqueline, the dead younger child, would often have seen Florence wearing the smock because she was at home during the day when her mother was working, Joanna would seldom have done so because she would have been at school while Florence was working.

Further events strengthened the parents' conviction when

the twins started school. At the time their older sisters were killed, Joanna had been at school for about five years and had learned to hold a pen and write properly. Jacqueline had been going to school for only about a year and held her pencil upright in her fist, though both teacher and parents had tried to stop her doing this.

When Gillian and Jennifer first learned to write at about the age of four and a half, Gillian was able immediately to hold her pencil properly; Jennifer, however, grasped it in her fist—just as her dead sister Jacqueline used to do. Even as an adult Jennifer would still occasionally hold her pen the wrong way.

When the twins alluded to their previous lives, their parents said they would just "burst out" with some remark but could never then be persuaded to enlarge on it or give more details. The impression one gets is that the twins certainly didn't have any continuous memory of a previous life; they would simply recall events in flashes, as though something had just jogged their memory. There was, for example, an incident when they were playing together near a lane behind their house. John Pollock heard them screaming hysterically and rushed out to find them crouched together in a corner, holding each other in terror and pointing at a car parked facing them in the lane, which had just started its engine. The twins were screaming: "The car! The car! It's coming at us!" On another occasion their mother saw them when they were in their playroom and thought they were unobserved, apparently re-enacting their death and talking about it in the present tense. Gillian was cradling her sister's head and saying: "The blood's coming out of your eyes. That's where the car hit you."

Was this truly a memory of their sisters' horrific death? Even if the twins had never been told formally how their sisters had died, might they not have absorbed from casual references or half-heard adult conversations at least something of the details of their sisters' tragic death?

John Pollock seems to have given more details than his wife to Ian Stevenson, and at times he seems to have elaborated some details that his wife did not remember. And some of the details that their parents felt were suggestive of reincarnation could have other, equally valid explanations: for example, the fact that all four of the children (in common with many little girls) enjoyed playing hairdressers and liked to comb other people's hair, especially their father's. Other events are more persuasive: his daughters' recognition of places in Hexham and, especially, Jennifer's apparent recognition of her mother's smock.

Finally, there is the question of the birthmarks, the cornerstone on which John Pollock's belief in his daughters' reincarnation was founded. When one thinks how often children fall and hurt themselves, the incident with the bucket must have been a trivial event in the panoply of childhood injuries and accidents (although Jacqueline did have to have stitches in the wound, which can be traumatic for a small child). But remember that both these children were killed in a horrifying accident in which they were thrown into the air by the car that hit them and suffered multiple injuries. Why should that one trivial scar be "remembered," rather than some mark indicative of Jacqueline's violent death?

The difficulty with the case of the Pollock twins is that families develop their own folklore. To anyone reading this story it would seem inconceivable that John Pollock did not to some extent impose his own belief in their reincarnation on the twins. But Florence Pollock was very insistent that the children should *not* be told about their father's beliefs, and their parents maintained that it was not until they were 13—long after the children had apparently forgotten all about their past lives—that they learned anything from their parents about their supposed reincarnation. John Pollock himself, taxed with this, agreed that it is a valid objection but argued that his openness about reincarnation meant that he was more likely than most Western parents to note and remember remarks and behaviour of his daughters that seemed relevant. John Pollock desperately wanted his daughters to return, and, indeed, the belief that they had returned must have been a source of immense comfort to both parents.

One can easily imagine how appealing the idea of reincarnation would be to anyone similarly bereaved. Kim and Margaret Sargeant (pseudonyms) already had two young sons when Elizabeth was born in December 1979. Their joy in their first little girl was sadly short-lived. The family was devastated when, at the age of only six months, Elizabeth became ill and died.

Margaret's mother was convinced that Elizabeth "would come back" and told her daughter so repeatedly. Then, two years later, in December 1982, after two miscarriages, Margaret had another little girl, Isobel. Isobel was blue-eyed, like her mother and her dead sister Elizabeth, whereas the two boys, and another little girl born subsequently, all have brown eyes.

When Isobel was just two years old, she happened to see photographs of Elizabeth's grave, with all the posies and flowers. She ran to her mother and cried: "Mummy, my flowers." "No, dear," replied her mother. "Yes, Mummy, my flowers. Dark, dark, me frightened, trees, trees, everyone crying. Me go 'way. But me come back again, me not go away again."

Isobel's grandmother, who told us this story, says that there was indeed an aisle of trees near the baby's grave. She says, too, that Isobel is a very clever little girl who at two seemed very advanced for her age and is now doing very well at school.

Isobel's mother and grandmother feel sure that Isobel *is* Elizabeth come back to them. Her grandmother says that when Isobel started school she did talk about her feelings to some of her school friends. But they themselves have not talked about Elizabeth to Isobel, or encouraged Isobel to talk about a past life. If she did have a past life as Elizabeth, they want her to forget it.

It is often assumed that in the West children are discouraged from talking about past lives because in this culture reincarnation is considered to be impossible. If a child claims to remember a past life it is assumed either that he or she is lying or at best creating fantasies that might evoke ridicule or disapproval from neighbours, teachers, etc. But the accounts we have been given suggest that many Western parents don't ignore what the child says or punish him or her for saying it. On the contrary, they listen sympathetically, and sometimes even try to follow up whatever sparse information the child is able to give. Steve's son Joe is now fourteen and has always felt that he has lived before. The first indication his parents had of Joe's past-life memories was when he was three and on a bus with his mother returning from a shopping trip in Bristol. Steve recalled:

> The bus leaves the A370 and takes the Long Ashton road, and on the left of this is open countryside. The land has been raised by landfill, and a park-and-ride now occupies the site.
>
> Joe pointed out of the window and said: "When I was a man I used to live over there."
>
> My wife was taken aback but just answered: "Did you, love?"
>
> Joe continued: "Yes, and I had a wife called Sally."
>
> We questioned Joe at the time but no further information was forthcoming. When Joe was ten, however, we were passing the site when Joe remembered more: "I could see that tree from my window."
>
> The tree was an old skeleton, long dead, and has now been removed. Joe also said he remembered being in the kitchen of a house, wore long boots and had something in his hands which he was cleaning. He also remembers the house was a farm and he was the owner; his wife had brown hair and a slightly largish nose. They also had a small dog.

From what Joe has told them they estimate that his memories are of a period within the last half of the nineteenth century and the first half of this. Although they would have liked to trace this "previous life," without a surname it seems impossible to do so. However, they have obtained a copy of a map of 1843 which does indeed show a building at the site indicated by Joe which was apparently a kennel farm.

Hindus regard memories of past lives as entirely natural, and, not surprisingly, there are many accounts of Indian children who seem to have past-life memories. It has been suggested that parents who believe in reincarnation (that is, nearly all Indian Hindus) may subtly encourage the development of pseudo-memories out of fragments of information a child might have uttered that could be interpreted as references to a previous life. However, Ian Stevenson and N. K. Chadha, who have investigated many of these cases in detail, found that Indian parents were much less inclined to offer such encouragement than is usually supposed—in fact, in nearly half the cases they studied parents actually tried to stop their children from talking about previous lives, sometimes even by punishing them. The most usual reason seems to be widespread belief that children who remember previous lives die young. They may also fear that they might lose their child to his or her other family—either the family might kidnap or entice him away, or the child himself might try to run away.

There may be other reasons too. The child may irritate or embarrass the family by making invidious comparisons between the present family and the remembered one, or claiming that his or her "real parents" loved him or her more than the present ones. If the child has memories of a life in a much lower class, or demonstrates lower-class habits acquired in a previous life, this may embarrass the parents so that they try to keep all accounts of such a life within the family. Finally, some children have publicly, and often loudly, claimed to have been murdered and to have named the murderers of their previous incarnation. When a child starts to talk like this, parents may fear reprisals.

Certainly, the parents of young Mahavir Singh did nothing to encourage his conviction that he had lived a previous life. On the contrary, their son's bizarre behaviour so maddened them that at one point they even employed an exorcist to rid him of his strange beliefs. This intriguing case was reported by Antonia Mills, Erlendur Haraldsson and Jurgen Keil in the *Journal of the American Society for Psychical Research* in July 1994.

THE CASE OF THE INFANT CAMEL DEALER

Mahavir Singh (pseudonym) was born in the Agra district of Uttar Pradesh in India in 1982. He began to talk when he was only a year old and straight away showed a great interest in animals, particularly camels. His father possessed cows but no camels, and no one else in the village owned a camel either. Although Mahavir liked the cows and would get up before anyone else in the family to go out and water them, he urged his father continually to buy a camel. From the time he was a toddler, whenever a camel dealer came by Mahavir would pursue them, taking hold of the camel's rope and insisting that the animal belonged to him.

He continued this peculiar behaviour until one day, when he was about two years old, he told his mother that he had seen his son (he used the word *lalu*, the term for either "son" or "brother's son") passing by. From then on he regarded this one particular set of camel dealers as his relatives.

From the age of about three Mahavir would put some of his food aside, saying: "This is for my children." When questioned, he said that he had five children and a wife, and that his brother also had five children. He added that a businessman named Teja had some of his money and had not returned it, and he made other statements about members of his family, and about his death near the Ganges.

It was Mahavir's frequent demands to be taken to his wife that annoyed his parents so much that finally they employed the exorcist to stop him talking about this. The attempt was unsuccessful. One day Mahavir told his father: "My brother has fallen from a camel." His father, assuming it was his elder son who had fallen, went to see and discovered that someone had indeed fallen from a camel, but it was not his son: it was Pathi Ram, a camel dealer. It was Pathi Ram's adult son whom Mahavir had called *lalu* on numerous occasions as he passed by with his camels.

When eventually they heard of Mahavir's claims, Pathi Ram and his family came to visit him. The families had not previously known of each other's existence—they lived in different communities and came from different castes. Pathi Ram had indeed had a brother, Khem Raj, who had had five children and died near the Ganges. He and his family were convinced that Mahavir was Khern Raj reborn. (Their belief may have been strengthened by the fact that Mahavir also recognised the businessman, Teja, who owed him money—and persuaded him to repay the debt to Khem Raj's family.)

Mahavir Singh's family remember seventeen separate statements he made about Pathi Ram's family, fifteen of which were later shown to be correct. It is possible that they had forgotten about, or failed to include, other statements he made which did not tally with the facts that emerged subsequently. This would certainly make his proportion of hits less impressive—although it wouldn't explain how he came to make any hits at all. On any reckoning, Mahavir seemed to know things about Khem Raj's life and death which he had no normal way of knowing.

Mahavir continued to visit Khem Rajs family regularly, though his initial urgency subsided after the first few visits. However, he continued to ask his father to buy him a camel.

It seems that once children believe they have "found" their previous life, their need to talk about it subsides. Elizabeth Paradise told us of a similar situation from her own childhood concerning her brother Andrew, eight years her junior. As a very young child Andrew began to talk about his "other mummy" and his "other house," and their mother was very upset by this. Andrew didn't give any indication of the period when he lived his other life but said that his "other mummy" wore a long dress with a big white apron. The house was old, with a big pond in front of it and lots of fields and trees all around. He said he was told not to play near the pond in case he fell in. There was no mention of a father or any other relatives. Mrs. Paradise continued:

> When Andrew was about five years old, my father drove us down to Devon on our first summer holiday in the area. Somewhere *en route* . . . Andrew, who was kneeling up on the back seat looking out of the window, suddenly shouted: "Stop, stop. There's my house. There it is!"
>
> My mother insisted that my father stop the car, and we reversed and pulled up outside a plain, fairly unattractive cottage, and sure enough it was surrounded by fields and trees with a roughly shaped pond to the left of the house. My mother wanted to knock on the door and ask some questions of whoever lived there then, but my father, extremely irritated by the whole "nonsensical business," wouldn't hear of it and drove

on. Andrew then settled down in the corner of the back seat and went to sleep. When he woke up he was bright and happy and never, ever mentioned his "other mummy" again. From then on the whole thing was dropped by all of us. Many years later . . . I asked Andrew what he remembered of it. He was highly amused and said surely I was making it all up, as he certainly remembered nothing. For myself, I always believe that he had lived before, probably dying as a young child, and that seeing the place had laid his ghosts.

Sometimes it is not the child's apparent memories that make a family wonder whether some long-gone relative has reincarnated in their child but some small, trivial-seeming incident or piece of behaviour. Susan Ashworth told us this story about her grandmother, who is now 101:

My grandma had two children, Kenneth (my father) and Brenda. Brenda died of whooping cough when she was two and a half. Before her death she had been particularly fascinated by my grandfather's bunch of keys and would always want to play with them, particularly when in her cot before settling down to sleep. This earned her the nickname "Bunch," as my grandfather would sing to her, "Brenda, Brenda, Bunch of Keys," to get her off to sleep.

In 1958 my sister Kathryn was born and closely resembled Brenda. One afternoon in August 1959 my grandmother was settling Kathryn for her afternoon nap. The two of them had a little game whereby every day Kathryn would ask to be called by a different name before being tucked up. The names Kathryn chose were always taken from stories with which she was familiar—Tinkerbell or Sleeping Beauty—or were names she'd heard during the course of the week. On this particular day when my grandma asked her what she wished to be called, she replied: "Call me Bunch." That particular day was 26 August—Brenda's birthday.

No one except Susan's grandmother knew that Brenda's nickname had been Bunch, or knew the significance of that particular date—Susan's father was away at the time and her grandfather had died a few years earlier.

It has to be admitted that the past lives of children, though convincing in their very simplicity, are fairly prosaic compared with the lives of Egyptian Pharaohs, American Indians, Aztec warriors, etc. that their elders so often remember. It is seldom that a young child's apparent past-life memories are dramatic enough to stop you in your tracks. That is why the account we were given by Mrs. C. Rodwell is so unusual.

Mrs. Rodwell's son Jonathan, now eight, was a bright child and started to talk early. Mrs. Rodwell recalls what happened one day when Jonathan was only two:

> My elder son came running out of Jonathan's room saying: "He's giving me goose bumps . . . He says he was leading the Roman army for weeks and his feet hurt." Jonathan was in his cot when I went to his room. I looked at the feet he was rubbing. They were all peeled. The doctor said they looked like "trainer feet" that she treats teenagers for that live in trainers. But Jonathan was still in Start-Rite baby shoes. He told me I was kinder than his first mum and had lovely eyes.

And, says his mother, every winter he complains that his feet hurt, and both big toes become peeled and sore.

Is Jonathan's story of leading the Roman army memory or the fantasy of a bright and imaginative child? If it is fantasy, one would expect it to be elaborated much further—Jonathan cannot, for example, remember what his name was, although he says he wishes he could.

Sometimes a family finds that the most convincing clues to a child's past-life identity seem to lie not so much in what they say but in how they behave. Ian Stevenson investigated the next case over the course of five years and talked to members of both the families involved. It hard to disagree with him that Gopal Gupta is one of the strongest cases for reincarnation.

A Case of Brahmin-Like Behaviour

Gopal Gupta was born in Delhi in August 1956 to lower-middle-class parents with little education. Soon after Gopal began to talk, when he was between two and two and a half, his parents were entertaining a guest, and Gopal's father asked him to remove a glass that the guest had used. His son replied: "I won't pick it up. I am a Sharma [a member of the highest caste in India, the Brahmins]." He then threw a temper tantrum.

When he was asked to explain his behaviour, Gopal started to talk about a previous life in which he claimed that he remembered living in a city, Mathura, about 100 miles (160 kilometres) south of Delhi. He said that he owned a company concerned with chemicals and even gave the name of the company—Sukh Shancharak. He talked about the large house he had lived in and about his wife and two brothers. He said that he had quarrelled with one of these brothers, who had then shot him.

Gopal's mother didn't encourage him to talk about this previous life. His father sometimes talked to his friends about Gopal's strange memories, and one of them told him that he remembered vaguely having heard about a murder in Mathura which he thought was similar to the one Gopal had described. Even so, it wasn't until 1964, six years after Gopal had first spoken about his Mathura life, that his father visited that city for a religious festival, found that it did indeed have a company called Sukh Shancharak, and that in 1948 one of the owners had shot and killed his brother, Shaktipal Sharma.

The two families belonged to different castes, lived in different cities, and each insisted that they had never heard of the other. But after Gopal's father's visit they made contact with each other, and some members of the Sharma family visited Gopal in Delhi and then invited him to visit them in Mathura. Gopal not only recognised various people and places in Mathura but seemed to know things about the family which only family members could have known. He described, for example, the basis of the quarrel between the two brothers, details of which had never been made public. The Sharma family were convinced that Gopal was Shaktipal Sharma reborn.

Shaktipal Sharma had been a member of a prominent family, and his murder had made headline news. If Gopal had been a few years older when he first produced these memories, one could easily have concluded that he was simply recounting events he had read about and forgotten. But at the age of two this simply isn't credible. Might his family, perhaps hoping there might be some benefits in claiming this strange kinship with a family of higher caste, have fed him information? Even if they had, there seems no way they could have known the details that convinced the Sharma family.

Gopal didn't show any particular desire to continue a relationship with his past-life family, though he did occasionally visit Shaktipal Sharma's two sisters, who lived in Delhi. But gradually all contact between the two families ceased. However, Gopal did continue his Brahmin-like behaviour for several years, insisting that he was of a superior caste to the rest of the family, refusing to do housework, which he regarded as servants' work, or to drink from a cup anyone else had used. Eventually, Gopal seems to have resigned himself to his more modest circumstances and talked less about his previous existence, though he did not entirely forget it. The last time Ian Stevenson was in touch with the family was in 1974, when Gopal was 18. Gopal's father believed that even at that age Gopal still had some memories of Shaktipal Sharma's life.

Nearer home, Albert Crow describes a similar example of "Brahmin-like behaviour" exhibited by his own grandson.

My father was a dogged person, dominant, intelligent and very forthright. My son, now forty, has one child, a boy of four, the image of my father, just as intelligent, just as dominant, and very adult. I was thrown completely when I had reason to chastise him. He turned to me with knitted eyebrows (Dad's habit), pointed his finger and said: "Don't talk to me like that—I am your father and if anyone's going to tell someone off it will be me!" Another time, my son chastised him for being demanding. He again turned to him and said: "Don't

you dare talk to me like that. I am your father's father
and I demand respect!"

Mr. Crow says that every time he looks at his grandson he
wonders if reincarnation is a fact. He adds that the boy's
mother claims she feels dominated by him, too, almost as if
she were married to him.

It is interesting that Mrs. J. Foster's (pseudonym) daughter
also produced her first past-life memory of her "other family"
when she had just been reprimanded. The child was a baby of
about a year and a half, able only to converse in baby talk,
when her mother had reason to speak sharply to her one day
for doing something a bit naughty. "She looked up at me and
said: 'You aren't my mummy. My mummy is a big lady, and
we lived in a big building, and they took my daddy and my
brother away. And my name is Bronski.'" The child never
mentioned this again, but the exchange convinced Mrs. Foster that reincarnation is a fact and that her daughter was a
child victim of the Holocaust.

The logic of "you're not being nice to me; therefore you're
not my mummy" is very understandable in a child of this age.
But only rarely does a sense of grievance seem to trigger a
child's comments about a previous life; on the contrary, what
evidence there is suggests that these are children who get on
well with their families and are not alienated from them in any
way (see page 250).

What happens to these children when they grow older? As
adults, do they retain anything of their past-life memories?
And perhaps most interesting of all, what kind of children are
they?

14

Children Who Remember

"When I first appeared I knew where I had been—now I have forgotten."

Ben

GOPAL Gupta (see page 240) is exceptional in retaining memories of a past life at least until he was in his late teens. Most children seem to forget their past life completely by the time they are seven or eight. At any rate, they no longer talk about it. This may be because they realise that it is something their families prefer not to discuss, or because as they grow older they themselves begin to realise the implications of what it is they are remembering and to be embarrassed by it. Stevenson has suggested that there is certainly a cutoff point for girls. Small girls will talk happily about their previous husbands or children, and everyone will be interested and amused. But once the child reaches puberty, other people's attitudes change and the child will very quickly realise this and stop.

There is also the straightforward explanation that all children get bored with an idea or a game after a while and that their accounts of a previous life are just another such game. Children will tell their parents, for example, that an imaginary friend who has been a constant companion for months has gone away, or grown up, or that they don't want to play with them any more. Or it may be that as they grow out of early childhood, children gradually come to accept an adult view of the world, and these memories, together with Father Christmas, the Tooth Fairy and the monster that lives in the back of the wardrobe, are acknowledged to be impossible and abandoned.

We know, too, that most adults have only limited or poor memory of their early childhood, and it may be that apparent past-life memories are simply forgotten, just as so many other early memories are forgotten. There is probably a psychological need to forget as well; too vivid memories, too strong an attachment to a supposed previous life might make it more difficult for individuals to deal with the people and situations they meet in this life—which is, after all, the one that has to be lived.

But even though most studies report that children forget their past-life memories within a very few years, many adults have told us that they have past-life memories they were first conscious of in childhood. Wendy McClymont feels she can remember the day she was born and has a memory of lying in her cot feeling very contented and thinking, So this is where I have come to. It is only recently that she realised that most other people do not have these very early memories—she says she can remember her first year as well as other years. "I seemed to have all the knowledge but needed to relearn how to use it. I can remember being pushed in my pram facing my mother and knowing that if I could manage to get on to my knees I could turn around to look the way I was going. I was so pleased the day I managed to do this."

When she was three Wendy was taken on holiday to Devon by her parents and shown Drake's Drum. She can remember being very interested in this as she knew that she had been Sir Francis Drake in a previous life. She says: "This seems amazing and impossible to me now, but I know that when I was three years I just accepted it without realising that there was anything strange about it. As a three-year-old I am sure I had never heard of reincarnation, and I doubt if I had hear of Sir Francis Drake until I got to Plymouth."

When adults report childhood memories it is difficult to know how much the original memory has been elaborated throughout a lifetime. Inevitably memories acquired in this life will become interwoven with the fabric of apparent past-life recall. Carolyn Silver (pseudonym) has described this process very well. Mrs. Silver's little girl Sophia was only two when she started, quite freely and spontaneously, to talk about "when I was Jenny." "At first," Mrs. Silver says, "I took this to be simply an extension of the 'mummies and babies' game that little girls play, as the first comments were simple remarks like, 'When I was Jenny, my children used to eat all their meals up and they used to say thank you, Mummy'."

However, details were gradually added in the same casual manner until quite a clear picture of a very ordinary, middle-class family began to come into focus. Comments were always about mundane, everyday experiences and very normal people, rather than fantasies about princesses and parties which a little girl might be expected to dream up. Mrs. Silver continued:

> Sophia's playschool is held in the village Old School and is known to her only as the venue for the Toddler Group, Tumble Tots and craft fairs. Her older sister and brothers attend the modern primary school built in the 1970s. One day, however, she told us that she went to the Old School for her big school when she was Jenny. She also told us that there were buses, but they were not like the buses now, and that no shops were open on Sundays then.
>
> "Jenny" was apparently married to Jim Harper, a local doctor, who died after a blow to the head while attempting to help men hurt in a mine. She said that this happened on Holcombe Hill (the dominant landmark in the town). I know of no mine in the vicinity, although I believe there is a quarry there used for the stone from which the monument to Robert Peel (which stands at the top of the hill) was made.
>
> At the time of Princess Diana's funeral, although the coffin was always draped and concealed by flags, and Sophia has never experienced a death in the family, she suddenly remarked: "I've been in one of those, but mine wasn't like that; it was black." She has also told us that she was in heaven and saw baby Jesus and that he had a black face.
>
> However, the natural, chirpy way in which she used

to recount all these strange ideas, and the subject-matter, so oddly at variance with Sophia's experiences and the stories which we read to her, so very far removed from any voluntary fantasy which such a little girl may be expected to have, seem to make the whole experience more remarkable.

Sophia is a perfectly normal, happy little girl. She is not a child prodigy and has not been exposed to ideas or experiences other than those usual for such a young child. A belief in reincarnation forms no part of our ethical or religious background, and this sort of experience is unknown for us in any other part of our family.

Sophia's mother has noticed that as Sophia has grown older and more aware, it is becoming much more difficult to be sure which of her memories are genuine and which have become elaborated with time. She is now four and, her mother says, "has become aware of the interest aroused by her comments, and was also deeply impressed by Princess Diana's death. Her comments are now becoming fewer, more self-conscious and muddled with the circumstances of Diana's death. Now, for example, she will maintain that she was killed in a car crash."

It is easy to see that the more interest a family shows and the more they encourage or reinforce the child's story, the more likely it is to become embellished in the telling, or to incorporate details the child knows would please the adults. If a family is expecting or hoping to see one of its erstwhile members reborn, this kind of reinforcement is almost certain to occur. In most cases, however, it does not. James Hamilton says: "I remember being conscious of a past life at the time of my birth; also I remember trying to tell my parents of my experiences when I was older—they did not believe me and became upset if I persisted. As I became older my memory of the past vanished, although from time to time I had flashbacks which I attributed to dream or tricks of the mind."

WHO REMEMBERS?

What kind of children are they, these children who remember past lives? Boys and girls show little difference in their ability to remember past lives, although Ian Stevenson has found that slightly more boys than girls report past lives in a ratio of 55:45, and in some cultures as much as 60:40. In our own sample of 20 children, this ratio was reversed; there were more girls than boys, 60:40.

Most people who have observed these children say that they are often more intelligent and more advanced emotionally than their siblings. Bright children are usually imaginative. They may also have parents who have stimulated their imaginations by talking to them a lot and telling them stories. But this doesn't provide a full explanation. Many parents have commented on the fact that when their child talks about a past life, he or she uses language, concepts and statements that seem to be incompatible with the age and stage of development of the child. This is particularly striking in the following case.

Ben is autistic. He didn't speak until he was five, and then only at a very simple level—"I five." At six he was still not speaking in proper sentences. Then, sitting in the back of the car one day, he suddenly said in a voice quite different from his normal voice, "I saw a little boy run over by a train," and a minute or so later, "That little boy was me." When she had overcome her surprise, his mother asked him if this was something he had seen on TV and he replied, no. Then he stopped talking.

Some months later the family were staying with Ben's grandparents in New Zealand when again, quite out of the blue, he announced: "When I first appeared I knew where I had been—now I have forgotten." Again, he did not elaborate, and again he spoke in this "different" voice.

These statements seemed to come from some quite different level of Ben's being; they had a content and form and meaning well beyond his actual level of language development. They also had a clarity and a lack of embroidery that Ben's mother felt might be at least partly due to his autism, although this matter-of-factness is exactly what many other parents have commented on.

Lesley Davies describes the following conversation she had with her small son when he was just over two years old. She remembers thinking at the time how long the sentences were. Now she has a grandson of a similar age, and talking to him has brought home to her that the length of sentences her son used would have been very adult for a child of that age.

> I was busy ironing and miles away in my thoughts, heavily pregnant with my next child, when my little boy, who must have been less than two years and three months, since that is the difference between my children, suddenly looked up from playing with his Dinky cars and said: "Mummy, when I was an old man, I was very, very sad."
>
> I suddenly realised he was talking to me and started to listen, and he said again: "Mummy, when I was an old man, I was very sad." When I asked him why, he said it was because his two little daughters had been burned to death when his house caught fire, and it had made him very, very sad.
>
> On questioning, he said that he had lived in Bedminster [an area of Bristol] in a terraced house, and that his house had caught fire and he had been outside on the pavement and seen his two little daughters at the bedroom window, where they had burned to death. He said they were wearing smocks and, on questioning, he said his wife's name was Annie. He might have said she was sad too; I am not sure.
>
> My son was only at the most two years and two months, possibly a little less, and I had to be very careful and gentle with the questioning. I did not want to frighten him, and there seemed a point when he did not want to carry on talking about it, and went back to playing with his Dinky cars. We never talked about it again, and this is all that I can remember.
>
> We lived near Bristol, and my son's grandparents lived in the area next to Bedminster, so he may have heard that name, but I cannot see how he could have known about "smocks," "terraced houses" or a name such as "Annie."

Professor Erlendur Haraldsson, of the University of Iceland, has studied the personalities of thirty children in Sri Lanka who claimed previous-life memories. In a few of these cases he found a striking fit between the child's statements and facts in the life of someone who had lived before he was born, sometimes in a distant community. But in most cases no one was found whose life corresponded to the child's memories. The question of verification was not, however, Professor Haraldsson's main concern—what he has tried to do is identify common characteristics in the children who have these memories. Did they have a particularly rich fantasy life, for example, or a need to compensate for social isolation? Were they more suggestible than most children—something especially likely to be important in a culture where reincarnation plays a major role? Did they show a tendency to dissociate, or attention-seeking behaviour? Finally, how did they get along with their parents? If this relationship was disturbed, the child might have good reason to claim that he or she actually belonged somewhere else.

What Professor Haraldsson found confirmed that these children are usually very bright. He asked the teachers and parents of two groups of children of the same age to answer questionnaires about their personality and behaviour. One group had at some time claimed to have memories of a previous life; the other, control group, had never done so. The most striking difference he found between the two groups was that those with past-life memories seemed to be more mature for their age, and more intelligent. They had greater verbal skills, better memory and were doing much better in school than their peers. This might have been at least partly due to the fact that they were also more demanding of themselves, feeling they had to be perfect. They were more serious, and tended to fool around less in school than other children.

Does this mean that children of high ability are more likely than other children to create stories of a previous life? Or that children who remember a previous life are more gifted? We don't know, but there certainly seems to be some association in children between past-life memory and intelligence. If one assumes for the moment that past-life memories are very common in early childhood, but that they are very quickly forgotten, then it could be that only those children who learn to speak particularly early would be able to talk about past-life memories before they vanish completely. On the other hand there are, of course, plenty of intelligent, early talkers who never speak a word about a past life.

Are these children more socially isolated than other children, so that they need to create this "other world" for their own comfort and companionship? Professor Haraldsson found no evidence that they were any more likely than other children to confabulate a fantasy life, and none that they were more socially isolated. Although they were often withdrawn and liked to be alone, they got along well with other children, and most had two or three brothers and sisters. None of them showed any signs that they felt rejected by their families. Neither were they any more suggestible than other children. Professor Haraldsson concluded that their past-life memories were much more likely to have arisen spontaneously than to have been generated by fantasy or suggestion.

So far as their behaviour was concerned, it was the parents rather than the teachers who tended to find this a problem. Their parents reported them to be argumentative and stubborn and said that they talked too much. It was also the parents rather than the teachers who commented on the children's apparent need to be alone. This suggests that the children are, in fact, socially quite competent, and no more isolated than their peers.

Whether this need to be alone is a cause or an effect of the child's feelings about a past life is debatable. Does a child's liking for solitude for example, arise because he wants to be alone with his past-life memories (especially if he is discouraged from talking about these within the family)? Or is it because he feels different, or has been made to feel different, from other children because of his claims? One also has to remember that it can be very discomfiting for parents to have their children persistently claim membership of another family. It would not be surprising if this sometimes caused friction. In many of the accounts that we have had the children, when speaking about their past lives, do seem to have been in some altered state of consciousness: they spoke differently, and then after the statement they went back to their normal manner again. This behaviour argues against the theory that past-life memories make the children want to be alone, as it seems that the past-life memories do not in any way consume or obsess the children; once they have talked about them they happily return to the normal play.

In another, more recent study Professor Haraldsson has tried to find out if these children showed a tendency to dissociate. He found that children who remember previous lives are more likely to show rapid changes in personality, to daydream more, to have intense outbursts of anger, and to refer to themselves in the third person. They are also more likely to claim that things they did actually happened to another person. They talk to themselves more often, are more likely to be sleepwalkers, and tend to deny or forget painful experiences.

However, these behavioural traits are not sufficient to suggest that the children are in any way abnormal. Their behaviour certainly shows a degree of independence which one might expect from highly intelligent children. But they certainly don't seem to stand out as a very special group or to be markedly different from their peers.

Professor Haraldsson did, however, find an interesting difference when he compared children whose cases were "unsolved"—that is, no one had been identified whose life corresponded to the child's statements—with children whose cases were solved, in that such a person had been identified. One of the tests he gave measured children's suggestibility. He found that on this measure the total scores of the "solved" cases were significantly lower than the scores for the "unsolved" cases. He concluded that the children who made verified statements about a previous life were less suggestible than those whose statements had not been verified, and, indeed, less suggestible than children in general.

What is quite clear is that *any* child may have apparent past-life memories, regardless of the culture into which they are born. In cultures in which reincarnation is accepted as entirely natural, such cases are found more easily. But whether they actually occur more frequently is much less certain. The anthropologist Antonia Miffs investigated several cases of children in India and found that cultural acceptance of the idea of reincarnation does not seem adequately to explain the claims of young children. Sri Lanka is a country where reincarnation is accepted, but only a few children can be found every year who claim to remember a previous life. Professor Haraldsson managed to find only twenty Sri Lankan children with past-life memories over a period of three or four years—probably no more than could be found in the West if a dedicated search was made for them. In our own search in England, response to a single newspaper article produced twenty cases of children with apparent past-life memories. Clearly neither cultural expectations nor religious faith can account for the occurrence of these experiences.

"Solving" Past Lives

Where there does seem to be a real cultural difference is in the number of "solved" cases of past lives. Few cases of apparent reincarnation in children are ever "solved" in the sense that some deceased person is found whose life convincingly matches the statements the child has made. Mahavir Singh (see page 235) and Gopal Gupta (see page 240) are among the small number of past-life cases that have been "proved" to the satisfaction of the families concerned, and both occurred in cultures in which a search was thought worthwhile because reincarnation was accepted as a possibility.

It would be virtually impossible to prove most of the British cases known to us in the same way, because the children seldom give the kind of information that can be verified. Ian Stevenson found the same difference when he was comparing the past-life memories of American and Indian children. While about three-quarters of the Indian children mentioned the name of the person whose life they remembered, only about a third of the American children he studied mentioned names that could help identify their previous incarnation. When they did so, the life they remembered was almost always that of a member of the child's own family. One child remembered the life of someone who had been a close family friend. This has to raise the possibility that these children may have elaborated a fantasy about a past life based on what they had learned in a normal way.

There are other problems in trying to "prove" whether or not a child is truly remembering a past life. In most cases there is no written record of exactly what a child has said before a case is "solved." It is impossible to know how much doctoring of the original testimony has taken place. All of us are prone to do a little rewriting of history when we have the benefit of hindsight. When people visit a fortune-teller or read their horoscope, for example, they retain whatever seems appealing or appropriate and mentally discount the rest.

Of the twenty-three children in Sri Lanka Professor Haraldsson studied who claimed previous-life memories, he managed, by dogged detective work, to find matches for two of these that are in many respects very convincing. In neither case did cultural beliefs about reincarnation encourage the parents to reinforce the children's claims. In fact, there was active discouragement. Dilukshi's parents did their best to stop her talking about her other family; Duminda's mother was very concerned about her son's claims to have been a monk in a previous life and about his wish to become a monk again, for she had no wish to lose him to a monastic life.

Dilukshi's story is especially interesting, because there are two written records of the statements she made before any attempt was made to verify her claims.

DILUKSHI AND SHIROMI

Dilukshi Geevanie Nissanka was born in Sri Lanka on 4 October 1984. A year and a week before her birth, in a village near Dambulla, 80 miles (129 kilometres) away, a little girl called Shiromi had died by drowning in a canal.

When Dilukshi was less than two years old she began to speak about a previous life near Dambulla, where a rock temple is one of the most famous places of pilgrimage in Sri Lanka. She made about 30 statements about this life, which included the fact that "my brother and I fell into the stream and I came here [that is, she died]."

To her parents' chagrin she refused to call them Mother and Father and demanded to be taken home to her other mother, saying: "My mother is not like you, aunt. She loves me very much." Not surprisingly, her parents did their best to stop the child talking about this other, idyllic family, but in the end, when Dilukshi was nearly five, they capitulated and set about trying to find them. Eventually, a journalist was contacted who wrote an account of the case, listing all the statements Dilukshi had made. The account was read by Shiromi's father, who contacted Dilukshi's father. The child was taken to Dambulla, and apparently led the way to her former home, some four miles (6.4 kilometres) away from the town. Here she was accepted as the former daughter of the house, after allegedly recognising various objects and people and making statements that the family verified.

How well did what Dilukshi remembered of her previous life correspond with Shiromi's? Some of her memories (that she played "boutique"—that is, shop; that she had a doll; that she slipped on a rock going up to the Dambulla temple) were either so general that they might have applied to almost any child or so trivial that witnesses would have been unlikely to remember them. But of the 17 statements that she made which Professor Haraldsson considered potentially verifiable, he concluded that twelve corresponded quite well with Shiromi's life, while only four were definitely wrong. Her memory of names—even of her own name, which she said was Suwanna—was particularly inaccurate, but her references to locations and places scored some hits and a few near misses. She had said, for example, that the roof of their house could be seen from the small Dambulla rock where she often played. There is indeed a rock, the only one, 30 or 40 yards (27 or 36 metres) from Shiromi's house, and both Shiromi's mother and her sister confirmed that she had called this the small Dambulla rock and had often played there. Professor Haraldsson climbed the rock and confirmed that, through the trees and bushes, the roof of Shiromi's house could indeed be seen. Her descriptions of the stream where she drowned, the footbridge over it, and the paddyfield nearby all matched these locations reasonably well. She remembered a public drinking cistern that had been near the Dambulla temple in Shiromi's lifetime, although it no longer existed. Dilukshi had stated that her mother wore a housecoat with beautiful buttons. Shiromi's mother told Professor Haraldsson that this was correct—she had used and still uses a dress called a housecoat, a garment that the interpreter said was not commonly worn by women in that area.

To a Westerner, the fact that Dilukshi listed so many topographical details that checked out more or less correctly and yet did not give her own name correctly, let alone the names of her close family members, seems to make the story less credible. Presumably a stream, a paddyfield, a footbridge, even a rock might be found in a good many villages. But how could she have known the name of the village itself—Dambulla? Professor Haraldsson points out that, in Sri Lanka, given names are very little used. Relational names are much more usual—an adult might address a boy or young man as "malle" ("younger brother"), for example. Dilukshi had said that she had a younger brother called Mahesh. Shiromi's brother had, in fact, a quite different name, but Shiromi did have a playmate whose name was Mahesh and she had called this boy "malle."

Dilukshi's parents had no connection with Dambulla and knew no one in the town. They had, however, visited it once in early 1984 on their way back from a pilgrimage. Professor Haraldsson makes no comment on this, but as Dilukshi was born in early October it is tempting to conjecture that this might have been around the time of her conception.

SEARCHING FOR THE ABBOT

Duminda Bandara Ratnayake was born in June 1984 of Sinhalese Buddhist parents. When he was about three years old he started to talk about his life as an abbot at the Asigirya temple and monastery in Kandy, one of the largest and oldest temples in Sri Lanka. His mother reported that he claimed that he had owned a red car, had taught other monks, had suffered a sudden pain in his chest, fallen on the floor, and been taken by some monks to a hospital, where he had died. Duminda claimed also to have owned an elephant and expressed a longing for a moneybag and a radio, which he said he had had in Asigirya (and which are both odd belongings for a monk to have).

Moreover, Duminda behaved in a curious way for a three-year-old. He displayed a most unchildlike calmness and detachment, wanted to carry his clothes in the fashion of a monk, and when his mother called him "son" protested and said that he wanted to be called "podi sadhu" ("little monk").

He said he wanted to be a monk, and when his mother allowed it (which was seldom) he liked to wear a monk's robe. He visited the temple regularly and went every morning and evening to a Buddhist chapel close to his house. He attached great importance to cleanliness, liked to be alone and didn't play with other children. Once, when his mother helped him wash his hands, he told her that she should not touch his hands (women are not supposed to touch men's hands). More bizarrely still, he would recite religious stanzas in Pali, the ancient language of Sinhalese Buddhism which is still learned by monks.

Duminda's mother sought advice from a monk residing in a nearby temple who agreed to meet Duminda. The little boy wouldn't answer the monk's questions, but he asked for a fan (a special piece of Buddhist religious paraphernalia used only by monks who preached). When he was given one, he held it in front of his face and recited one of the Buddhist stanzas, just as a preaching monk would do at the beginning of any formal sermon.

If one sets aside the odd, monkish behaviour of this small boy and looks only at the statements he made, was there anything to identify a particular monk out of the many who had lived and died at the Asigirya temple? Duminda had made several statements that Professor Haraldsson decided were specific enough to make a search for such a monk worthwhile—that he had a red car, died of a heart attack, died in hospital, had a radio, preached and owned an elephant.

Duminda had used the Sinhalese word meaning "abbot" or, less frequently, a word meaning "big monk" to describe himself. And until the 1980s, no monks other than the abbot owned a car, or possessed a moneybag (or, at any rate, the money to put in it). Professor Haraldsson therefore checked out Duminda's statements against the five abbots who had lived between 1921 and 1975. One of these—Gunnepana, who died in 1929—matched five of the six statements. Only one statement fitted each of the other abbots.

Only two abbots had owned a car, Godmunne, who died in 1975 and owned a white Mercedes, and Gunnepana, who had owned a car variously described as red or brownish. Only these two abbots had also died of heart attacks, though neither had died in hospital. Gunnepana himself hadn't owned an elephant, but one of his disciples had done so, and Gunnepana was said to have taken an interest in the animal. Neither had he owned a radio, but of all the abbots he was said to be the only one to own a gramophone on which he often played records of Buddhist chanting. Now, Duminda had never seen a gramophone, so it is possible that he did not recognise the difference between a radio and a gramophone. Gunnepana was also one of the only two abbots who preached.

When Professor Haraldsson last saw Duminda, at the end of 1990, he was six years old, and although his memories seemed to be fading he was still much more interested in religion than is a normal six-year-old, and still retained his unusual calmness and dignity (in contrast to his normal, noisy, active brothers). His mother had at last agreed that he should enter the monastery when he was seven, the earliest permissible age.

REMEMBERING PAST LANGUAGE

Unlike many past-life children, Duminda is not outstandingly intelligent. At the age of five he was performing like an average five-year-old at school and didn't show any special ability for memorising. What makes his story particularly puzzling and interesting was his reported ability, at the age of three, to chant religious stanzas in clear and faultless Pali. This is the equivalent of a three-year-old Roman Catholic reciting a Latin Mass. Rather in the manner of *Thought for the Day*, Sri Lankan radio broadcasts a recital of some of these stanzas at 5 a.m. each morning, and this was, Professor Haraldsson thought, one obvious source. However, Duminda knew one stanza ("Worship of the Tooth Relic") which the director of the religious programme said had never been broadcast. Duminda's mother and grandmother both knew this stanza, but both affirmed that the boy had not learned it, or any other stanza, from them. In fact, they claimed to have learned one stanza from him. If the account is accurate, how can we explain the fact that this three-year-old, quite apart from the number of hits he scored, apparently spoke faultless Pali? The only rational explanation is that he was taught the stanzas, probably by his mother and grandmother, but the evidence is that this did not happen.

Very rarely, an adult who claims to have experienced a past life seems to be able to speak a language he or she has apparently never been taught—the phenomenon known as xenoglossy (see page 209). But children, even when they seem to have memories of life in a foreign country, show no ability to speak the language. Duminda is the only exception to this rule that we have come across. Ian Stevenson has studied a group of twenty Burmese children who claim to have been Japanese soldiers in the Second World War. (For most Burmese this would be an unwelcome incarnation in view of the atrocities committed by the Japanese-occupying army in Burma at that time.) These children can't say where they lived in Japan or even remember their Japanese name.

However, in a few of these children Professor Ian Stevenson has suggested that there *are* memories of another language, and that these may interfere with the child's ability to learn their mother tongue—something he calls glossophobia. One such case is that of a Burmese woman, Ma Win Tar, who believed that she had a past life as a Japanese soldier.

Ma Win Tar claimed that she had been captured and killed by Burmese villagers (probably in 1945 as the Japanese army in Burma was retreating before the advancing British forces). She certainly showed some masculine behaviour—she liked to keep her hair cropped short, like a boy's, and wear boy's clothes, she was fond of firearms, and once or twice said she wished to become a soldier. She also showed various traits said to be more Japanese than Burmese (her food preferences, a relative insensitivity to pain, and a streak of cruelty—she would kill insects, for example, although Burmese Buddhists normally try to avoid doing so). She was also in the habit of slapping her playmates on the face—something the Burmese seldom do but which was said to be the usual way in which the occupying Japanese soldiers showed their displeasure to the villagers.

She did not show any knowledge of Japanese, although Ian Stevenson was told that when she was young she seemed to show a resistance to learning Burmese. As a young child she would sing songs in what her parents said sounded like a foreign language. When she was learning to speak she would say a foreign-sounding word instead of the Burmese word she had just been told. Even at the age of 16 she would sometimes develop a slight foreign accent when she was angry.

Stevenson suggested that Ma Win Tar might be "remembering" Japanese and that this interfered with her ability to learn Burmese. The evidence for this looks thin. Language development in children varies enormously. And virtually any young child's first words sound more like a foreign language than their own—early attempts at language are always an approximation, and a child asked to repeat a word for the first time seldom makes a very accurate attempt. If Ma Win Tar's language development really was significantly worse than that of other children of the same age and intellectual ability, then one might be justified in looking for some special explanation, but we don't know if this was so. Neither, on the face of it, does her behaviour seem sufficiently odd to need a past life to explain it. However, she was clearly a family deviant, sufficiently so to bring her to the attention of Stevenson, and for the family to search for some explanation. Stevenson saw her within her culture and within her family, and perhaps in that setting her behaviour did seem more than just odd and unconventional and demanded more than a rational Western explanation.

MEMORY AND IMAGINATION

How do we know that children's past lives are not simply the product of imagination or false memories? Children take a long time to learn the difference between reality and fantasy, and certainly up to the age of about five the boundary between the two is very blurred. Recent studies of child abuse suggest that the evidence is that children who *spontaneously* report current or recent abuse are usually telling the truth. However, children who have not been abused but are repeatedly questioned about supposed abuse may confabulate to please the interviewer, and may come to believe their own imaginings.

The children who report past lives virtually always do so spontaneously. Almost all the parents who wrote to us about their children's memories mentioned this. The children will talk only when they want to: they can't usually be persuaded to do so.

Stevenson's subjects varied widely in their apparent need to talk about their previous lives. Some talked about them only occasionally, when something sparked off a memory; others talked so incessantly that they drove their present families almost to distraction. Most of our sample seemed to make only occasional remarks, and, when they had said what they wanted to say, couldn't usually be persuaded to elaborate. Lesley Davies said of her son: "there seemed a point when he did not want to carry on talking about it, and went back to playing with his Dinky cars." Tammy's mother, too, says that the initiative always has to come from Tammy—whenever they have tried to persuade her to talk about her other life, or to elaborate on what she has said, she doesn't respond. The parents of the Pollock twins also said that when their daughters talked about their previous lives, they would just "burst out" with some remark but could never then be persuaded to enlarge on it or give more details. There is some evidence that when they were alone the twins talked about the car accident that killed their sisters, but there is no way of knowing whether they were truly sharing a mutual memory or whether they had learned about the accident in a normal way in this life and were simply acting out the drama.

The impression given is that none of these children had continuous recall of a previous life but occasionally, as though something had jogged their memory, would have a sudden flash of memory, like a window opening on a particular scene but allowing no hint of what lies beyond the field of vision.

These memories don't *seem* like fantasies. The children talk about their "other families" in a very matter-of-fact way. When children are using their imagination, it is usually pretty clear. Of course, children fantasise, but if they are fantasising then why aren't their stories more fantastic? In adults, the element of fantasy is very evident in many, perhaps even most, past lives. But in children, never. None of the children claimed to have been a famous person or to have performed extraordinary or heroic deeds. This may reflect their more limited memory bank of images and experience. But what it *seems* like is that they are describing what they remember, no more, no less. In nearly every instance—in both Stevenson's cases and those we have studied—what we see are glimpses of the apparent memories of ordinary children leading ordinary lives.

Another obvious difference between children and adults is that while adults, especially under hypnosis, tend to present strings of past lives, children, with very few exceptions, remember only one. Ian Stevenson says that although a small number of his subjects do remember more lives than one, the second life is nearly always an intermediate life about which few details are remembered. He has found only one case in which two previous lives are remembered with enough detail to enable them both to be verified.

Another indication that these children are not fantasising is that their stories remain consistent, even over long periods of time. And this is odd, because children like to please. One would expect them to embellish their stories if only to interest or get attention from adults. They don't seem to do this. Joe (see page 234), for example, can't remember what his name was although he says he wishes he could, and his parents have indicated that if he could remember a name they would be willing to try to trace his previous identity.

Other aspects of these past-life memories in children need to be explained. The first is the fact that they occur at all. Newborn infants do have a capacity for some sort of memory. Babies can pick up sounds while they are in the womb; they respond selectively to their mother's voice after they are born, and to the smell of her milk. But this is simple primitive memory, more feeling- and experience-dominated than intellect-dominated.

Most people have very limited memories before five or six years of age. "Episodic memory"—the ability to associate an event with a context and hence locate it in time and place—does not develop until after the age of four. Few people seem able to remember events that took place much before they were three years old. And it is highly unlikely that any adult can recall genuine memories from the first year of life, because the hippocampus, which plays an important role in the forming and storing of long-term memories, is not yet mature. So far as we know there is no neural substrate before the ages of one or two for the kind of elaborate verbal memories that some young children report. So how do we explain these very early memories?

Déjà vu probably explains many past-life experiences in adults. Might this be a possible explanation for childhood experiences? For various reasons this seems unlikely. *Déjà vu* is a complex cognitive experience that emerges only at a certain stage of mental development, seldom before the age of seven. The child has to be able to compare the present with the past, to relate present experiences to images in his memory and recognise a sense of familiarity in the comparison. He also has to recognise that he should not be feeling this sense of familiarity.

However, *déjà vu* can occur in children younger than seven. Dr. Vernon Neppe has collected three examples of children well below this age who have described this kind of experience. Two of the three were of above-average intelligence; the third was average.

> I was only five years old. I can assess this because this was when we went on a holiday including Lake Tanganyika. Maybe that was the reason it stuck in my mind—because I was quite small. We went on a little launch on Lake Tanganyika. The adults were trying to catch crocodiles. I felt great excitement and was also a little afraid. My child mind worried that the crocodiles would turn over the launch. We went only to a little island actually in the lake. You can imagine how small it was. As I walked on it, it looked familiar. I thought I had been there before. The whole scene seemed familiar, no specific features. I had never been on an island like this. The feeling was quite ridiculous, because there probably weren't even any houses.

Dr. Neppe suggests that when it occurs at such an early age, *déjà vu* may be being used as a defence mechanism against anxiety.

> My first *déjà vu* experience happened before I was six years old. I can work that out because we had just moved from Zastron to Ladybrand. I noticed the koppies around the area, and I felt I knew every little fact, of them—extremely intense, like reliving. Of course, Zastron has its own koppies, yet it was not just another koppie—this one was of a specific kind, with its own special features, and I had never seen one like it.

Dr. Neppe points out that although in each case the experience was quite intense—intense enough to be remembered many years later—it was very simple: the whole scene seemed familiar to the child, and yet he could not enlarge on this and say exactly what it was that seemed familiar. Dr. Neppe suggests that this is a reflection of the limited cognitive development of the two children. In the third example he quotes, the child is slightly older and the description given more detailed.

> I was six or seven at the time. I know that because my grandmother was holding my hands, and I would not have let her hold in hands if I were older. My grandmother took me to visit an old friend. Her house had an arched gateway. I knew what was in the house. I knew about the courtyard and about the cat. It evoked a feeling of familiarity as if I had been there before. I went past the house many times subsequently. It never reevoked the feeling of familiarity.

In each case, what the children described could be interpreted as being a past-life memory or dismissed as *déjà vu*. But *déjà vu* cannot explain how children who are so much younger than those Dr. Neppe describes can have such detailed experiences.

Most of the children we have heard about seem well able to distinguish between their two lives, to separate the past from the present without becoming confused: Lesley Davies's

little boy—"when I was an old man, I was very, very sad"—
Sophia Silver—"when I was Jenny"—Joe McCafferty—
"when I was a man I used to live over there." They do,
however, sometimes expect their present families to share
their memories. Robert Killwick's little girl, from the age of
two until she was five or six, for example, would often start a
conversation with, "Do you remember when I was a little girl
before and I used to wear long dresses that dragged in the
mud?"

In a *déjà vu* experience the tag of familiarity is put on to
an ongoing experience. Most people know what it is like to
have a weak *déjà vu* experience, when they suddenly feel that
they have experienced what is going on in front of them before. In temporal-lobe epilepsy these *déjà vu* experiences can
be very strong, so strong that you know with total conviction
what is going to happen as it occurs. This mislabelling of a
current experience, such as is shown in Dr. Neppe's examples
above, is very different from most of the childhood past-life
memories described in this chapter. In the reincarnation experiences there is no mislabelling of the current experience; they
appear as true memories. Thus, it is highly unlikely that *déjà
vu* is an explanation.

IMAGINARY FRIENDS

Between the ages of three and seven, many children acquire
imaginary friends. Quite often they are only children; often
they are socially isolated. The friends, who come to play a
major role in their lives, are usually given definite personalities, habits and preferences, and sometimes assume some aspects of the child's own personality. They may act as a
scapegoat for the child ("It was Tim that did it") or as a way
in which the child can project his or her own needs or feelings
("Tim doesn't like it when you're cross"). These imaginary
friends are usually dismissed by adults as simply that—figments of the child's imagination.

However, it is sometimes suggested that these imaginary
friends, who are so real and important to many young children
but who then finally disappear, might be remembered fragments of a past life. Certainly, many of the people who have

told us of their past-life memories had imaginary friends as children. Tammy had an imaginary friend called Peter, and Lynn Lowe (see page 267) remembers having an imaginary friend called John. When she was three years old Wendy Mc-Clymont (see page 244) had an imaginary friend called Billy Boy and wonders now whether he was a memory from a past life (though she doesn't say that he seemed like this at the time). Nicola Gilpin's daughter Sophie (see page 225) for a long time had two imaginary friends called Ben and Henry— Ben looked like a soldier and Henry had no hair. Sophie still remembers Ben and Henry but has forgotten the rest.

Occasionally, these invisible friends seem to be more than a mere figment of the child's imagination. Lorraine Herbert's daughter Joanne is now twenty-six. When she started to talk at about the age of two she would go behind the settee and say she was going to see "Dotty," or that "Dotty" was coming to tea. The family dismissed Dotty as an imaginary friend but became more intrigued when, on questioning, Joanne told them more about Dotty. She said that Dotty was about eleven years old, with black hair and eyes, and had lots of brothers and sisters. Asked where Dotty lived, she described what sounded like a gypsy caravan, although she had never seen one. After about six months or a year Dotty wasn't mentioned again, and everyone forgot about her. Some years later, however, they discovered that "Dotty" was indeed an old Romany name.

Mrs. D. Wright (pseudonym) also gives an account of an imaginary friend who seemed to have at least some ghostly substance. "When my eldest son was eighteen months old, he would constantly talk to an old door in our home. On asking him who he was talking to, he said a little girl called Black. I put this down to an imaginary friend until by chance I was talking to a neighbour, and she was shocked at this story and told me of the people that lived in the house before the people we bought the house from. Apparently, their surname was Black and they had one young daughter, who had died of cancer."

What can we deduce from the existence of these imaginary friends? Sadly, very little. No one knows what proportion of all children have imaginary friends, and how many of those children also have past-life memories. When children talk about their imaginary friends, they act as though their invisible companion is very much part of their present life, someone who is living alongside them in the here and now, and is a quite different person from themselves. Children who talk about a past life seem very clear that it is *in* the past. In talking to Tammy we tried to find out whether "Peter" seemed to be part of her "other life." Without "leading" her, it was difficult to get the idea across to her simply enough for her to understand. In the end we asked her mother whether when Tammy talked about Peter, and about her other life, the other life seemed to be more real to her. She said very decisively that it did, and Tammy then agreed with this.

One of the only cases in which there does seem to be a substantial link between a child's imaginary friend and his memories of a past life is that of Thomas Mather (pseudonym) whose story is described on page 95. Thomas was born in British Columbia, but almost as soon as he could talk he would frequently refer to "when I lived in San Francisco." Thomas occasionally mentioned an imaginary friend called Bowdey, and when he was four he told his mother that Bowdey was a friend of his who lived in San Francisco.

So for the moment the relationship between past-life memories and imaginary friends has to be left open. But it is clearly an area where further research is feasible, and one in which one might even find a definite answer.

THE LINK WITH VIOLENT DEATH

Dr. Satwant Pasricha is a researcher who has investigated many children in India who claim to have past-life memories and has often collaborated with Ian Stevenson. Pasricha and Stevenson found that many of the children they studied remembered the mode of death, that the death was usually violent, and that often the child has a phobia relating to the mode of death. Ian Stevenson believes that there is a link between violent death and retained memories of a past life (see page 49). However, he acknowledges that in the cultures he has studied, the incidence of violent death is in any case much higher than in a general Western population.

Although far fewer Western children are available for comparison, they seem to be less likely to remember, or at any rate to talk about, their mode of death. A few do seem to have died violently, or at least prematurely. The Pollock twins seemed to have some memory of the car crash that killed their sisters, for example, and Sophia Silver has a memory of being in a coffin. Lynn Lowe recounts an apparent past-life memory that automatically brings to mind the Tay Bridge disaster. She remembers that when she was a young child she would ask her mother when they were going to Scotland again, and she was always told that they had never been there. But Lynn has a memory of being in a railway carriage with a dark-haired woman whom she knew was her mother. It was as if she were looking down on herself, watching the end of her life. She wore a reddish-brown coat with a kind of cape around the shoulders, and a bonnet, and was reading a book. The last thing she remembers is that she was seeing the metal criss-crosses of a bridge and then feeling a sudden lurch and tumbling as the train spun.

It could be that most of the other children in our sample didn't talk about their death because they did not want to, or because they had picked up on the prevalent Western attitude that it is not a matter for discussion. It may also have something to do with the fact that while Stevenson's and Pasricha's subjects commonly remembered life as an adult, and the death they remembered was usually the violent death of that adult, most of the children in our sample remembered their previous life only as children; few had memories of life as an adult. Whatever the reason, in our sample there was no clear relationship between violent death and past-life memories.

PAST-LIFE MEMORIES AND SELF-HYPNOSIS

All hypnosis is self-induced, in the sense that no one can be hypnotised against his will; people have to allow themselves to be put into a trance state. Adults often report that they first become aware of past-life memories when they are in a meditative or relaxed state, or a state of self-hypnosis. Ian Stevenson has noticed that a few children "become abstracted from their immediate surroundings as they talk about the previous life. They may appear to onlookers to be in a partial trance, though . . . they are readily brought back to awareness of their surroundings." In a few cases parents have reported to us that their child seems to go into a state very similar to a trance state when these memories are triggered.

Mrs. Cunliffe's description of her son Nicholas (see page 226) sounds very much as though he was temporarily in an altered state of consciousness. "Nicholas's eyes seemed fixed and slightly glazed when I glanced in the driver's mirror, but when I turned to face the back seat his eyes were back to normal." Tammy's mother (see page 221) also commented: "Most of the time she would be playing like a normal two-year-old, but now and again she would just get this vacant look on her face and say to me, 'Mummy, can I tell you something?', and I'd know she was going to tell me about 'years ago'." The "different voice" that Ben's mother (see page 247) says that he used also seems to indicate a different level of consciousness.

It is difficult to put a name to this experience. What is clear is that it indicates some sort of break in the flow of consciousness. It is reminiscent of other conditions when images come into consciousness in such a way that they are disjointed from the current conscious stream. In post-traumatic stress disorder, for example, flashbacks of an accident may suddenly come into mind and take over consciousness. In these children there was this same imperative quality to the experience but, interestingly, without the same emotional tone. The experiences seem to pre-empt the stream of consciousness, need to be spoken about, and then disappear without leaving the child at all disturbed or distressed. Intrusive memories in adults almost always leave an emotional mark. These childhood experiences are clearly only fragments of memory, and they seem to come without a strong emotional tone.

Children who have past-life memories are usually very young, and yet often the memories have a very strong structure of before and after, and of time passed. Might the children simply be confused about time and about the pattern of family relationships, so that when they claim to have been the father of one of their own parents, for example, this is just a reflection of this confusion? Although this is a possibility, most of the children seem to be able to make a clear distinction between the "now" of their present life and the "then" of their remembered past, and usually (though not always) to understand that their present family relationships are distinct from those they seem to remember. Sometimes, though, the two worlds evidently overlap, as in the case of Robert Killwick's little girl, who used to say: "Do you remember when I was a little girl before and I used to wear long dresses that dragged in the mud?"

So what are these memories? Are they a part of normal childhood development? Probably not, though normal children certainly have them. Are they pathological? It doesn't seem to be so. These children are intelligent, well-integrated children with no apparent psychological problems except a tendency to be argumentative. A feeling of "not belonging" is certainly quite common in childhood; many children feel or claim to feel that they are adopted and don't really belong to the families. Is the "other life" simply another way of expressing the same feelings? Again, it doesn't sound like it. There is no suggestion that these children feel alienated from their present-day families, nor is there an element of the fantasy you might expect if the child were simply making up an ideal family to replace the everyday one, which was for some reason temporarily failing to come up to scratch.

Wherever these memories spring from, everyone who studies these children is convinced that in nearly every case the children are not fantasising. And they are certainly not lying. They are simply reporting what seem to them to be real memories of a life they think they have lived before. Our Galilean science persuades us that reincarnation is impossible. With the advances that have been made in physics and our better understanding of the nature of the universe in which we live, we can no longer say with the same certainty that past-life memories cannot exist. Perhaps these children are right. Perhaps they have lived before.

15

Stretching Coincidence

If I believed in reincarnation, I'd come back as Warren Beatty's fingers.

Woody Allen

CHARLES Porter was a native North American Indian from Alaska, a member of the Tlingit tribe. Until he was eight years old he would often talk about how he had been killed by a spear in a Tlingit clan fight. He knew both where he had been killed and the name of the man who had killed him. He gave his own name in this previous life. And when he told the story he pointed to his right side to indicate where the spear had struck him. Charles Porter had been born with a birthmark—a pigmented area about an inch and a half long and half an inch wide (3.8 by 1.2 centimetres)—on his right flank, just at the spot he always indicated when he talked about the spear thrust that had killed him.

A belief in reincarnation is part of the traditional religion of the Tlingit. They also believe that when someone is reincarnated his body may bear some trace of its past life. Many cultures in which reincarnation is accepted, such as Burma, Thailand, Sri Lanka and the Tlingit of Alaska, regard birthmarks or birth defects as proof of a specific link between past life and present incarnation. Others, the Hindu-Buddhist cultures, don't require a specific explanation for a birth defect—the doctrine of karma is explanation enough. A malformation will be attributed by the parents to some event in one of the previous lives of their child; they will not be interested in or look for any particular event that might have caused that particular defect.

Professor Ian Stevenson is one of the few scientists who has made a serious attempt to discover whether birthmarks or birth defects really can be related to experiences in a remembered past life. He has investigated and described over 200 cases of people who have been identified as particular persons reborn, and who have physical birthmarks or defects which seem to confirm this identification. The results of his work are published in a mammoth two-volume work, *Reincarnation and Biology*. For the less intrepid reader a condensed (and cheaper) version, *Where Reincarnation and Biology Intersect*, is also available. It is easy to pick out and pick holes in many individual cases, but in fairness to Stevenson it must be said that he urges readers not to express an opinion about his conclusions without studying the larger work, which gives a much more detailed account of each case, pointing out its weaknesses as well as its strengths.

Stevenson is interested in reincarnation because he is interested in the reasons for the differences between individual people. He doesn't deny that individuality comes from both our genes and our environment, but he suggests that there may be another contributory factor—our uniqueness may also derive from reincarnation. He suggests that sometimes mental images in the mind of a deceased person can survive death and can influence the form of an embryo or fetus so as to cause birthmarks and birth defects. The effect of mental imagery interacts with the influence of other factors, such as genetic and cytoplasmic ones, that contribute to the final form of a baby. He admits that the evidence for this is not compelling; his claim is only that it provides a rational, and not a religious, basis for a belief in reincarnation. And if he is right, he has found what might be the missing link between persistence of memory and persistence of personal identity. For Ian Stevenson, the evidence from birthmarks and birth defects provides one of the strongest rational reasons for a belief in reincarnation.

Birthmarks are areas of discoloured skin which are present from birth and are the result of some developmental defect. The most common are freckles and moles; others are malformations of the blood vessels in the skin, forming the red patches ("stork's beak marks") often seen above the bridge of the nose or on the nape of the neck after birth, or bright red strawberry naevi, which at birth may appear as tiny red dots, grow into raised, red lumps during the first months of life, but then usually shrivel and disappear altogether by the time the child reaches school age. Port wine stains are dark red, permanent marks with a sharply defined margin. Finally, there are the brownish, pigmented areas, often called *café au lait* patches, sometimes associated with a genetic condition called neurofibromatosis.

Birth defects are abnormalities such as spina bifida or cleft lip and palate, which are also present from birth. Birth defects have many recognised causes, of which genetic factors, viral infections and chemicals such as alcohol and other teratogenic drugs are the most common. But these recognised causes account for fewer than half of all birth defects. Stevenson suggests that reincarnation can not only account for the defects of "unknown cause" but can explain why a particular *person* has a defect, and why this defect is in one place and not another, or takes one form and not another. Cleft lip and palate, for example, have a genetic component. Identical, monozygotic twins have the same genetic make-up. If one of a pair of identical twins is born with the condition, in 38 percent of cases the other will have it too (this figure is only 8 percent if the twins are non-identical). And yet that also means that in 62 percent of cases the other twin *won't* have the condition. The genetic make-up is the same, the environment is the same and yet some other factor is clearly also involved.

One can't attach much significance to a birthmark or birth defect alone, especially as most of the cases Stevenson has studied are from cultures where parents often expect their child to be a reincarnation of some family member and look for proof in the form of birthmarks or birth defects. But when children also have memories of their previous life which can be verified, as in the following case, it is easy to understand how convincing this proof can seem.

THE OEDIPAL BRIGAND

U Thet Tin was a Burmese brigand who died at the hands of government troops who had shot him in the knee and lower abdomen. Some time after his death his widow, Daw Unt, dreamed that her dead husband had appeared to her and told her he was coming to protect her. Shortly afterwards she became pregnant, and when the child, Maung Tin Win, was born she saw that he had three birthmarks. One was on his right knee, and of the other two one was on the right side of his abdomen and the other, larger one on the right side of his lower back. These latter two could be said to correspond to the entrance and exit holes of the bullet that killed U Thet Tin.

One day when the little boy was about three or four years old and looking at a snapshot of U Thet Tin, he suddenly remembered his previous life. "I asked where Ma Unt was . . . I remembered Ma Unt and was feeling lonely for her. Suddenly I knew that my mother was my previous wife."

Ian Stevenson met the family in 1979, when Maung Tin Win was a young man. Maung Tin Win insisted that nobody had ever told him about his previous life, and he did not dream about it. His family recounted how, when he was a child, he had described his previous life and how he had died. They also reported that he showed various personality and behaviour traits (not particularly attractive ones) which made it feasible that he might be the reincarnation of a man who had lived and died a bandit. As a child he was interested in guns and playing robbers, for example, and later in alcohol and gambling. However, none of these traits need a past life to explain them—his father in his present life was a heavy drinker, for example, and alcoholism is known to be an inherited characteristic. As for his interest in guns, most small boys, however pacific their parents, regard any long stick as a potential kalashnikov.

Perhaps more interestingly, until the age of about ten Maung Tin Win seemed to be very jealous of his father for marrying his previous spouse and unusually hostile and aggressive towards him. In his previous life his present father had been a member of the band insurgents U Thet Tin had led, and the child Maung Tin Win refused to address respectfully someone he said was a subordinate. But perhaps Freud would have an explanation for that.

Two Fishermen's Tales

Many people believe not only that they will be reincarnated but that they have some control over where they will be born again. In some cultures the body of a child who has died is marked in some way, in the expectation that when the child is reincarnated a corresponding mark will be found on the re-born body. Birthmarks serve a similarly useful purpose of identification. So sometimes, Stevenson suggests, someone who dies a natural death and wants to be identified on rein-carnating may draw the attention of relatives to any scars or birthmarks that he may have. There is, after all, little satisfaction in being reborn unless your chosen family recognise and honour you for it.

William George Sr. was a Tlingit fisherman who claimed repeatedly that he would reincarnate as the son of his own favourite son. He had two birthmarks, one on his left shoulder and one on his left forearm, and he predicted that in his next incarnation his body would have the same two birthmarks at the same two places. As a second test, in the summer of 1949 he gave his son a gold watch and asked him to keep it for him, William George, to have after he was reborn. The watch was put away in a jewellery box, where it remained for the next five years.

In August 1949 William George disappeared from the fishing-boat of which he was captain; it was presumed he had fallen overboard and drowned. Soon afterwards his daughter-in-law, Mrs. Reginald George became pregnant. During her labour, she dreamed under anaesthesia that her father-in-law appeared to her and said that he was waiting to see his son, and on 5 May 1950 the baby, William George Jr., was born. It should come as no surprise to any of us that William George Jr. had two prominent birthmarks, one on his left shoulder, one on his left forearm.

Between the ages of three and five William George Jr. said and did several things that suggested to his parents he had some memory of his grandfather's life. The most impressive of these was his recognition of the gold watch when he was about four and a half years old. His mother happened one day to sort through the various objects in her jewellery box and spread them out in her bedroom. William George Jr. picked up the watch and said: "That's my watch." He was very possessive about it, and, in fact, they had some difficulty in persuading him to give it back. From time to time afterwards he would again demand that his parents give him "his watch."

The child also referred to his aunts and uncles as his sons and daughters, and expressed paternal concern about their welfare. Members of the family entered into the spirit of the thing at first and called him "grandfather," but his father eventually decided that his son was becoming too preoccupied with his previous life and discouraged him from talking about it. They noticed other things too. He had a mild phobia of water, which is perhaps unexpected in a reincarnated fisherman, even one who had drowned at sea, and an odd gait, turning his right foot outwards: his grandfather had had an ankle injury as a young man and walked with his right foot turned out in a similar way.

Birthmarks are not inherited, so one cannot argue that the child had simply inherited his grandfather's birthmarks. It is certainly odd that in this one child out of the ten in the family should have been born with a birthmark as if in accordance with the grandfather's prediction. But on the facts as we are given them, the birthmarks form a real stumbling block to belief, largely because there is some doubt about exactly how many birthmarks grandfather had. Reginald George, the old man's son, remembered his father having only one birthmark, though his wife, Mrs. Reginald George, was certain that her father-in-law had had two. This is quite a significant point. Birthmarks are common; by chance two people might each have a birthmark at the same site, but that they should each have *two* corresponding birthmarks raises the odds considerably. Reginald George thought that his father's birthmarks had been slightly raised, whereas the baby's were not. Again, his wife didn't remember this. However, both agreed that the baby's birthmarks were smaller—about half the size—of his grandfather's.

One would be inclined to think that Reginald George

would have had the more intimate knowledge of his own father's skin blemishes. In any case, there must have been some family discussion about the birthmarks if William George Sr. had indeed been so insistent that they would be the means to identify him in his next incarnation. It is odd that Mr. and Mrs. Reginald George could not agree about how many birthmarks there really were.

Mrs. Reginald George seems to have had the most emotion invested in this reincarnation. Her announcing dream of her father-in-law's impending birth suggests that she was very ready to accept her baby in this guise. Given her acceptance, and the fact that it was quite within the cultural norm for grandfather to return in this way, she may well have encouraged the young lad to play father to his uncles and aunts. It was certainly she who allowed young William George to find "his" watch, and if she wanted him to be a reincarnation of his grandfather she must have been sorely tempted at the very least to draw his attention to it among the various contents of her jewellery box. Finally, it was her husband, not she, who finally decided that enough was enough and put a stop to any more talk about reincarnation.

Another case of identification by birthmark also concerns a Tlingit fisherman, Victor Vincent, who died in the spring of 1946. Victor was very fond of his niece, Mrs. Corliss Chotkin, the daughter of his dead sister Gertrude. Victor was convinced that Gertrude had already been reincarnated in the person of the Chotkins' young daughter, and it was with a nice sense of family feeling that he decided he, too, would like to rejoin the family. About a year before he died he said to his niece: "I'm coming back as your next son. I hope I don't stutter then as much as I do now. Your son will have these scars." He then showed her two scars that he had from minor operations, one on his right upper back, the other on the bridge of his nose, the result of an operation to remove the right tear duct.

In the spring of 1946 Victor died. Eighteen months later his niece gave birth to a boy who was named Corliss, after his father. According to his mother, the young Corliss did indeed have two birthmarks at exactly the sites of the two scars on his great-uncle's body.

When Corliss was thirteen months old, his mother was trying to get him to repeat his name. The child said to her: "Don't you know who I am? I'm Kahkody [Victor Vincent's tribal name]." Later he spontaneously recognised several people Victor Vincent had known and also made two statements about events in his great-uncle's life which his mother did not think he could have obtained normally. Corliss Jr. showed other traits that reinforced the family's belief that he was the reincarnation of his great-uncle. He, too, was a stutterer, and, like his uncle, he had a strong interest in boats and in being on the water. Corliss Sr. had no interest in engines, but Victor Vincent had had considerable mechanical skill, and Corliss Jr. had the same ability.

Unfortunately, we can't really regard the birthmarks as providing the sort of clincher this story needs. To begin with, by the time Ian Stevenson came on the scene, when Corliss was fifteen, he was told that both the birthmarks had migrated downwards since the boy's birth. The mark that should have been on the bridge of his nose was now on the lower part of the right side of his nose; the mark on his back had also moved downwards.

We consulted Professor Sam Schuster, Professor of Dermatology at the University of Newcastle, about these apparently mobile birthmarks. He confirmed that birthmarks never migrate, although they may change in size and shape. If the lad's birthmarks were at exactly the sites of his great-uncle's operations when he was born, that is where they would remain.

The mark on the boy's back Ian Stevenson described as particularly interesting because it was "scarlike," "darker than the surrounding skin and slightly raised . . . Its resemblance to the healed scar of a surgical wound was greatly increased by the presence at the sides of the main birthmark of several small round marks that seemed to correspond to positions of the small round wounds made by needles that place the stitches used to close surgical wounds."

Ian Stevenson tried to confirm the presence of the original scars on Victor Vincent, but while he was able to find hospital records of an operation to remove the right tear duct he wasn't able to obtain any medical report that related to the scar on Victor Vincent's back. He did learn that Vincent had

had pulmonary TB of his right lung, and conjectured that the scar might have been the result of some procedure relating to this. But there is no independent evidence that Victor Vincent ever had an operation on his back. We have only the family's unsubstantiated account that this occurred. Some strawberry naevi may look indistinguishable from healed wounds, and it seems most likely that Corliss Jr. had this kind of birthmark on his back, although this type of birthmark often fades in early childhood.

The evidence for reincarnation here looks thin—in fact, almost threadbare. The first problem is the mystery of the migrating birthmarks. The second is the doubt about whether great-uncle ever even had a scar from an operation on his back. The third is the very high expectation within the family that young Corliss would be the incarnation of his great-uncle and would have the birthmarks to prove it. Fourthly, the testimony seems to have emanated largely from the mother, who probably felt under some personal obligation to her uncle to recognise him in this, his next incarnation.

THE JAPANESE SOLDIERS

In his book *Reincarnation and Biology* Ian Stevenson describes four cases of Burmese people who remember a previous life as a Japanese soldier killed in Burma during the Second World War.

Ma Win Tar was born in Upper Burma in 1962. She was born with severe defects of both hands. Several fingers were missing; others were only loosely attached to her hands and had to be amputated. Around her left wrist were three depressions, which looked as though a rope had been tightly wound around her arm.

Ma Win Tar began to talk when she was about eighteen months old, and when she was about three began to talk about a previous life as a Japanese soldier. As she grew older she became fervent in her insistence that she was Japanese and started to behave in a way that seemed more appropriate to this previous life than to her present life as a young Burmese girl. She liked to dress like a boy and keep her hair short. She complained that Burmese food was too spicy and refused to eat it, preferring sweet foods and pork. She also had a streak of cruelty which is said to be rare in Burmese children. She would slap the faces of her playmates—something apparently typical of the behaviour of Japanese soldiers but which the Burmese rarely do. She was also said to be relatively insensitive to pain and more hard-working than most Burmese children.

Ma Win Tar's memories of her previous life included being captured by some Burmese villagers, tied to a tree and burned alive. Although Ma Win Tar has no memory of her fingers being damaged, Stevenson suggests that a soldier resisting capture might well put his hands up to ward off a blow, so that his fingers might well have been struck by a sword. But that can only be conjecture.

Maung Aung Htoo first spoke of his life as a Japanese soldier when he was just over three years old. Like many other Burmese subjects of Stevenson, he tended to think about his past life more on cloudy days than on sunny ones. He preferred to wear shirt and trousers and boots rather than the traditional longyi (a cloth tied around the waist) and sandals. Like Ma Win Tar he had a Japanese taste in food, disliked the traditional spicy Burmese food, preferring sweet foods, and liked to eat raw or partly cooked fish and meat. And, like her, he was hard-working and relatively insensitive to pain. He had the same prominent streak of cruelty, liked hunting and killing small animals, and would slap and kick his younger brothers. He seemed to be hostile towards Burmese people and rejected Buddhism.

Maung Aung Htoo had deformed hands and feet—birth defects attributed to his memory that he was murdered by mutinous soldiers of his own unit, who tied him to a tree and tortured him by chopping off his fingers and toes. This is unusual; most Burmese who remember being Japanese say they were tortured by Burmese villagers, and this method of torture is one that was more characteristic of the Burmese than the Japanese.

Another of these past-life Japanese, Ma Win Yee, showed no Japanese behaviour traits—her only unusual behaviour was a preference for strong tea (the Burmese like to drink very weak tea, the Japanese, in general, drink strong tea). She was feminine, and showed no desire to look, dress or behave like a boy. She did, however, have deformed hands and feet, and this was attributed to her past-life memory of being tortured, before being killed, by having her fingers and toes chopped off.

The fourth case is that of Maung Hla Hsaung, born with deformed hands and feet. When he was not yet three he started to refer to a previous life in Japan. He spoke in a "strange language" for a time, but then learned Burmese normally. He explained the defects of his hands and feet as the results of torture after he had been captured. As a child he would sometimes ask for money so that he could go to Japan. And he, too, showed many of the "Japanese" traits described in the first two cases—a liking for long trousers instead of the Burmese longyi, a preference for sweet foods, a certain insensitivity to pain and a tendency to cruelty towards insects, though not humans. Unlike his two brothers, he liked to play at being a soldier when he was a child.

If we simply look at the data Stevenson presents, quite independently of the family and the culture in which it has been collected, then this combination of past-life memories and the physical evidence of the birthmarks do seem to make a good case for reincarnation. Unfortunately, we can't consider the data in isolation. The cases he describes occurred in a culture where reincarnation is accepted as a fact, and where birthmarks and birth defects are regarded as strong evidence for it. One can easily imagine the mother of a child born with a birth defect discussing this with friends and family, wondering about the possibility that it might have occurred as the result of something that had happened in a previous life. The child would inevitably hear such discussions even if he did not fully understand them. The family would unwittingly allocate the child a role, and the child would be likely to act out that role in subsequent behaviour—thus confirming the family's belief. We have to wonder whether the birthmark is the result of a past life or vice versa—that the parents assume that there must be a past life to explain the birthmark and set out to find or create one that fits. Certainly, we have not come across accounts ftom other cultures of children who have birth defects and corresponding past-life memories to explain them. But this may, of course, simply be because no one has looked for them.

We could only really test this hypothesis by finding children from these cultures who had birth defects but had been adopted at birth into a different culture. If, in the absence of family and cultural reinforcement, such children produced past-life memories that seemed to explain their defects, it would go a long way to confirming Stevenson's theory.

Violent death is a recurring theme in a great many of these cases. In fact, it figured so prominently in the cases Ian Stevenson studied that he feels such a death must play an important part both in the occurrence of recovered past-life memories and in that of birthmarks and birth defects. Violence, he says, may act through concentrating attention and fixing memories.

Whenever he investigated such cases, Ian Stevenson tried to verify claims that a birthmark corresponded to a wound acquired in a previous life by examining the medical records of the dead person. A single birthmark may not be very convincing. But Stevenson describes several instances of people who claimed to remember a previous life in which they had died by shooting, and had birthmarks corresponding to both the entrance and exit holes of the bullets that had killed them. The odds against this happening by chance are, he says, only 1 in 25,000. One such case is that of Cemil Fahrici.

REINCARNATION OF A BANDIT

Cemil was born in Turkey in 1935. The night before his birth his father had dreamed that a distant relative, Cemil Hayik, entered the house. Cemil Hayik had been a bandit, on the run since killing two men who had raped his sisters. Just a few days earlier, Cemil Hayik had reached the end of the line; surrounded by police and with no hope of escape, he had placed the muzzle of his gun beneath his chin and pulled the trigger.

The dream convinced the parents that the bandit Cemil would be reborn as their son and, indeed, when he was born they noticed a prominent birthmark on the right beneath his chin, a scar-like area that bled for a few days and required stitching in hospital. On the left side of the top of his head was

a second birthmark, a hairless area about 0.8 inches long by
0.08 inches wide (2 centimetres by 2 millimetres). These
marks corresponded to the entrance and exit holes of the bullet that had killed Cemil. From the time he was two, the child
began to talk about his life and death as Cemil Hayik, and
until he was six or seven used to have nightmares about fighting the police. Although he had been christened "Dahham,"
the boy refused to be called by any other name but Cemil. He
developed a markedly hostile attitude towards the police and
would throw stones at them, and he once tried to take his father's rifle and shoot some soldiers with it.

The biggest barrier to belief in this case is the timing. A
baby is most vulnerable to any kind of damage during the period its major organs and systems are being formed—which is
largely during the first three months of pregnancy. Birthmarks
are developmental abnormalities in the skin. The skin is one
of the earliest body organs to develop—in fact, by the third
month of pregnancy a baby's skin will already be growing
hair and nails. By the end of pregnancy, any birthmarks or
birth defects will be long established. And yet it was only a
few days before the baby's birth that Cemil shot himself,
causing the wounds that were supposedly reproduced in the
baby's birthmarks.

One rational explanation would be that the relationship between the birthmarks and the wounds occurred by chance,
that there is no causal relationship between the two. Once
they had seen the birthmarks, however, the family would be
almost bound to make the connection, and the scene would
then be set for the child to play out his expected role as Cemil
reborn. Another possible explanation is that the facts of the
case became distorted over time so that by the time Stevenson
met the family, some years after Cemil's birth, there had been
some rewriting of history.

But assuming that the facts are indeed as reported by
Stevenson, the only way, using our current scientific understanding, that we can link Cemil's death, apparent rebirth and
the birthmarks is through a parapsychological explanation.
We would have to say either that the child's developmental
blueprint had some foreknowledge of Cemil's future death
and rebirth, which caused the birthmarks to develop, or that

Cemil "chose" this particular baby to be reborn into because it had already developed the appropriate birthmarks. We have to remember, too, that Cemil was a *distant* relative, not someone who might perhaps have close psychic ties to the family. Does it seem feasible?

Even more spectacular, and more convincing, was the case of Necip Unlutaskiran, a child born with seven birthmarks who remembered a previous life as a man who had died of multiple stab wounds in corresponding places.

Necip was born in Turkey in 1951. Some time before his birth his mother had a dream in which she saw a man she did not know standing before her with bleeding wounds. This dream seemed to make sense to her when she saw, after her son was born, that he had seven birthmarks.

Unlike most children who remember previous lives, Necip was a late talker, and it wasn't until he was six that he started to tell his mother that he had lived in Mersin, a city about 50 miles (80 kilometres) from his home, that his name then had also been Necip, and that he had been stabbed. As he described the stabbing, he pointed to various parts of his body to indicate the stab wounds. He also began to ask his mother to take him to see "his" children in his previous home.

At first his parents paid little attention to his story. But when he was about twelve years old his mother took him to meet her father, and Necip met, for the first time, his grandfather's second wife. To everyone's astonishment, Necip suddenly said that he recognised her as someone he had met in his previous life. This woman said that she had indeed known a man in Mersin named Necip Budak, a quarrelsome type who had died after being repeatedly stabbed in a drunken brawl.

On the strength of this, Necip's grandfather agreed to take him to Mersin, where he recognised several members of the family of Necip Budak, who confirmed Necip's statements about his previous life. The most convincing of Necip's claims was that "his" (Necip Budak's) wife had a scar on her leg, the result of a stab wound he had once given her. Necip Budak's wife admitted this and is said to have shown a scar on her thigh to other people, though whether Ian Stevenson himself saw this is not made clear. Ian Stevenson did not meet

Necip Unlutaskiran until he was thirteen, by which time a few of his birthmarks had faded. Stevenson did, however, see the hospital notes made when Necip Budak was admitted after the stabbing, and was able to confirm that six of the birthmarks did indeed correspond to stab wounds.

It's very difficult for the sceptic to find a way out of this case if the facts are as reported. There is the correlation between the multiple stab wounds and the birthmarks. There is the family's reluctance to accept the story. And finally there is the confirmation of Necip's statements about his previous life, about which there seems to have been no previous family knowledge. The best the sceptic could do is to argue for multiple coincidences, which in this instance makes a very weak case.

It is interesting that one of the few instances in the West where a birthmark has been cited as evidence of reincarnation does not follow the pattern of most of Stevenson's cases, in which birthmarks usually represented past-life injuries that were either fatal or at least caused by extreme violence, usually at the time of death. This is the case of the Pollock twins, whose parents believed them to be the reincarnations of their two older daughters, killed in a tragic accident (see page 228). The twin Jennifer was identified as the reincarnation of Jacqueline largely because when she was born her father noticed that she had a birthmark on her forehead, just above her right eye. It was in this very same place that Jacqueline had had a scar, the result of an accident when she was three years old and had fallen and hit her face on a bucket.

Jacqueline was six when she died—three years after this incident, which is a long time in a small child's life; long enough for her to have recovered, long enough for it to be more or less forgotten. It seems odd that this relatively minor injury should have been perpetuated in a subsequent life, especially when one remembers that she received horrific injuries in the accident in which she met her death. If Jennifer were to bear any mark at all which related to a previous life as Jacqueline, why did it not relate to the injuries that caused her death?

Ian Stevenson has also suggested that Jennifer's birthmark

is significant because Gillian, her identical twin with an identical genetic make-up, did not have a similar birthmark. But identical twins do not have identical birthmarks—birthmarks (as opposed to some birth defects) are developmental and have no genetic basis. Identical twins are no more likely to have similar birthmarks than any other two siblings.

If we are even to begin to accept Stevenson's suggestion that birthmarks may be indications of injury in a past life, we have to explain how marks acquired during the lifetime of one body might be passed on to another. The genes provide the only mechanism of inheritance that we know of, and the genes do not allow for the inheritance of characteristics acquired during an individual's life. Lamarckism, the theory of evolution that did allow for this by suggesting that, for example, the giraffe's long neck evolved because the animal continually had to stretch to reach the tops of trees, is now largely rejected as a serious scientific hypothesis, though it surfaces occasionally on a folklore level, as it seems to have done in this case. And even that hypothesis would not explain those cases in which there is no relationship between the two people involved: for example, the case of Necip, described above. In almost half of the cases Ian Stevenson has studied, the two families concerned lived far apart, had never met and had no knowledge of each other. Even Lamarckism could not explain how a member of one family could have inherited characteristics acquired by another.

We have to remember that most of the cases Ian Stevenson has studied are from cultures where parents often expect their child to be a reincarnation of some family member, and look for proof in the form of birthmarks, birth defects or announcing dreams. When such a child talks about a past life, how do we know that he has not simply picked up the information about his past personality in the normal way from his parents, even if they have not intentionally fed it to him?

Stevenson and Jorgen Keil, a psychologist at the University of Tasmania who has studied past-life memories in a group of children in Turkey, Thailand and Burma, both claim that there is some indirect evidence that this doesn't necessarily happen. They cite the "silent cases"—the children who don't claim past-life memories despite the strong belief of their parents that they have been reincarnated. In these cases there is no evidence from the children for reincarnation, only the belief of the parents that it has occurred. Clearly, these cases are quite different from those in which the child has a past-life memory. However, their interest lies in the fact that some children will not take on board their parents' beliefs about reincarnation. Stevenson estimated that about 12 perent of his 225 cases were "silent"; Keil found rather fewer—5 percent of "silent" children in a group of 112 cases. Keil found nothing in these children's personalities which would explain why they were less likely to talk about past lives even though they were expected to do so.

Ian Stevenson believes that he has found many cases in which there is indisputable correspondence between wounds or birthmarks on a deceased person and birthmarks and other features (including statements about a previous life) of a child. One explanation he advances is reincarnation. But he considers alternative hypotheses too. One is that the birth-marks occurred by chance and that the child acquired his claimed memories through extrasensory perception. How-ever, he has found no evidence that any of these children show any paranormal ability at any other time.

Stevenson has also suggested that attention concentrated on a part of the body before death in a previous life may be a factor in generating birthmarks and birth defects in the present life. He cites the case of a child, Ruvan Ranatunga, who had a very deformed left ear. Ruvan Ranatunga remembered the previous life of Sampath, a child who had also had an abnor-mality of the left ear. Sampath's mother had tried repeatedly to reshape his ear into a normal form by massaging it. This undue concentration on the ear must, Stevenson concludes, have focused so much of Sampath's attention on that organ that the deformity was generated again in his next incarnation. In essence this is no different from his argument that the marks of a violent death can be reproduced in a subsequent body because of the attention focused on them at that time.

An alternative explanation Stevenson considers is that of "maternal impressions"—the theory that images in a pregnant woman's mind can have a physical effect on her unborn child. We know that beliefs and mental images about the body can induce the physical changes known as stigmata. Suggestible people can develop stigmata under hypnosis as well as by self-inducing them at will. Under hypnosis, it is possible to suggest to someone that a cold penny placed on their palm is red-hot, and a weal and blister characteristic of a burn will develop under it. One gifted sensitive, Olga Kahn, has even been able to self-induce stigmata through telepathy. Various researchers conducted telepathy experiments with her in which a "target" image (a letter or simple design) was transmitted telepathically to her, and an image approximating to this (she sometimes made mistakes or produced a distorted image) would appear as red lines on the skin of her arm and upper part of her chest.

In 1946 a London psychiatrist, Dr. Robert Moody, published in the *British Medical Journal* the account of Alec, a twenty-six-year-old army officer serving in India four years before the outbreak of the Second World War. While he was in hospital for a minor infection, it was discovered that he repeatedly walked in his sleep. To prevent him injuring himself, the nurses sometimes tied his hands behind his back while he slept. In spite of this he managed to slip away one night and wandered around the countryside.

Alec's sleepwalking grew worse and was sometimes accompanied by aggressive behaviour for which he had no memory when he awoke. He was admitted to a psychiatric unit for observation, and one night was seen to thresh about for an hour as if trying to free himself from imaginary bonds. He then crept out of the hospital, with his hands held behind his back as if they were still tied. But even more astonishing was the fact that when Alec returned to the ward deep weals could be seen on his arms, as if he had, in fact, been bound tightly by ropes. The matter was reported to the consultant in charge, Dr. Moody, who decided to watch the patient himself one night. Exactly the same thing happened, and this time Dr. Moody saw deep indentations appearing on both Alec's forearms, and finally oozing small quantities of fresh blood. Even the next morning the marks were still clear enough to show up in photographs.

An impressive case of induced stigmata was described by Morton Schatzman in his book *The Story of Ruth*. Ruth was a young woman with a gift for creating very strong mental imagery that appeared to her as external hallucinations. She could make the hallucination slap her, and red fingermarks in the form of weals would appear on her skin. She could hallucinate her daughter putting hallucinatory hands over her eyes, and then, when a light was flashed into her eyes, her brain would respond as if she were in fact unable to see it. If Ruth hallucinated biting into a lemon, her mouth would pour saliva, but if she merely *thought* about eating it, then the saliva would scarcely flow.

We know, then, that the mind has an extraordinary ability to influence the body. Stigmata may develop, blisters be raised by suggestion, wounds revived by vivid memories. The mechanism of transfer of imagery from the brain to the body surface is thought to be by the autonomic nervous system. But the action of the autonomic nervous system so far as we know does not cross the placenta. So it is much more difficult to understand and explain how a mother's mental images can cause physical changes in her baby's body, which is what the theory of "maternal impression" suggests.

In *Reincarnation and Biology* Ian Stevenson describes several cases where there is an almost identical correspondence between a sight seen by a pregnant woman and a subsequent deformity in her child. He quotes, for example, a woman whose brother's hand was torn off by machinery and his forearm later amputated above the wrist: her baby was later born with a congenital deformity of the same arm, the hand and forearm absent.

Unfortunately, virtually all of the cases he describes occurred in the nineteenth or very early twentieth centuries, when knowledge of the causes of birth defects was more limited. The only relatively modern case quoted dates from 1949 and concerns a woman who saw a man with only one external ear (the other having been cut off by a sword during the war) when she was only one to two months pregnant. She later gave birth to a baby with a congenitally absent left external ear. The French physician who delivered the baby also knew the soldier whose ear had been cut off. His report did not, unfortunately, mention which of the unlucky man's ears had been lost.

The belief that if a pregnant woman sustains a severe shock or sees a distressing sight, then this can somehow affect her unborn baby and produce some mark or defect, is one of the oldest old wives' tales in the business. One can understand why a mother coming to terms with a deformed child and looking for an explanation should attribute the deformity to her own experience. But in the West maternal impression is a notion that has been subject to general medical derision for several centuries. There is no known mechanism by which mental imagery could be transmitted from a woman to her unborn child. And while the number of women who suffer traumatic events or see distressing sights during pregnancy must be considerable, the number of major birth defects and birthmarks is relatively small and constant—about two percent. If there really is any substance in the theory, it is hard to explain why no more modern cases have been published, or why no papers have been published to suggest an increased incidence of such cases after a major catastrophe or war where large numbers of women must have seen horrific sights. However, we can't be certain that there is no correlation until we actually look for it: for example, by doing a prospective study in, say, Bosnia or Ruanda, to correlate birth defects with prior exposure to such incidents.

However, there are at least one or two reports in modern times which suggest that the power of the mind may have played at least some part in the causation of a birth defect. One of these was intriguing enough even to have made its way into tha astion of medical respectability, *The Lancet*. The case concerns a sixteen-year-old Australian girl who, in an effort to gain parental consent for her marriage to a man they strongly disapproved of, became pregnant by him. Far from giving her blessing, the enraged mother cursed her daughter, saying that if she continued with the pregnancy the baby would be born without arms and legs, and blind. Several people witnessed the cursing, which took place during the fifth or sixth week of the pregnancy and was then repeated in letters to the hapless daughter every two or three weeks for the rest of the pregnancy. When the baby was finally born, its lower limbs were absent, and only a small part of the right arm was present. The left arm was normal, but the left hand had only two fingers and the thumb.

In this case the timing at least was right—the cursing occurred during the first trimester of pregnancy, the time when a baby is most vulnerable to damage. The physician who reported the case, Dr. Elizabeth Turner, found no factor other than the stress induced in the woman by her own mother's curse. Clearly, straightforward explanations won't do, but current scientific data, which shows that prayer (in the sense of a positive intention to heal at a distance) can influence people at a distance even though they do not know they are being prayed for, could be applied in this case. All the studies relate to positive intention, but there is no reason why a negative intention might not be as effective, and in this case the mother's will could be directly imposed on the developing fetus.

In Sri Lanka Ian Stevenson found another, very similar case of curse-induced deformity. In August 1980 a young Sri Lankan woman, Leelawathie, and her husband Sompala gave birth to a son, Sampath Priyasantha. He was born without any arms and with severe deformities (talipes) of both feet. Stevenson was sent photographs of the baby and decided to go to investigate, but unfortunately the little boy had died before Stevenson could reach the remote village in which the family lived. The child was about twenty months old when he died, and just beginning to speak, but he had said nothing that suggested he remembered a past life.

Indeed, the parents themselves did not mention it either, and it was left to Stevenson himself to raise the subject. "It occurred to me that Sampath might have been the reincarnation of someone known to his family who had died after having his arms badly injured, perhaps in an industrial accident. I therefore asked the baby's father whether he knew of anyone who had died after having his arms injured."

The man's reply perhaps explains his unusual reluctance to cite reincarnation as an explanation for his son's deformities. "Yes," he replied. "There was a man I killed by cutting off his arms and legs with a sword."

We needn't be too horrified at this admittedly rough justice. The murdered man, Yasapula, was a notorious bully from what we can only regard as a dysfunctional family. His brother described to Ian Stevenson how he personally had killed three of his family's enemies and how their own father had died when a bomb he was preparing slipped out of his hands and blew him to pieces. The murder of Yasapula had been precipitated over a quarrel about the murdered man's dog, which had strayed on to the property of Sampath's father and eaten some food. Sampath's father, with the aid of his own brothers, had got their victim drunk and then cut off his arms and legs (some slight exaggeration here: the postmortem report, according to Stevenson, described the limbs as "dangling" rather than actually severed).

The murdered man's mother was outraged. She repeatedly cursed the murderer and his family. Stevenson's informants differed about the exact nature of the curse, but the baby's mother certainly believed that she had been told that she would have a deformed baby.

If this were a case of reincarnation, there is an odd logic and an odder sense of justice about it. Would Yasapula have chosen (if there is considered to be any choice in the manner of one's rebirth) to be reborn to the family that had butchered him so cruelly in his previous life? Certainly, Yasapula's own family regarded Sampath's birth as just retribution to Sompala for killing Yasapula, but they didn't consider that Yasapula had been reborn as Sampath. Yasapula's mother, Ian Stevenson says, could not accept the possibility that her son, who had "done nothing," should be condemned to reincarnation in a deformed body. In this case a more plausible explanation than reincarnation, he suggests, might be maternal impression, which implies that Sampath's mother saw the mutilated body and this imprinted itself on the developing child by some parapsychological mechanism. If we are to assume a parapsychological mechanism, though, perhaps even more plausible is the possibility that the curse of Yasapula's mother did indeed affect the developing fetus, as apparently happened in the previous case.

In summary, Stevenson suggests that the physical form of a dead person can influence the form of a living and often unrelated person who seems to be his reincarnation and may have memories of his life. He suggests that these past-life memories are carried by some intermediate vehicle (he calls this the *psychospore* to avoid using a term with any religious connotations) between death and presumed rebirth.

He has no explanation of why, if reincarnation does occur, only a few people remember a previous life. Although he believes that violent death figures so prominently in the cases he has studied that it may play a part both in the occurrence of past-life memories and of birthmarks and birth defects, some of the instances he gives do not seem to merit the description "violent." He cites, for example, the case of someone who had red medicine spilled on his face while he was dying, who was reborn with a red birthmark on his face. There are also many cases, such as that of the Pollock twins, where a violent death is remembered, and there are birthmarks that are thought to correspond to much more trivial injuries.

For Stevenson, birthmarks provide valuable extra evidence to support the possibility of reincarnation. But for many people they simply add an extra barrier to belief. Reincarnation already implies acceptance of some as yet unknown method by which memory can survive death and be transmitted to another brain within another body. That physical characteristics, too, can survive death and be transmitted to another physical body is for many people beyond the boggle threshold.

16

The Psi Hypothesis

Eternity is a terrible thought. I mean, where's it going to end?

Tom Stoppard

IAN Stevenson's work on birthmarks and birth defects is important because, whether it succeeds or not, it is a valiant attempt to forge a scientific link between persistence of memory and persistence of personal identity—something which is essential if "proof" of reincarnation is ever to be found. Without such a link, all we are left with are memories. Can these ever be evidence enough for the persistence of individual identity? Martin Gardner examines the question of persistence of identity in *The Whys of a Philosophical Scrivener* and quotes John Locke's *Essay Concerning Human Understanding*:

> For Locke, persistence of memory is the basis for persistence in time of a person's identity, and this is independent of whatever material substances make up the body. If he could recall Noah's Ark and the Flood as vividly as he recalls having seen the Thames overflow its banks last summer, Locke writes, he would assume it was he himself who had once occupied a body in Noah's time.

This sounds persuasive, and yet Locke's assumption fails on two counts. First, we have seen how untrustworthy even the

most vividly recalled memories can be, and, secondly, even if
we accept that these are genuine memories of a past life, does
persistence of memory inevitably imply persistence of personal identity?

The experiences described in this book are memories. The
people who have them seem to be aware of past events, usually through "visions," sometimes in dreams. Often the vision
is evoked by an encounter with a particular person or place.
Sometimes these events can be explained rationally; occasionally they seem to be beyond the range of any existing scientific explanation. But even if we look for a possible
paranormal explanation, does that explanation have to be
reincarnation?

Apparent past-life memories may or may not have anything to do with reincarnation. Alternative, non-scientific
theories might explain the phenomenon of past-life memories equally well, though this is not to say that they would
confirm that reincarnation is a fact, let alone suggest a mechanism for it.

There is now considerable scientific evidence (sum-
marised very well in Dean Radin's book *The Conscious Universe*) that parapsychological—psi—effects such as telepathy
(the effect of mind on other minds), psychokinesis (the effect
of mind on matter) and precognition (the ability of mind to
gain information across time) do occur. As yet we can't understand or explain them, let alone fit them into any coherent
model of the human mind. At present they still remain outside
the main body of scientific knowledge.

It is never satisfactory to explain away one set of phenomena we don't understand by invoking another set of phenomena we don't understand. Nevertheless, philosopher Stephen
Braude has argued that an equally plausible explanation for
the fact that some people seem to remember past lives is that
they are people who have very special paranormal abilities.
They acquire their memories through a form of "super-psi,"
that is, through a combination of parapsychological effects
such as telepathy and precognition.

Parapsychological experiments have recognised characteristics. To begin with, they are not repeatable in the way that is
usually demanded by science. Quite often an experiment

starts positively and then the effect decays with repetition. This is not surprising because parapsychological experiments involve consciousness, and one of the important aspects of consciousness is motivation. As people become bored or their motivation changes during an experiment, the results of the experiment are likely to alter. Secondly, the experimenter has an effect on the experiment. And, thirdly, there is what is known as a "sheep/goat" effect—that is, some people can and others cannot carry out the experiment successfully. If parapsychological phenomena are involved in past-life memories, these characteristics might provide one explanation for why it is that only a few people (usually those who already have some belief, or motivation to believe, in reincarnation) experience these memories.

Psychic phenomena are well known to occur independently of time. It is possible to influence an event that has already taken place, providing the outcome of that event is not known to anybody. For example, it is possible to change the distribution of numbers generated by a computer after they have been generated, providing they have not been looked at. From our scientific knowledge of parapsychological events, we can postulate that memories of a past life are nothing but the picking up of events that have already occurred in the past and experiencing them in the present. Reincarnation need not enter the picture. And this theory does seem to fit the fact that such memories don't seem to be available as continuous experiences over long periods of time but as a series of highlights picked out of a life.

Another explanation that is often advanced for people's apparent ability to acquire knowledge of the past is telepathy. Telepathy was suggested as an explanation for the strange collective memory of Arthur Guirdham's group of reincarnated Cathars (see page 152), for example, with Guirdham himself unwittingly transmitting his own knowledge of the Cathars to other members of the group.

In the case of the Cathars, at any rate, several things make this improbable. Even if we assume for the moment that there is unequivocal evidence that telepathy exists (and there is accumulating evidence that it does) it is still a pretty ineffective means of communication. Among the Cathars a great deal of information was accurately transmitted. It would have necessitated mind-reading on a heroic scale to achieve quite so many telepathic buff's-eyes—more than even the best telepathic subjects have managed to produce. Telepathic information seems most usually to be transmitted as flashes, or images, often only approximate. The acquisition of such a wealth of detailed knowledge as the Arthur Guirdham group displayed is so far unprecedented in psi research.

Secondly, we would have to assume that the Guirdham Cathars, as a group, had astoundingly good telepathic ability. Not everybody has, and in fact those laboratories that have carried out serious experiments on telepathy have found that people who are consistently successful ESP subjects are very rare. To find a whole group of people who could communicate happily in this way stretches credulity to snapping-point.

Ian Stevenson has considered the possibility that some of the children he has studied who feel they have had past lives might have picked up information about a previous personality through ESP, but he has found no evidence that they have done so. He argues that if it were through ESP that these children had picked up information about a previous personality, there is no reason why their ESP should be limited only to this. One would expect them to show evidence of telepathy or precognition in their ordinary, present life, and they do not.

Nevertheless, the majority of convincing past-life memories are experienced as the kind of isolated flashes of imagery which are characteristic of telepathy. There is certainly some evidence of a link between belief in reincarnation and psychic experiences. Haraldsson and Houtkooper, in a multinational survey of human values, found that a belief in reincarnation was one of the best predictors of psychic experiences. Certainly, of the adults in our own sample who remembered past lives, a great many also believe that they are psychic or sensitive in other ways. Kathleen Cliff (see page 110), for example claims that she often sees events before they happen as did her mother and grandmother. K. Holsman (see page 101) had precognitive dreams about Gandhi's assassination on two consecutive nights, five days before the assassination took place. Mrs. Elizabeth Royce has had two very detailed past-life experiences (see page 182). She is a healer who has had psychic experiences since she was a child and says that many of the healers she knows have also had past-life memories. Barbara Conduitt, an American who has lived in England for twenty-five, has often experienced episodes of thought transference with her sister in America. If thoughts can be transmitted between two people separated by 4,000 miles (6,450 kilometres), might this not, she wonders, happen also across time? She feels that some of her own past-life memories might be explained in this way. Barbara has memories of two past lives, the first of which is described on page 23. Of the second, she says:

> My second life is that of a man living in London. He's a fat, happy man, wearing a wig (with lice or fleas under it), riding down a busy street in a carriage. There are crowds of people on the streets and he's excited and happy about his journey. He sits in the corner of the carriage, which is open-topped, leaning his right arm on the top of the carriage and waving his left about. I know he's fat because I can see his pudgy legs, crossed, and see a red ribbon tied around the top of his trousers, which end at the knee. He is wearing white hose and shiny shoes.
>
> Bless him, he's a cheery soul, and I meet him almost every time I go to London! There are certain areas of the City (mostly around the Embankment) that I can feel the lice itching under my wig, and I find myself sitting in the exact way he sits. That's how I became aware of him. It has happened so many times—each time in a little more detail. He is so happy. I'd love to know why—and where he is headed.

Researching the family tree, Barbara's sister discovered an ancestor, one Thomas Larkin, periwig-maker, who lived in London in the seventeenth century. Was this, Barbara wondered, her "cheery soul"? And if so, might her apparent memories of him be due not to reincarnation but to thought transference?

Stewart Paxton often has strong flashes of a previous life as an eighteenth-century French landowner (his final memory is of seeing the sun glinting on the guillotine blade that was to end his life). He, too, says that he has some psychic ability: "I can see, psychically in some people, their past lives, their anxieties, and can offer psychic help."

Sarah David (pseudonym) says that she is a spiritual person who likes to look into all aspects of the unknown, and is psychic in the way she senses things and gets premonitions. She has often felt that she has met someone or been to a particular place before:

> One such strange incident was when I was visiting a friend in Fulham. I met him at his office, which is on the corner of a road which felt familiar. The actual interior of the office felt even more familiar. I kept getting a peculiar feeling about the place having been something like a shop before and that I had been there many times. But the oddest thing was a familiar warm, musky, delicious smell that I seemed to catch from time to time (sort of downwind) but that no one else could smell. I couldn't really work out what it could be and forgot all about it.
>
> A couple of weeks later I went into a baker's in Wimbledon Village with my sister and recognised the same smell. I told my friend when I saw him again what the odour I had experienced in his office had been like. He told me that at one time many years ago there had been a baker's shop there, where they had baked all their bread on the premises all day and night long. After making some enquiries I found out that the shop had been built some time early this century and was knocked down some twenty years ago. It was quite the strangest thing.

Heather Charles had a past-life experience (see page 98) and also recounts the following experience which she had one morning in 1987:

> I sensed a terrible earthquake one morning as if it were about to happen in my bedroom. The hair on the back of my neck stood up. I looked at the window and felt as

if a pressure wave were building up and the window would implode. I thought the house may be about to be hit by lightning, and I decided to dash downstairs quickly. As I moved, the oppressive atmosphere and the shaking of the floor ceased. I looked out and all was normal. I questioned my neighbours about thunder and any strange sensations they may have had in their homes that morning: everything was normal to them. It worried me all day, and later that day we heard on the news about the earthquake in Los Angeles and the descriptions of the earthquake with windows imploding was the same as the sensory experience I'd had that morning.

For many people ideas of "super-psi" or telepathy are probably easier to believe than the idea of reincarnation. A. J. Ayer writes in *The Concept of a Person and Other Essays* (page 127):

> ... even if someone could convince us that he ostensibly remembered the experiences of a person long since dead, and ... this were backed by an apparent continuity of character, I think that we should prefer to say that he had somehow picked up the dead man's memories and dispositions rather than that he was the same person in another body: the idea of a person's leading a discontinuous existence in time as well as space is just that much more fantastic.

THE COSMIC MEMORY BANK

A different approach to the puzzle of past-life memories is to postulate a kind of cosmic memory bank in which all life experiences are recorded and into which any living mind can tap. If this were done without the person being consciously aware that he or she was doing so, the memories would seem to be personal memories of a previous life.

This is an attractive theory, as it fits in with our everyday perception of time as flowing only one way. Again, the problem is that we lack a mechanism. We can't explain how the memories of thoughts, feelings, emotions are stored, as these are usually considered to be evanescent and transient. Neither do we know of any way in which events long in the past could be accessed and extracted from the memory store. We need a theory that could explain the possibility that mind can exist or memories be stored outside brain processes.

Such theories do exist. The first group are the "field theories," which suggest that there is in the universe some "field force" that links individual minds. Jung's concept of the collective unconscious is one such field theory. He suggested that part of the mind exists beyond individual brains and is a reservoir of human experience inherited from ancestors and contributed to by the current generation, independent of time and place.

A universe with this kind of structure has also been suggested by biochemist and cell biologist Rupert Sheldrake in his theory of morphic resonance. Sheldrake's theory has the advantage that it does not differ violently from our current world view. He suggests that there is a field, which he calls the morphogenetic field, which interpenetrates the universe, is beyond time and space, and exists everywhere at once. Matter in widely separated areas can therefore be influenced by the field. He suggests that information relating to a pattern of behaviour can be transmitted from the brain to the morphogenetic field and modify it. The field in turn will modify other, similar brains so that they become more likely to reproduce this particular pattern of behaviour. The more similar the forms, the greater will be the resonance. Morphogenesis could explain why scientists in different laboratories who have no contact with each other often tend to make the same discoveries at more or less the same time.

Morphogenesis would also provide a mechanism whereby individual experiences in some way come to modify the structure of the morphogenetic field. If memories (information) are held in this way they would exist independently of the brain and therefore be accessible to another brain which "resonated" with them. Although this theory does not suggest that personal consciousness need necessarily continue, with a slight modification of the theory it is likely that a mechanism for the continuation of personal consciousness after death could be postulated.

Is this theory (which at the moment is just a theory with no real evidence to support it) any more successful than a theory of reincarnation in accounting for apparent past-life memories? It could explain how it is that occasionally more than one person remembers the same past life (though such duplicated memories are usually those of some famous or notorious person, which makes them dubious). It could also explain why young children who remember a past life remember it only as a child, not as an adult. There is considerable structural difference between the brains of a child and an adult, and it seems unlikely that the brain of any two-year-old can have such "structural similarities" with the brain of a deceased adult as to induce "morphic resonance." Presumably, a child's brain "resonates" more easily with the brain of another child, although we don't know what "resonate" really means.

The theory would also explain why most past-life memories have a "snapshot" quality. It would certainly explain telepathy, because if past-life memories are accessible via a morphogenetic field, memories from living individuals should be accessible in exactly the same way. Telepathy seems particularly to exist between people who are empathic to each other and whose brains might therefore be supposed to "resonate" with each other.

However, it wouldn't explain why only a very few people pick up memories in this way, or why some children (Shanti Devi, page 11, for example) who have past-life memories do remember life as an adult. Neither would it satisfactorily explain the very few cases such as Laurel Dilmen, the Spanish Antonia (page 129), where the past-life experience has continuity and detail which give it the quality of a continuous life rather than of isolated random snapshots of memory. For the "best" cases of past-life memory, reincarnation is probably a better explanation than morphic resonance.

THEORIES OF DISCARNATE MINDS

One serious problem about accepting telepathy as an explanation for acquired knowledge is that telepathy requires a sender as well as a receiver. The knowledge has to be transmitted by someone living, unless one takes a further step away from rationality and postulates possession by a dead person in the form of a discarnate personality. In essence, invasion by a discarnate entity is the same as reincarnation, except that the "invasion" of the body takes place after birth rather than at birth or before it. There is no logical reason to consider possession as a quite different phenomenon from reincarnation.

If we assume that some part of a human being, which we call "soul" or "spirit," exists independently of the physical body, then memory of a previous existence can be attributed to this "spirit" rather than to the physical brain of its current human body. But in making this assumption we enter tiger country, tracking anecdote rather than evidence. There are many anecdotal accounts, for example, of out-of-body experiences during the near-death experience, when people feel that "they" (their soul or spirit) have separated from their body and been able to see themselves and their surroundings from some vantage-point outside their body. Several prospective studies are taking place to test this in hospital theatres or intensive-care units to see how many patients who have been resuscitated after being near death report leaving their body, and whether those who do can indeed gain information that they could not have got through their ordinary senses. If they can, it would strongly reinforce the concept that mind and brain are separate although interconnected.

More unusual is the following account by a New Zealand friend, a doctor who has seen many deaths, but on one particular occasion is convinced that he was aware of the moment a soul actually left the body.

> I was . . . on the golf course about eight years ago when I was called over to the next foursome to someone who had collapsed. He had probably arrested after an MI [heart attack] and his colour was initially OK, although he had no pulse. I then "saw" something leave, starting from his legs and travelling up his body. It was harder to define what happened at his head. I have always regretted not doing CPR [cardiopulmonary resuscitation]

at the time, as it may of course have brought him back.
I have seen other deaths but nothing like that.

If we accept the concept that a soul or spirit does indeed leave
the body at death, it opens up the possibility that memories of
past lives are nothing to do with reincarnation but are simply
communicated by these discarnate spirits, in much the same
way as it is claimed that they communicate with spiritualist
mediums. Mediums do not claim the memories they receive
as their own, but they are quite clear that they are being used
only as a channel through which these discarnate souls communicate. If we could prove that mediums are able to communicate with discarnate souls, it would offer no proof of
reincarnation, but it would certainly prove what one might
call the first principle of reincarnation—that a soul can survive the death of a physical body and carry the memories of
that physical body within it.

ONE WHITE CROW

The problem is that the history of mediumship, is littered with
self-deception, frauds and charlatans. However, there have
also been a few men and women whose paranormal abilities
as well as their personal honesty are widely regarded as being
above suspicion. If we can show that *one* human being is able
in some way to pick up information from the dead, even if we
can offer no explanation about how they do it, then we have
also to accept that because nothing in nature occurs singly,
this may be an ability that other human beings also have to a
greater or lesser extent, even though they may not be aware of
it. As William James, Professor of Psychology at Harvard
University, memorably said: "To upset the conclusion that all
crows are black, it is sufficient to produce one white crow, a
single one is sufficient."

The one white crow of the spiritualist world is usually considered to be Leonore Piper of Boston. Born in 1859, Mrs.
Piper discovered her own ability as a medium when she went
into a trance state while attending a seance conducted by a
clairvoyant, J. R. Cocks. In the history of mediumship Mrs.
Piper stands head and shoulders above the rest, a medium so

successful that she could have earned a personal fortune, but who instead chose to devote her career to assisting psychical research. She was investigated both by Professor William James, on behalf of the American Society for Psychical Research, and then by Richard Hodgson. Richard Hodgson, a confirmed sceptic, was a founder member of the British Society for Psychical Research and had already investigated, and exposed as fraudulent, other mediums, including Madame Blavatsky, founder of the Theosophical Society and at that time the best-known mystic in the world.

In 1887 Hodgson went to Boston with the expressed intention of unmasking Mrs. Piper, and he tried every trick in the book to do so. He invited strangers off the street into her sittings at the last moment; he introduced all her sitters as "Mrs. Smith"; he hired private detectives to intercept her mail and read her letters; he had members of her household followed to make sure that they were not collecting useful information or setting up sittings. During her sittings he held lighted matches against her arm to see if she was genuinely in a trance state (she did not flinch, though her spirit guide, a Dr. Phinuit, complained of a slight feeling of cold). It was all to no avail. Mrs. Piper continued, through Dr. Phinuit, to tell her sitters intimate details about themselves and enabled them to speak with dead friends and relatives. Even when she was persuaded to visit England, where she knew no one and had no contacts who might have helped her gather information, her sittings were said to be equally astonishing.

Eventually, after four years of research, Hodgson put in his report to the SPR. He was forced to acknowledge that Mrs. Piper was not a fraud. At this stage, however, he still did not accept that she was in touch with the spirits of the dead, and he did not believe that her spirit guide, Dr. Phinuit, was genuine. Instead, he concluded that she was obtaining information about dead people telepathically from the minds of her sitters, and then unconsciously impersonating them.

Mrs. Piper apparently accepted Hodgson's conclusions without complaint—she herself didn't know what happened during a trance, so this seemed as good an explanation as any. Dr. Phinuit, however, was said to be furious, and at his next appearance insisted: "I am real. I once lived in a body and if those cranks weren't so stupid they could find me."

For Hodgson this was not quite the end of the matter. In February 1892 George Pellew, a Bostonian lawyer and a friend of Hodgson's, was found dead outside a house. According to newspaper reports he was suffering from an eye infection that affected his vision and led to his accidentally falling down the area steps and striking his head.

Within a few weeks of his death. "GP" appeared at one of Mrs. Piper's sittings, introducing himself to an old friend ("Mr. Smith") who happened to be there. Asked if he could produce any proof that he really was Pellew, Mrs. Piper's hand wrote a message that convinced the sitter of his identity. Hodgson immediately started to introduce Pellew's old friends into the sittings, all under the name of Smith. Pellew recognised and spoke to 30 of them, picking them out from at least 150 other people who attended these sittings. What he said about his death confirmed the newspaper reports. He told his father he was alone when he died, and at one sitting said: "I fell down the steps, you know, accidentally. You know how I passed out . . ."

Hodgson was at last convinced, not just of the psychic ability of Mrs. Piper but of the ability of the human soul to survive death. In 1897 he produced a second report for the SPF, and this time his conclusions were unequivocal. He wrote: "I cannot profess to have any doubt that the chief communicators are veritably the personages they claim to be, and that they have survived the change we call death, and that they have directly communicated with us, whom we call the living, through Mrs. Piper's entranced organism."

Hodgson's conversion was complete, but like many converts he abandoned immediately his critical faculties. He does not seem to have taken account of the fact that by the time "GP" first appeared, a few weeks after his death, Mrs. Piper could have picked up a good deal of information about Pellew simply from reading his obituaries. In his second report he mentioned that "GP" had been hesitant in his recognition of only one sitter—a young woman who had been a child when Pellew had last seen her. He failed to mention several other nonrecognitions, including someone who had been one of

Pellew's closest Harvard friends. Security surrounding these later sittings also appears to have been pretty lax. Many sitters knew each other, or knew Mrs. Piper in her non-trance state. It was no secret to Mrs. Piper, for example, that Hodgson was bringing friends of Pellew to the sittings to meet "GP." And by this time Mrs. Piper was mixing socially with at least one of the sitters, Lilla Perry, who attended nearly all the sittings involving "GP." Pellew had boarded with the Perrys for three years while he attended Harvard Law School, and there is strong evidence that he and Lilla had been in love.

But probably the most significant relationship was between Mrs. Piper and Hodgson himself. At first this had been at best uneasy, probably even hostile. Hodgson distrusted Mrs. Piper; she was said to be furious when she discovered she was under surveillance. By the time of his second report to the SPR in 1897, however, they had known each other for ten years and their relationship must have changed considerably as she gradually earned his respect. She would not have been human if she had not wanted to build on this respect, and the death of George Pellew may have provided her with just such an opportunity. Did she, perhaps unconsciously, want both to please him and to offer him irresistible proof of her mediumistic powers?

There seem to have been plenty of opportunities during the seances themselves for Mrs. Piper to have acquired information. Mrs. Piper's hearing was acute, but people who were not sitting near her tended to whisper among themselves, assuming that they would not be overheard. Sitters were also advised to treat "GP" as if he were a living person, and indeed often seem to have fed him information. The transcripts of sessions during October and November 1896, for example, reveal Hodgson himself chatting informatively away to his dear departed friend, confiding that he had received a letter from Tom Perry to say they had changed their minds and were "not coming over now . . . Edith is here in Boston staying with some friends, but I haven't seen her yet".

> Hodgson: Just before you go, George, I want to tell you that I've seen Edith and will bring her, not the next time nor the time after, but the time after that.

GP: Good, good, good.

RH: You'll be surprised to see her. She's an enormous great
        thing . . .

RH   [two days later]: You'll be ready for Edith tomorrow?

GP: You bet!

And with that amount of priming, you bet he would be.

Even more intriguing are the facts surrounding Pellew's
death. His death certificate showed that he did not die where
his body was reported to have been found, but in a far less
salubrious area of the city, outside one of the gambling dives
he was in the habit of frequenting. The coroner's report gave
as the cause of death "dislocation of axis [that is, a broken
neck] and Haemorrhage into Brain." No autopsy was performed on the body, and without an autopsy there is no way
the examining doctor could have known either whether the
axis was dislocated or whether there was any haemorrhaging
into the brain unless there was some obvious external injury
to the skull. The report does not, however, mention any such
injury. Why? James Munves, in a reassessment of the transcripts and the circumstances surrounding the whole Pellew
affair, has pointed out that the Boston coroner's office at that
time was notoriously corrupt. Charles Pellew, George's
brother, led a life more respectable and far less louche than
George. The sordid circumstances of his brother's death
might have been so potentially embarrassing to Charles that
he persuaded the coroner to issue a false report, concealing
both the location where the body was found and the existence
of any head injury that might indicate foul play. The newspapers did not know this. The sitters at the seances did not know
this. Most significantly, even "GP" himself did not appear to
know this, or if he did he wasn't prepared to share the information with anybody else.

So where does this leave our one white crow? Mrs. Piper
was undoubtedly a remarkable woman, and by all accounts an
honest one. She had hundreds of sitters, many of whom returned only a few times, sometimes with intervals of several
years. And yet in her trance state Mrs. Piper would be able to
pick up with them just where she had left off, remembering
trivial personal details about them. One possibility is that she

was able to pick up what was in her sitters' minds through telepathy, though it is claimed that often sitters themselves were unaware of things she told them. But it is also feasible that in her trance state Mrs. Piper was able to access a wealth of stored information in the same way as cryptomnesic memories are accessed under hypnosis. We've seen how impressively cryptomnesia can operate in the pastlife regressions of, for example, Blanche Poynings and Joan, the Chelmsford witch. Imagine a state of consciousness in which could be recovered not just one particular set of forgotten memories but virtually any impression, any fact that has ever been registered in our memory banks. If Mrs. Piper's memory operated in this way while she was in a trance state, it is no wonder she was so often able to astonish those who attended her sittings.

But was she truly able to communicate with the spirits of the dead? Certainly, before Hodgson's conversion, he had carried out a thorough assessment of Mrs. Piper and was unable to find any glaring evidence of fraud. But from the evidence of the George Pellew sittings (which are, after all, the ones that made a convinced spiritualist of the sceptical Richard Hodgson) there has to be real doubt about this. It does look as though there are at least a few black feathers in the plumage of our one white crow.

17

Science and the Soul

I think I may say that for my part I should be slightly more annoyed than surprised if I should find myself in some sense persisting immediately after the death of my present body. One can only wait and see, or alternately (which is no less likely) wait and not see.

Professor C. D. Broad, philosopher, 1962

"BEING born twice," said Voltaire (always one to question orthodoxy), "is no more remarkable than being born once." Scientists, or at any rate orthodox Western scientists, would beg to disagree. Science knows exactly how it stands on man's capacity to survive death and on the possibility of reincarnation. The scientific view is simple. Our consciousness of the world is generated by brain function. Memory is located entirely within the brain. Reincarnation involves the continuation of memories independently of a brain, something that, from the point of view of science, is impossible. There is no mechanism that science knows for storing or accessing memory outside the body or in the absence of a brain. When, at death, the brain dies, so do our memories and so does our consciousness of the world. There is nothing beyond this, and any step in this direction is into the unproven and speculative.

Reincarnation is the belief that we do not live one single life, but many. With each new incarnation we acquire a new body. What distinguishes a belief in reincarnation from other beliefs centred on the immortality of the soul is the importance attached to personal identity, and the belief that this, too, can survive and be reborn with many of our physical traits from previous lives.

Even if we accept that, whatever terminology we use, some part of us, our essence, or spirit, or soul, or psychosphore, can survive death, there are still intellectual stumbling blocks to accepting reincarnation. Why doesn't everyone have past-life memories? If we exclude those cases for which there is a clear scientific explanation, at the most—the very most—there are probably only a few hundred cases that demand some explanation, whether or not reincarnation is that explanation. Against those we have to set the billions of human beings of whom the only lasting trace is the legacy of their genes.

Then there is the question of arithmetic. The numbers simply do not add up if reincarnation involves a one-to-one transmission of a human soul that has already lived. In the last 2,000 years the population of the earth has increased from 200 million to something approaching 6 billion, and it is still rising. This makes a nonsense of the argument that every one of us has lived another human life before. If one argues that reincarnation is not everyone's lot, what is it that determines that some of us have lived before and will live again, and some of us haven't and won't? Is violent death the criterion, as some cultures believe?

Many other cultures and communities believe reincarnation to be possible because they are not restricted by a Western scientific framework. And in the Middle Ages, before science gained a firm foothold in our culture, the Western world, too, believed in the existence of a soul that inhabited the body and survived its death. So how did we get ourselves into this scientific straitjacket which allows for no soul and no survival? Simply because of the way that scientific thinking has developed.

An excellent review of this process can be found in Richard Tarnas's book *The Passion of the Western Mind*. At the time of the Greeks the soul was considered to be an integral part of nature; there was no question of the separation of physical reality and soul. The split started to develop in the thirteenth and fourteenth centuries as Western thinkers began to question the nature of the soul, and became complete in the sixteenth and seventeenth centuries under the influence of Descartes and Galileo.

The philosophy of Descartes was a dualist philosophy based on the notion of God as separate from the world. Descartes defined two substances: the *res extensa* and the *res cogitans*. The *res extensa*, or "the extended thing," had a precise location in space and was synonymous with the body. The *res cogitans*, or "the thinking thing," was synonymous with the mind and the soul, and had by definition no spatial location, although it was connected to the body by the pineal gland. It was, so to speak, outside the world. This splitting off of body from mind has caused endless difficulties, as it is not clear how the two are meant to communicate and where the mind and soul are located.

In saying this, Descartes set in motion a train of thought that has led our current scientific story into great difficulties when mind and consciousness need explanation. This view was very helpful to Descartes because it protected him from the wrath of the Church. The mind and the soul were split off from the body, and given to the Church to do with what they would, and the body became an objective entity in space.

Galileo changed the way in which we viewed the world. It was in the seventeenth century, at the dawning of the Age of Enlightenment, that he formulated the belief structures that underpin our science and on which it is based today. He suggested that objects existed in their own right and had properties that could be weighed and measured and, more fundamentally, that objects would remain even if they were not observed.

This idea of the permanence of objects is so common today that we hardly give it a second thought, but in Galileo's time it was a radical concept and led to a totally different way of thinking. Until then, objects and the person perceiving them had been linked together, forming a unity. Galileo split this unity and produced a disunited world. On the one hand was an external, objective world that was independent of its observer. Objects in this external world had what he termed primary qualities because even when the object was unobserved these qualities (weight, mass, etc.) would continue unchanged. But he also recognised that there existed a second, subjective world, the world of sense perception. When an object was perceived, the very act of perception bestowed what he called secondary qualities on it—secondary because these qualities were dependent on the individual observer and disappeared when no observer was present. No object is red unless it is seen to be red, or hot unless it is felt to be hot.

Newton's theory of colour was based on the concept of an external world independent of the observer. In his experiments on colour, Newton showed that a thin pencil of white light passed through a prism produced a much expanded beam of light divided up into different colours. He argued that the splitting of this beam was due to a different angle of refrangence (now called refraction) for each colour, and he had various theories about why this should be different for different colours. We know now that Newton's theory was correct, that different coloured lights vibrate at different frequencies, are slowed by the prism by different amounts and are therefore refracted differently.

However, the whole of Newton's theory was based on the fact that he did indeed *perceive* different colours. The outside world was constructed in his subjective consciousness. If Newton had been colour-blind, he would have perceived the extended pencil of light which came out of the prism as different shades of grey; looking at this grey spectrum, it would have been almost impossible for him to have defined a coherent theory of colour. Obviously, then, secondary qualities are very important to our science; in fact, most scientific theories start as observations—that is, they are secondary-quality theories, and later become primary-quality theories only when they are made more formal, usually by mathematics.

And yet in Galileo's view it was the external, independent world, with its own qualities, uncontaminated by our perception, which was primary. The internal, subjective world was of little value because in the last resort its secondary qualities are temporary, existing only for as long as they are perceived.

The stage was now set. Before Galileo made his astonishing perceptual breakthrough, the world was a unity. Afterwards the world was defined as something outside ourselves, something objective from which could be culled the truths about its structure and behaviour which we call scientific facts. It was a dead world, a random world, a world without meaning and purpose. It was also a world which had no ethics and no moral values because those are purely subjective, secondary qualities, and the secondary-quality world of perception was unimportant and subordinate.

The science of Galileo and Newton was quite brilliant and has been highly successful. Without it, modern science would not have flourished or modern technology developed. There would have been no cars, no microchips, no understanding of the flow of electrons in wires, leading to radio and television. There would be no theories of the universe. It has allowed us to set up hypotheses, form theories and make predictions apparently quite independently of ourselves and to achieve deep insights into the structure of nature.

Galilean science has helped us understand the brain, the way neurons fire, how they group together in pools, how features of the outside world are extracted from the stream of neuronal firing which makes up the information entering the brain. It has helped us understand some of the rules governing the way in which the brain puts together a sensory picture of our environment, both external and internal. Modern neuroimaging has shown that the brain deals with different functions in different areas. It is common knowledge that hearing, vision, smell and sensation all take place in separate brain areas. Even the transcendental feelings of being at one with God and the universe are being mapped on to the brain. Neuroimaging pictures taken while the person is under the influence of hallucinogenic drugs such as cylocybin, LSD and ketamine, which induce such transcendental feelings, show that specific brain areas are activated. Even God appears to manifest in a particular brain area.

Correlations between subjective experience (for example, seeing an angry face) and neuronal firing (for example, amygdala response) abound in the brain. But nowhere in this picture is there any theory which suggests how you get from neuronal functioning to conscious experience. And this is our dilemma. For without a proper understanding of the nature of consciousness and the way in which that consciousness interacts with brain function, we cannot even begin to approach the question of a soul and the possibility of reincarnation. Galilean science has told us almost everything about the nature of the world—and almost nothing about the nature of our own consciousness as, *by definition*, its theories exclude consciousness (secondary qualities).

And yet there is little truth in the idea of an independent, objective world. The whole scientific enterprise can take place only in the consciousness of the human mind. Without consciousness, there would be no theories and no science. Galileo argued that matter was the primary quality of the universe and consciousness was secondary, but it is now clear that consciousness is primary and that the material world takes on the form that it does only because this is the way in which it is structured in our consciousness.

Reincarnation is another belief system and it, too, is dependent on our consciousness. Because it depends more on thoughts and feelings than on objective Galilean evidence, it is impossible, without a secondary-quality science, either to prove or disprove. The science of the Reformation denied the possibility of either a soul—that is, the continuation of personal consciousness after death—or the possibility that reincarnation could take place. There is thus little point in looking to Galilean scientific theory for validation of ideas concerning reincarnation. All we can do is to suggest the kind of worldview that would make reincarnation a possibility, even though we might still have no idea of its *modus operandi*. For example, is the world as fixed and are objects as separate as Galilean science would suggest?

A SCIENCE OF CONSCIOUSNESS

Theories of reincarnation, as we have seen, require a comprehensive theory of consciousness, an explanation of the way in which the brain interacts with conscious processes and some general mechanism for storing individual experience. There is not one word about consciousness, except descriptions of the way it is reflected in neuronal firing, in any scientific theory of the brain. It is only the correlates of consciousness that are mentioned. The process involved when the colour "red" comes to consciousness, for example, is not—cannot—be described; all we know is that a particular set of neurones fire in response to light at that particular wavelength.

At the moment physicists are way in front of biologists in

beginning to form a general theory of consciousness. Theories such as quantum mechanics are beginning to be developed in which consciousness is an integral property of the world, and these theories are being applied to the brain. If consciousness is an integral property of the world, then there is no reason why individual consciousness cannot exist outside the brain. This is getting very close to saying that some component of man exists outside the body. If brain processes could be shown to modify structures beyond the brain, or could themselves be modified by such structures, then there is the possibility of a soul outside the brain. There is also the possibility that this soul could be released by death.

It has now been recognised that what is needed is a new science of consciousness, a totally subjective science which recognises the primacy of conscious experience. This new science would set about healing the rift produced by the Galilean/Newtonian revolution. It would *include* consciousness within its theories. One suggestion is that matter should be regarded as having two "faces," a subjective, internal face, and an objective, external face. The scientist, viewing objectively, sees the external face of matter; the internal face has to be experienced, and is seen subjectively. Patterns of vibrating air particles are heard as music, because brain processes extract the internal face of matter and allow it to become conscious. There need no longer be a divide between an objective, external world and a subjective, internal world because they are both simply different views of the same thing.

A QUANTUM LEAP IN THE SEARCH FOR THE SOUL

In the early twentieth century two major new advances—the theory of relativity (dealing with very large masses) and the theory of quantum mechanics (dealing with the atomic world)—have shown that matter may indeed be highly interconnected. These theories have shown not that Newton and Galileo were wrong but that their view was incomplete, and that the simple Newtonian view of the world needs to be expanded.

One of the most important and earliest quantum-mechanical experiments showed that light could exist as either waves or subatomic particles (photons). If an experiment were so set up that the track of the photons could always be known—for example, if a beam of light were passed through one small pinhole—then light behaved as a particle. On the other hand, if there were two pinholes so that it was impossible to know which pinhole light had passed through, then light behaved as waves. These waves of light interfered with each other and produced an interference pattern on the screen behind the pinholes.

In quantum mechanics, then, particles can be defined as either a wave or a particle. When the wave description is used, then every wave is connected with every other in the universe. At the everyday level (the macro level), matter behaves as particles and the interconnectedness is less apparent. This suggests that although the Galilean view of independent objects is correct at the macro level, from the point of view of each individual particle the universe is highly interconnected.

An important quantum-mechanical concept is that until the precise position of the particles is measured the state of the system is undefined, The significance of this finding is that in order for the world to become manifest, it has to be acted on in some way. Until then, it remains in a virtual form. Measurement in a quantum-mechanical experiment can be carried out by a remote sensor or by a human observer. The important point is that the measurement has to be made before the quantum-mechanical state collapses into a defined physical state. This is the closest that any physical theory has come to incorporating consciousness.

This is an intriguing theory, but, because it deals with atomic and subatomic particles, can we really apply it to a macro object like the brain? The recent cosmology which states that the universe at its inception was smaller than half the size of the electron, but yet contained everything that has flowed from it, has linked together the very large and the very small, so that the distinction between them no longer applies. For many years it was thought that the brain was also too large, too hot (too much thermal noise or too much atomic movement) and too wet for quantum-mechanical events to take place. However, recently a doctor, Stuart Hammeroff, and a mathematician, Roger Penrose, have suggested that there are areas inside the brain cells, the microtubules, in which it is possible for quantum-mechanical events to take place. If this is indeed so, then these effects are certainly widely distributed throughout the nervous system, and it is likely that the whole brain and nervous system work as a quantum-mechanical computer.

The implications of this are exciting. If the brain *did* work as a quantum-mechanical computer, then the rules governing information transfer within it would be quite different. Because quantum-mechanical events are spread throughout the universe, it can be argued that brain function would be extended in space beyond the skull.

If we take these ideas and use them as quantum allegory— that is, extending precise quantum-mechanical concepts outside their strict scientific frame of reference—we could postulate that the soul exists as a virtual field. This field need not even have a spatial location. When the field interacts with a brain, it would collapse from its virtual form into that of a defined soul. At death, the field would return, modified by life experience, to its virtual form. This would then await its interaction with another brain to again become manifest. One could argue that only in a small number of cases would there be sufficient overlapping of the two soul states for previous memories to condense from the field. This would explain why not everybody has a previous-life memory. Virtual fields would also solve the problem of location of memory outside the brain, and the apparent "population problem" of soul transfer, as you could argue for a field with extensive properties that are not significantly diminished by the condensation of a single soul. The morphogenetic field of Rupert Sheldrake (see page 300), although not identical to this concept, contains several similarities and points in a similar direction.

Quantum mechanics contains another important key concept which is related to the amount of information it is possible to get from quantum states. The usual example is that of a particle. If you wish to know its position accurately, then quantum mechanics will not allow its velocity to be precisely known, and vice versa. This is called the Heisenberg uncertainty principle. It is as if nature puts a limit on the information it will give. Again, using quantum allegory, it is possible to postulate a theory whereby soul "stuff" is of such a quality that it falls below this theoretical level of detection, and thus cannot be "found." It could, however, still have effects in the Galilean world of the brain. This idea then removes the stumbling block of having to define the location of the soul.

A new quantum mathematical theory, developed by Amit Gotswarni, a physicist at the University of Oregon and described in his book *The Self-Aware Universe*, postulates that the basic structure of the universe is consciousness, not matter. From this, a number of surprising and interesting features arise. First, that there is only one observer in the whole universe. If you wish, you can call this observer God, although it might be better described as part of the universal conscious process. A further consequence of this is that all individual consciousnesses are one, a belief already held by the mystics, who see no division between individual consciousnesses.

Consciousness then becomes a realm of possibilities that exist, out of which the actual "matter" of the world arises. There is no difficulty in incorporating either souls or the possibility of reincarnation into this theory, as the soul, on its transition from actual (interacting with a brain) to virtual (re-entering the realm of possibilities) could carry with it any amount of information that it had "acquired."

Next, there is the concept of parallel universes. The concept here is that a virtual quantum state observed in different ways can lead to different results. This means that whenever an observation is made, a whole set of results may flow from it. The idea of parallel universes is that different observations will lead to different results, moving you from one universe to another. Either universe is equally possible, but they are slightly different. To put this more simply, using quantum allegory you could decide to take the left-hand fork on the way to town, which will lead you into a universe where a whole set of experiences arise. But it doesn't exclude the possibility of another universe that you would have entered, with a different set of experiences, if you had taken the right-hand fork. The argument here is that universes branch every time, an observation is made. On this scale, using this idea, the concepts of soul and reincarnation would fall easily into place as they would simply be in another universe.

There is now a huge amount of data which shows that, as your level of consciousness changes, the perceived world alters. There are descriptions of mystical experience in which the world is totally transformed. People who have had these experiences say that when they are in this altered state of consciousness the world has a quite different structure. Often, they will describe the world as being composed of love, and say that every element of the universe is alive and conscious.

One way of interpreting these observations is to postulate a transcendent reality which coexists with and interpenetrates our ordinary reality. We see one reality when the brain is working one way, and another when it is working differently, Taking this as the model, it would not be too difficult to assume that there are other realities which interpenetrate our usual world and of which we may never be aware. If this were the structure of the universe, then the idea that souls coexisted with us would be perfectly tenable. An interpenetrating, transcendental reality would also provide an answer to the problem of what happens to the soul after the death of the body; it allows a location for the soul, coexistent with the material universe and yet outside it.

We could make some predictions from this model. On page 302 for example, is an eyewitness account by a doctor who saw something apparently leave the body at the moment of death. The theory of interpenetrating realities would suggest that what he saw was the transition of the soul from one, material universe to another. What is interesting about his account is that he seemed to find it harder to see what happened towards the end of the process, as if there were a gradual change in materiality of whatever it was he saw, with a parallel change in its visibility.

This theory has further predictions. It suggests that there may be people who have differently functioning brains and who are able to be aware of a different level of reality. This, at least, is testable—and in an experiment we did some years ago we set out to test it. Twenty mediums agreed to be given tests of brain function. We compared the results with those of a control group of people who were given similar tests. For various technical reasons we predicted that the right temporal lobe would be functioning abnormally in the mediums, probably because it had been damaged. And this is precisely what we found.

There are two ways of interpreting this. First, one can say simply that a damaged, malfunctioning brain produces a distorted view of the world. But equally valid is the suggestion that such a brain allows a *different* view of the world, opening a "window" through which a different reality could be seen. Recently, two patients in a head injury unit run by one of the authors of this book reported that after their head injury they developed some unwelcome precognitive ability; often when they passed people in the street they could see that something unpleasant was going to happen to them in the future. Both were upset by this, one so much that she would never go out.

Modern experiments in parapsychology certainly provide evidence for precognition. But what kind of universe would we have to postulate to allow for knowledge of the future or the possibility of time travel? Causality would be quite different in a universe in which the present could influence the future and the future influence the past. Events would not be random, as at any point the present might be interrupted by the future; synchronicity would be a normal characteristic of such a world. Reincarnation might also be a possibilty, with future lives running concurrently with present lives.

Life After Death

If one accepts that a soul can exist independently of the brain, then it is merely a matter of choosing the form of survival which seems either the most appealing or the most intellectually credible.

One can acquire a belief in the possibility of life after death through either faith or experience. Many people have the intuitive certainty, which we call faith, based on no objective evidence, that the soul can survive the death of the body. Others acquire the same degree of certainty through some kind of personal experience (revelation)—the near-death experience, for example. Reincarnation is a particular case of this general belief in survival. There are people with faith who "just know," who seem to have been born with a belief in reincarnation, and there are others who believe because they have experienced what seem to them to be past lives.

What we believe does seem to structure the world that we create for ourselves. Most Westerners are now disinclined to believe in miracles in the New Testament sense. R. Gardner, in the 1983 Christmas issue of the *British Medical Journal*, writes a most attractive article on miracles in which he quotes the following story, which illustrates the power of belief.

> When modern missionaries left some gospel books behind in Ethiopia and returned many years later, they not only found a flourishing Church but a community of believers among whom miracles like those mentioned in the New Testament happened every day—because there had been no missionaries to teach that such things were not to be taken literally.

It is easy to look around us and say reincarnation doesn't exist when it is our culture that has made it disappear. To come to a wider conclusion on reincarnation we need to stand well back from our culture so as to be able to take a different view. Because our current belief systems,do not allow for miracles, we do not either experience them or see the evidence to support them. We have been converted to the new faith of science by scientific missionaries.

The fortunate few have some personal experience to guide them; for the rest of us there is only uncertainty. But perhaps we need some uncertainty about our chances of survival. As Martin Gardner, in *The Whys of a Philosophical Scrivener*, points out: "If we knew that the celestial Emerald City were around the bend of death, and knew it with the kind of certainty that we know the existence of London or Paris, our lives would be disrupted by our impatience to get there. You must travel a road to reach the end of it, but jumping out a window will get you off the earth in just a few minutes."

Bibliography

Akolkar, V. V., *Search for Sharada: Report of a Case and its Investigation, Journal of the American Society for Psychical Research*, July 1992, vol. 86, no. 3.

Anderson, Roger, *On Novels and Reincarnation Memories*, letter in *Journal of the American Society for Psychical Research*, April 1993, vol. 87.

Anderson, Roger, *Commentary on the Akolkar and Stevenson Reports, Journal of the American Society for Psychical Research*, July 1992, vol. 86, no. 3.

Ayer, A. J. *The Concept of a Person and Other Essays*, St. Martin's Press, 1963.

Bernstein, Morey, *The Search for Bridey Murphy*, Doubleday, 1956.

Cockell, Jenny, *Yesterday's Children*, Piatkus Books, 1993.

Currie, Ian, *You Cannot Die*, Element Books, 1995.

Flournoy, Théodore, *From India to the Planet Mars*, Princeton University Press, 1994. Originally published 1899.

Gardner, Martin, *The Whys of a Philosophical Scrivener*, Harvester Press, 1983.

Gardner, R., *Miracles of healing in Anglo-Celtic Northumbria as recorded by the Venerable Bede and his contemporaries:*

A reappraisal in the light of twentieth-century experience,
British Medical Journal, December 1983, vol. 287.

Gershom, Rabbi Yonassan, *Beyond the Ashes: Cases of Reincarnation from the Holocaust,* A.R.E. Press, Virginia,
1992.

Gotswani, Amit, *The Self-Aware Universe,* Simon & Schuster,
1998.

Guirdham, Arthur, *The Cathars and Reincarnation,* The C.W.
Daniel Company Ltd, Saffron Walden, 1990. Originally
published 1970.

Guirdham, Arthur, *We Are One Another,* Neville Spearman,
London, 1974.

Guirdham, Arthur, *The Lake and the Castle,* C. W. Daniel,
London, 1976.

Haraldsson, Erlendur, *Children Claiming Past-Life Memories: Four Cases In Sri Lanka, Journal of Scientific Exploration,* 1991, vol. 5, no. 2.

Haraldsson, Erlendur, *Personality and Abilities of Children
Claiming Previous-Life Memories, Journal of Nervous
and Mental Disease,* 1995, vol. 183, no. 7.

Haraldsson, E., and Houtkooper, Joop M., *Psychic Experiences in the Multinational Human Values Study: Who Reports Them? Journal of the American Society for
Psychical Research,* April 1991, vol. 85, no. 2.

Harris, Melvin, *Sorry, You've Been Duped!,* Weidenfeld &
Nicholson, 1986.

Harrison, Vernon, *Some of the Automatic Scripts and Drawings of Matthew Manning,* Proceedings of the Society for
Psychical Research, October 1994, vol. 58, part 218.

Iverson, Jeffrey, *In Search of the Dead,* BBC Books, 1992.

Iverson, Jeffrey, *More Lives Than One?,* Souvenir Press, 1976.

Jarmon, Robert, *Discovering the Soul,* A.R.E. Press, 1997.

Keeton, Joe, and Moss, Peter, *Encounters with the Past,* Sidg-
wick & Jackson, 1979.

Lancaster, Evelyn, and Poling, James, *Strangers in my Body,*
Secker and Warburg, 1958.

Lishman, Alwyn (ed), *Organic Psychiatry*, Churchill Livingstone, 1982.

Lowes Dickinson, G., *A Case of Emergence of a Latent Memory under Hypnosis*, Proceedings of the Society for Psychical Research, 1911, vol. 25.

Manning, Matthew, *The Link*, Colin Smythe, Gerrards Cross, 1974.

Mills, Antonia, *Nightmares in Western Children: An Alternative Interpretation Suggested by Data in Three Cases, Journal of the American Society for Psychical Research*, October 1994, vol. 88, no. 4.

Mills, Antonia, Haraldsson, Erlendur, and Keil, Jurgen, *Replication Studies of Cases Suggestive of Reincarnation by Three Independent Investigators, Journal of the American Society for Psychical Research*, July 1994, vol. 88, no. 3.

Moody, Raymand, *Life After Life*, Mockingbird Books, Atlanta, 1975.

Munves, James, *Richard Hodgson, Mrs. Piper and "George Pelham': A Centennial Reassessment, Journal of the American Society for Psychical Research*, October 1997, vol. 62, no. 849.

Neppe, Vernon, *The Psychology of Déjà Vu*, Witwatersrand University Press, Johannesburg, 1983.

Pasricha, S., *Claims of Reincarnation: An Empirical Study of Cases in India*, Harman Publishing House, New Delhi, 1990.

Pasricha, S., Stevenson, I., *Indian Cases of the Reincarnation-type Tvo Generations Apart, Journal of the Society for Psychical Research*, 1987, vol. 54, no. 809.

Prince, Moreton, *Dissociation of a Personality: The Hunt for the Real Miss Beauchamp*, Longman, Green and Co. Originally published 1905.

Radin, Dean, *The Conscious Universe*, Harper Edge, 1997.

Rogo, D. Scott, *The Search for Yesterday*, Prentice-Hall, 1985.

Schatzinan, Morton, *The Story of Ruth*, Duckworth, 1980.

Selfe, Lorna, *Nadia—A Case of Extraordinary Drawing Ability in an Autistic Child*, Academic Press, 1977.

Sternman, Roy, *Reincarnation*, Piatkus, 1997.

Stevenson, Ian, *A Preliminary Report of a New Case of Responsive Xenoglossy: The Case of Gretchen, Journal of the American Society for Psychical Research*, January 1976, vol. 70.

Stevenson, Ian, *American Children Who Claim to Remember Previous Lives, Journal of Nervous and Mental Disease*, 1983, vol. 171, no. 11.

Stevenson, Ian, *Unlearned Language: New Studies in Xenoglossy*, University Press of Virginia, 1984.

Stevenson, Ian, *Children Who Remember Previous Lives*, University Press of Virginia, 1987.

Stevenson, Ian, *Can Children Be Stopped Speaking about Previous Lives?, Journal of the American Society for Psychical Research*, January 1990, vol. 56, no. 818.

Stevenson, Ian, *Reincarnation and Biology: A Contribution to the Etiology of Birthmarks and Birth Defects* (two volumes), Praeger Publishers, Westport, CT, 1997.

Stevenson, Ian, *Where Reincarnation and Biology Intersect*, Praeger Publishers, Westport, CT, 1997.

Stevenson, Ian and Pasricha, S., *A Preliminary Report on an Unusual Case of the Reincarnation-type with Xenoglossy, Journal of the American Society for Psychical Research*, July 1980, vol. 74.

Tarazi, Linda, *An Unusual Case of Hypnotic Regression with some Unexplained Contents, Journal of the American Society for Psychical Research*, October 1990, vol. 84, no. 4.

Tarnas, Richard, *The Passion of the Western Mind*, Ballantine Books, New York, 1991.

Treffert, Darold, *Extraordinary People. An exploration of the savant syndrome*, Bantam Press, 1989.

Turner, Elizabeth, *Teratogenic effects on the human fetus through maternal emotional stress: Report of a case, Medical Journal of Australia* 1960, vol. 47.

Wilson, Colin, *Afterlife*, Grafton

Wilson, Ian, *Mind Out of Time*, Victor Gollancz, 1981.

Index

Adams, Dom, 196–8
Adaway, Annette, 41
agnosia, 81
Akolkar, V. V., 82, 85, 89, 91, 214–5, 218
Alevis, 52
Alexander, June, 57–8
ancient places, 19–21
Anderton, Judith, 94
Andrews, April (pseudonym), 226
animal reincarnation, 51, 53, 57–8
Aristotle, 23
Ashworth, Susan, 238–9
autism, 207, 208–9, 247
automatic writing and drawing, 200, 201
Ayer, A. J., 299

Bailey, Stan, 111
Balaam, Mary, 199
Bedford, Helen, 167–8
Beecham, D., 37
behaviour and personality traits, xi–xii, 50, 61–2, 242, 273
Ben, 247, 268
Bernstein, Morey, 2, 3, 5, 7, 116

birth defects, 47–48, 51, 53, 55, 270–1, 272, 278, 279–81, 285, 286, 288–92
birthmarks, 47–8, 51, 53, 55, 155–6, 229, 232, 270, 271–8, 280, 281–5, 286, 289, 292
Blavatsky, Madame, xv, 304
Bloxham, Arnall, 7–8, 9, 124
Bond, Sharon, 106–7
Bose, Sushil, 14
Bowen, Olwen, 159–62, 164–7
brain, 313, 316–7, 319
    child's brain, 301
    damage, 79, 160, 207–8, 319
    death, 309
    hippocampus, 67, 76, 79, 160, 262
    left hemisphere, 66–7, 75, 207–8
    split-brain patients, 66
    temporal lobe functioning, 22, 35–6
    see also memory
Braude, Stephen, 202–3, 294
Britain, 55, 252
Brown, Rosemary, 203–5
Bryant, David, 183
Buddhism, xii, xv–xix, 48, 52, 57
Burgess, Tom, 22–3

Burma, 47, 48, 51, 53, 217, 258, 270, 278
Buzzard, Ronald J., 36
Byfield, Karen, 92–3

Caddick, Rex, 25–6, 117–19
Callaghan, Katherine (pseudonym), 190–2
Cape, Nicholas, 224
Carter, Pauline, 21
Carter Beaumont, Ivy, 149
Cathars, xiv–xv, 152–61, 295–6
Chadha, N. K., 235
Chamberlain, Denise, 184
channelling, 199–205
Charles, Heather, 98–100, 298–9
children
    childhood trauma, 79, 142
    déjà vu experiences, 262–4
    dreams, 94–6, 110–12
    gifted children, 204–5
    imaginary friends, 243–4, 264–6
    nightmares, 96, 104, 179–82
    past-life memories, 32–4, 56–7, 219–69, 285–6, 296–7
    personality type, 247, 248–51
    repeater children, 53
    sexual abuse, 65, 79, 142, 259
    trance state, 226–8, 268
    and violent death memories, 266
Christianity, xiv, 54
Chu, Wesley, 204
Clark, Paul (pseudonym), 26, 32
Cliff, Kathleen, 110, 296
Cockell, Jenny, 33, 120–3, 145
collective unconscious, 63, 76, 300
colour theory, 312
Conduitt, Barbara, 23–5, 297
consciousness, 28, 44, 309, 314, 315, 316, 318
consciousness, stream of, 268
Corkell, Bridie, 6
Cornwall, John, 17–18
cosmic memory bank, 299–301

Courtnadge, Terry, 110
cross-cultural reincarnations, 59
Crow, Albert, 36, 241–2
cryptomnesia, 6, 9, 10, 68, 74, 112, 113, 128, 143, 144–5, 192, 200, 214, 219, 308
cultural patterns, 46–63
Cunliffe, Nicholas, 226–8, 268
Curran, Pearl, 201–2, 203
curse-induced deformities, 289–92

Dalai Lama, xvii, xviii, xix
David, Sarah (pseudonym), 298–9
Davies, Lesley, 247–8, 260, 263
Davis, J., 41
De Prado, Antonia, 130–45
death-to-rebirth time interval, 47
deathbed scenes, 25–6, 27
déjà vu, 18–23, 61, 81, 153, 160, 262–4
depersonalisation, 81
depression, 79
derealisation, 81
Descartes, René, 310–11
Devi, Shanti, 11–15, 16–17, 25, 145, 301
Diana, Princess of Wales, xi, 245, 246
Dilmen, Laurel (pseudonym), 129–45, 168, 217, 301
discarnate possession, 214, 301–3
dissociated states, 61
Dobson, Professor Barrie, 9
Donald, R., 120–1
Dowding, Lord, xi
Dowling, Ann, 177–9
dreams, 75, 92–114, 150, 188
    announcing dreams, 47, 51, 53, 55, 285
    dream memory, 110
    dream neologisms, 150
    dream-recognition, 112, 113–14
    hypnagogia, 107, 109
    hypnopompia, 107
    lucid dreams, 94
    past-life recall, 93–5, 97–114

random dream imagery, 112
recurrent dreams, 93, 179
sleep paralysis, 104–5, 171
smell imagery, 99–100
telepathic dreams, 105–6
unintelligible dream-language,
    101–2, 103–4
see also nightmares
Druidism, xiv
Druse, 53, 68

Edmonds, Christina, 28
Egyptians, ancient, xii
eidetic memory, 73–4, 200
Elawar, Imad, 60
empathy, 163
English, V., 32
Ennius, xiii
epilepsy, 84, 159–60
    temporal-lobe epilepsy, 22, 160, 264
ESP, 296
Evans, Jane, 7–9, 10, 11

Fahrici, Cemil, 281–83
fantasy and imagination, 22, 61, 117,
    119, 128, 139–40, 188, 219, 259,
    260
Feldman, David, 205
Fermor, J., 41
field theories, 76, 300
Flournoy, Théodore, 151
Ford, Henry, xi
fraud, 141, 146
fugue states, 78–9
Funnel, Margaret, 66

Galilean science, 310, 311, 312–13,
    314
Gallagher, John, 37
Galloway, Donald, 196–7
Gardner, Martin, 293, 321
Gardner, R., 321
gender, reincarnation and, 53–4, 246–7
    see also sex changes

George, William, 274–6
Gershom, Rabbi Yonassan, 42
ghosts and apparitions, xx, 50
Gilpin, Sophie, 225–6, 265
glossolalia, 150–1
Gnostics, xiv
Goddard, Gillian, 182
Gordon, Jo (pseudonym), 195
Gotswami, Amit, 318
Gottlieb, Gretchen, 211–14
Grant, Joan, 153
Greek writings, xii–xiii
Greene, Charlton, 204
Gregory, Richard, 77
Grimmer, Tessa, 41
Guirdham, Arthur, 152–62, 295–6
Gunn, Battiscombe, 148, 149
Gupta, Gopal, 239–41, 243, 252

Haddur, Uttara, 83–91, 214–16
Hadfield, Elizabeth, 21
Haida, 53
Hamilton, James, 246
Hammeroff, Stuart, 316
Haraldsson, Erlendur, 151, 248–9, 250,
    251, 252, 253, 255, 256–7, 296
Harris, Lynda, 157
Harris, Melvin, 10, 11
Harris, Sue, 224–5
Harrison, Vernon, 200, 201, 202, 204
Heisenberg uncertainty principle, 317
Herbert, Joanne, 265
Hinduism, xii, xv–xvi, 48, 51–2, 57,
    234
Hird, David, 34
Hodgson, Richard, 304–5, 306, 307,
    308
Holocaust, 41–4
Holsman, K., 101–2, 296
Hornig, Heidi (pseudonym), 179–81
Hornsby-Smith, Michael, 55
Houghton, Martin, 38
Hulme, Alfred, 146–9
Hunter, B., 94

Hurst, Harry, 124
hypnagogia, 107, 109
hypnopompia, 107
hypnotic regression, 16–17, 67, 115–45
  enhanced capacity for imagery and
    role enactment, 115, 117
  regression therapy, 181–93
  self-hypnosis, 117, 267–8
  suggestibility, 115, 116
  trance logic, 116
hysterical dissociation, 78–9, 82, 90–1,
  142, 219

icons and preoccupations, 38–45, 59
Igbo, 48, 51, 53, 62
imaginary friends, 243–4, 264–6
immortality, xx
India, 47, 51, 54, 56–7, 234–5, 252
Inquisition, 132–4, 135–6, 144
Israel, 52
Iverson, Jeffrey, xvii, 9

Jainism, xvi, 51
jamais vu, 18
James, William, 304
Jarmon, Robert, 186–7
Jay, Dolores, 211–14
Jones, Anne (pseudonym), 100–1
Jones, Jeanne, 38–40
Jordan, 52
Jung, Carl Gustav, 76, 300

Kahn, Olga, 287
Kama, 202
karma, xvi, xx, 51, 270–1
Keeton, Joe, 124–5, 177, 216–17
Keil, Jorgen, 285–6
Killwick, Robert, 264, 269
King, Olive (pseudonym), 32
King, Paul, 92–3
Koshy, Valsa, 204

Lamarckism, 285
lamas, xvi–xviii

language, 85–6, 209–18
  archaic speech, 126–7, 202, 209,
    215, 217
  dream jargon, 101–2, 103
  glossolalia, 150–51
  xenoglossy, 209, 210–18, 258
Lawrence, Ruth, 204
Lebanon, 52
Lee, Raymond, 55
life after death, 320–1
Lloyd George, David, xi
Lobsang Lungrig, xvii
Locke, John, 293
Locke, Susan, 34–6
Loftus, Elizabeth, 64–5
Lowe, Lynn, 25, 265, 267
Lowes Dickinson, G., 69, 70–1, 72–3,
  74

Ma Win Tar, 258–9, 278–9
Ma Win Yee, 279–80
McCafferty, Joe, 233–4, 261, 264
McClymont, Wendy, 163, 244, 265
MacLaine, Shirley, xi
Mahler, Gustav, xi
Mancey, Suzanne, 30–1
Manichaeans, xiv
Manning, Matthew, 200–1, 202
Mather, Thomas (pseudonym), 95–7,
  266
Maung Aung Htoo, 279
Maung Hla Hsaung, 280
Maung Tin Win, 273–4
meditation, 17, 31, 117
memory, 64–76
  in babies and children, 260
  cosmic memory bank, 299–301
  dream memory, 110
  episodic memory, 261
  false memories, 65–8
  flashbacks, 27, 29, 30–1, 32, 44,
    107, 260
  forced reminiscence, 81
  forgotten memories, 68–75, 219

function, 75–6
genetic memory, 61–2
implanted memories, 67
memory pool, 63
misinformation, 64–5
photographic (eidetic) memory, 73, 200
savant memory, 207–8
storage outside the brain, 76, 309
migraine-induced mental disturbances, 22, 80–2
Mills, Antonia, 95, 179, 251
miracles, 321
Moody, Raymond, 14
Moody, Robert, 287
morphic resonance, 63, 76, 300–1, 317–18
Morse, Grace, 94
multiple personality, 61, 77–8, 82
see also hysterical dissociation
Murphy, Bridey, 2–7, 145, 209
musical channelling, 201, 203–5
Myers, Frederic, 23
mystical experiences, 318

Nadia (a savant), 205–7, 208
Napoleon Bonaparte, xi
near-death experiences, xi, xx, 14–15, 25, 26–7, 28, 223–4, 320
Neppe, Vernon, 262–4
neuroimaging, 313
neuroscience, 45
New Age beliefs, 55
Newson, Elizabeth, 205
Newtonian science, 312–13, 315
Nigeria, 48, 51, 53, 62
nightmares, 96, 104–5, 177–8, 179–82
nirvana, xvi
Nissanka, Dilukshi Geevanie, 253–5
North American Indians, 47

objective and subjective world, 311, 312, 314–15
Ouspensky, Peter, 23

out-of-body experiences, 23–6, 26–7, 302

Pafford, Ronald James, 33–4
Panchen Lamar, xviii–xx
Paradise, Elizabeth, 112, 237
parallel universes, 76, 318
paramusicology, 201, 203–5
parapsychology, 56, 62–63, 113, 294–99, 319
Pasricha, Satwant, 266–67
past-life therapy, see regression therapy
Patton, General, xi
Paxton, Stewart, 297–98
Pearn, Marion, 184
Pellew, George, 305–6, 307–8
Penrose, Roger, 316
personal identity, persistence of, 293–4
Philo Judaeus, xiv
phobias, 38, 50, 55, 57, 181–2, 184
Pidgeon, Joan, 98
Piper, Leonore, 303–7, 308
planchettes, 71
Plato, xiii
Pollock twins, 228–32, 260, 267, 284–5, 292
"population problem" of soul transfer, 310, 317
Porter, Charles, 270
possession, xx
Poulter, Beatrice, 29–30
Poynings, Blanche, 68–75
Pratley, Philip, 113–14
precognition, 112–13, 294, 296, 319
Preston, Frances Marie, 163–4
Prince, Morton, 78
Pring, Alan, ix–xi, xx
psychiatric illness, 22
psychic ability, 296, 298
psychoactive drugs, 16
psychokinesis, 294
Pye, Christine, 190
Pythagoras, xiii, 23

quantum mechanics, 76, 315–18

Radin, Dean, 294
Ranatunga, Ruvan, 286
Ratnayake, Duminda Bandara, 255–8
Ray, John, 149
rebirth, predictions of, 47, 55
recognition, spontaneous, 49, 55
regression therapy, 181–93
   see also hypnotic regression
reincarnation
   in ancient writings, xii–xiv
   characteristics, transmission of, xii,
      50, 61–2, 242, 275–6
   cultural patterns, 46–63
   importance attached to personal
      identity, 309
   non-scientific theories, 61–3
   principal features, 47–50
   scientific view, xx–xxi, 44–5, 61,
      309
   verifying past-life memories, 58–60,
      123–5, 252–3
relationships, past-life, 163–76
remote viewing, 112
retribution, xv–xvi
Rhodes, D. E., 27
Robertson, Alice (pseudonym), 95
Robinson, Neil, 189–90
Rodwell, Jonathan, 239
Roman literature, xiii
Royce, Elizabeth (pseudonym), 182–3,
   296–7
Rushton, Alan (pseudonym), 19

Sacks, Oliver, 81
Sai Baba, xv
Saltman, Maureen, 21
Sargeant, Isabel (pseudonym), 232–3
savant syndrome, 205–9
Schatzman, Morton, 287
Schonberg, Vera, 19–20, 23
self-delusion, 61, 146, 161, 219
Selfe, Lorna, 205–6, 208

sex changes, 49, 50, 51, 53–4, 57, 225
sexual behaviour, odd or inappropriate,
   50
Sharpe, Anne, 40
Sheldrake, Rupert, 76, 300
Sikhism, xvi, 51
Silver, Sophia (pseudonym), 245–6,
   264, 267
Singh, Mahavir (pseudonym), 235–7,
   252
Sizemore, Chris, 77
skills and talents, 50, 55, 194–218
sleep paralysis, 104–7, 171
smell, 35, 99–100, 298
Smith, Dorothy, 210–11
Smith, Hélène, 151
socioeconomic status, change in, 54
soul, xii–xiii, 54, 302–3, 309–10, 311,
   314, 317, 318, 319, 320
   immortality of, xiii, xiv, 54
   moment of death, 302, 319
   transmigration, xii, xiv
soul mates, 163–76
soul-splitting, 53
spiritualism, xx, 71, 147, 302–8
Sri Lanka, 52, 151, 248, 251–2, 253,
   270, 290
Stevenson, Ian, 23, 44, 46–7, 49, 53–4,
   55–6, 57, 58, 59, 60, 82, 85, 95,
   97–8, 179, 211–13, 214, 215,
   217–18, 224, 225, 231, 235, 239,
   241, 243, 247, 252, 258, 259, 261,
   266–7, 271, 272, 273–4, 277–8,
   279, 280–1, 283–4, 285–6, 288,
   290, 291, 292, 296
Stewart, A. J., 79–81, 81–2
stigmata, 287–8
Strickland, David, 42–4
sub-personalities, 188
suggestibility, 115, 116, 219
super-psi (parapsychological) effects,
   294–9
Syria, 52

Tammy, 220–3, 260, 265, 266, 268
Tarazi, Linda, 129, 134–9, 140–1, 143, 145
Tarnas, Richard, 310
telepathy, 105, 158, 287, 294, 296, 299, 301, 304, 308
retrospective telepathy, 63
Thailand, 46, 47, 51–2, 270
Theosophy, xv, 202
Thomas, N. R., 104–5
Thompson, Peter (pseudonym), 107–9
Tibet, 47
Tidy, Chris, 150
Tighe, Virginia, 2, 5–7, 116
time
    linear time, xii, 62, 113
    non-linear time, 113
Titanic, 40–1
Tlingit Alaskans, 47, 48, 51, 52–3, 270–1
Treffert, Darold, 207–8, 209
tulkus, xvi–xvii
Turkey, 47, 52
Turner, Elizabeth, 290

United States, 55–7, 252
universe, theories of the, 311–13, 317–18
Unlutaskiran, Necip, 283–4

Vincent, Victor, 276–7, 278

violent death, 26, 44, 49–50, 54, 55, 57, 226, 266–7, 281, 284, 292, 310
Virgil, xiii

Waddington, Alan, 37–8
Wagner, Richard, xi
Wall, Jean, 112–13
Wallace, Simon (pseudonym), 34
Wambach, Helen, 117, 199, 185
Warner, Chris, 164
Waterhouse, Joan, 125–8, 217
Weiss, Brian, 164
Williams, Davina, 21–2, 92
Williams, M., 31
Willin, Melvyn, 201, 203
Wilshire, Stephen, 209
Wilson, Colin, 157
Wilson, Ian, 80, 81, 126, 127, 148–50, 157
Wilson, Stephanie, 194–5, 198
wishful thinking, 54, 118–19, 219
Wood, Frederick, 147–8, 149–50
Woolger, Roger, 186, 187–8
Worth, Patience, 201–2, 203
Wright, D. (pseudonym), 265

xenoglossy, 209, 210–18, 258

Yogananda, Paramahansa, 34